Memoirs Of
The Private Life, Return,
And Reign Of Napoleon
In 1815
Vol. I

by

Baron Pierre Alexandre Édouard
Fleury De Chaboulon

Double 9
BOOKS

Memoirs Of
The Private Life, Return,
And Reign Of Napoleon
In 1815
Vol. I
**by Baron Pierre Alexandre Édouard
Fleury De Chaboulon**

ISBN: 978-93-59329-82-6

Published by

DOUBLE 9 BOOKS

2/13-B, Ansari Road
Daryaganj, New Delhi – 110002
info@double9books.com
www.double9books.com
Tel. 011-40042856

This book is under public domain

ABOUT THE AUTHOR

Baron Pierre Alexandre Édouard Fleury de Chaboulon (14 April 1779 – 28 September 1835) was a French politician. He was the Special Secretary to Napoleon Bonaparte's Cabinet. At the age of 16, he assumes command of a battalion of the National Guard and, on October 5, 1795, leads an insurgency against the National Convention. Given his young age, he was apprehended and imprisoned. The minister Fermont then asks him a question and gives him detailed financial management advice. As a result, he was appointed as an auditor to the State Council in the field of management. Later, he became the sub-prefect of Château-Salins (Meurthe), where he distinguished himself not only by his ability, but also by his great goodness, and Napoleon entrusted him with several tasks. Then named Reims's deputy mayor during the invasion in 1814, he fought the Allies with vigour and determination throughout the French campaign. During the restoration, he will travel to Italy to prepare for the Hundred Days and then to the Isle of Elbe. When Napoleon returns to France, he appoints him as Special Secretary, and he uses this position to carry out sensitive missions, including those at Bâle and with the Emperor of Austria.

CONTENTS

TO THE READER.. 7

MEMOIRS, &c. &c... 12

HISTORY OF THE REVOLUTION OF THE 20th OF MARCH. 47

TO THE READER.

The revolution of the 20th of March will form unquestionably the most remarkable episode in the life of Napoleon, so fertile as it is in supernatural events. It has not been my intention, to write the history of it: this noble task is above my powers: I have only attempted, to place Napoleon on the stage of action, and oppose his words, his deeds, and the truth, to the erroneous assertions of certain historians, the falsehoods of the spirit of party, and the insults of those timeserving writers, who are accustomed to insult in misfortune those, to whom they have subsequently paid court.

Hitherto people have not been able to agree on the motives and circumstances, that determined the Emperor, to quit the island of Elba. Some supposed, that he had acted of his own accord: others, that he had conspired with his partisans the downfal of the Bourbons. Both these suppositions are equally false. The world will learn with surprise, perhaps with admiration, that this astonishing revolution was the work of two individuals and a few words.

The narrative of Colonel Z***, so valuable from the facts it reveals, appears to me to merit the reader's attention in other respects. On studying it carefully, we find in it the exhibition of those defects, those qualities, those passions, which, confounded together, form the character, so full of contrasts, of the incomprehensible Napoleon. We perceive him alternatively mistrustful and communicative, ardent and reserved, enterprising and irresolute, vindictive and generous, favourable to liberty and despotic. But we see predominant above all, that activity, that strength, that ardour of mind, those brilliant inspirations, and those sudden resolves, that belong only to extraordinary men, to men of genius.

The conferences I had at Bâle with the mysterious agent of Prince Metternich have remained to this day buried in profound secrecy. The historians, who have preceded me, relate, without any explanation, that the Duke of Otranto laid before the Emperor, at the moment of his abdication, a letter from M. de Metternich; and that this letter, artfully worded, had determined Napoleon to abdicate, in the hope that the crown would devolve to his son. The particulars given in these Memoirs will entirely change the ideas formed of this letter, and of its influence. They confirm the opinion too, pretty generally prevalent, that the allied sovereigns deemed the restoration of the Bourbons of little importance, and would willingly have consented, to place the young Prince Napoleon on the throne.

It had been supposed, that the famous decree, by which Prince de Talleyrand and his illustrious accomplices were sent before the courts of justice, was issued at Lyons in the first burst of a fit of vengeance. It will be seen, that it was the result of a plan simply political: and the noble resistance, which General Bertrand (now labouring under a sentence of death) thought it his duty to oppose to this measure, will add, if it be possible, to the high esteem, merited on so many accounts by this faithful friend to the unfortunate.

The writings published previously to this work, equally contain nothing but inaccurate or fabulous reports, with regard to the abdication of Napoleon. Certain historians have been pleased, to represent Napoleon in a pitious state of despondency: others have depicted him as the sport of the threats of M. Regnault St. Jean d'Angely, and of the artifices of the Duke of Otranto. These Memoirs will show, that Napoleon, far from having fallen into a state of weakness, that would no longer permit him to wield the sceptre, aspired, on the contrary, to be invested with a temporary dictatorship, and that, when he consented to abdicate, it was because the energetic attitude of the representatives disconcerted him, and he yielded to the fear of adding the calamities of a civil war to the disasters of a foreign invasion.

It was perfectly unknown too, that Napoleon was detained a prisoner at Malmaison after his abdication. It was presumed, that he deferred his departure, in the hope of being replaced at the head of the army and of the government. These Memoirs will show, that this hope, if it dwelt within the breast of Napoleon, was not the real motive of his stay in France; and that he was detained there by the committee of government, till the moment when, honour outweighing all political considerations, it obliged Napoleon to depart, to prevent his falling into the hands of Blucher.

The negotiations and conferences of the French plenipotentiaries with the enemy's generals; the proceedings of the Prince of Eckmuhl; the intrigues of the Duke of Otranto; the efforts of those members of the committee, who remained faithful to their trust; the debates on the capitulation of Paris, and all the collateral facts, connected with these different circumstances, had been totally misrepresented; These Memoirs establish or unfold the truth. They bring to light the conduct of those members of the committee, who were supposed to be the dupes or accomplices of Fouché; and that of the marshals, the army, and the chambers. They contain also the correspondence of the plenipotentiaries, and the instructions given to them; documents hitherto unpublished, which will make known, what the politics and wishes of the government of France at that time were.

Finally I shall observe, in order to complete the account I think it right to give the reader of the substance of this work, that it furnishes elucidations of the campaign of 1815, the want of which has been imperiously felt. The causes, that determined Napoleon, to separate from his army at Laon, were not known: I point them out. General Gourgaud, in his narrative, could give no explanation of the march of the corps of Count Erlon at the battle of Ligny, of the conduct of Marshal Ney on the 16th, of the inactivity of Napoleon on the 17th, &c. All these points, I believe, I have elucidated. I show also, that it was not, as General Gourgaud and other writers assert, to raise the spirits, and excite the courage of the French army, that its leader announced to it the arrival of Marshal Grouchy. It is a certain fact, that Napoleon was himself deceived by a brisk firing, which took place between the Prussians and Saxons; and it is falsely, that he has been charged with having knowingly deceived his soldiers, at a moment when the laws of war and of humanity presented to him, to think rather of a retreat, than of continuing the battle.

I had at first rejected from these Memoirs such official papers, as had already been made known: but have since thought, that they ought to be inserted. This work, which embraces all the events of the reign of a Hundred Days, would be imperfect, if the reader were obliged to refer to the papers of the day; to read or consult the act of the congress of Vienna, that placed the Emperor Napoleon out of the pale of the law of nations; the Additional Act, which occasioned his loss of popularity; and the eloquent speeches and nervous declarations by which Napoleon, his ministers, and his counsellors, sought to explain and justify the 20th of March. I have thought, besides, that perhaps the reader would not find it uninteresting, to witness the contests exhibited, at that important period, between the legitimacy of nations and the legitimacy of sovereigns.

The colours under which I represent Napoleon, the justice I do him for the purity of his intentions, will not please all the world. Many persons, who would blindly have believed any ill I could say of the ancient sovereigns of France, will give little credit to my eulogies: they are wrong: if praises lavished on power be suspicious, those bestowed on the unfortunate will be true; to doubt them would be sacrilege.

Neither can I conceal from myself, that the men, who, from principle, see nothing but a hateful conspiracy in the revolution of the 20th of March, will accuse me of having embellished facts, and designedly distorted the truth. No matter: I have depicted this revolution as I saw it, as I felt it. How many others are pleased, to tarnish the honour of the nation, to represent their countrymen as composed of rebels or cowards! For my part, I think it the duty of a good Frenchman, to prove to all Europe, that the king was not guilty of abandoning France:

That the insurrection of the 20th of March was not the work of a few factious persons, who might have been repressed; but a grand national act, against which the efforts and volitions of individuals would have been vain:

That the royalists were not cowards, and all other Frenchmen traitors:

Lastly, that the return from the island of Elba was the terrible consequence of the faults of ministers and the ultras, which called to France the man of fate, as the conductor draws down the lightning from heaven.

This sentiment naturally led me, to conclude these Memoirs by a philosophical examination of the Hundred Days, and a refutation of the reproaches daily bestowed on the men of the 20th of March: but considerations, easy to divine, held my pen. It was my duty, to content myself with placing a statement of the facts before the eyes of the grand jury, the public, and leave it to decide. I know, that the question has been determined in the fields of Waterloo; but a victory is not a judicial sentence.

Whatever opinion the impartial reader may form of this work, I can protest beforehand, that I have not allowed myself to be influenced by any private consideration, by any feeling of hatred, affection, or gratitude. I have followed no impulse but that of my conscience, and I may say with Montaigne: "This is an honest book."

Too young to have participated in the errors or crimes of the revolution, I began and ended my political career without blot, and without reproach. The places, titles, and decorations, which the Emperor deigned to bestow on me, were the reward of several acts of great devotion to his service, and of twelve years of trials and sacrifices. Never did I receive from him any favours or gifts: I entered his service rich, I quitted it poor.

When Lyons opened to him its gates, I was free: I spontaneously embraced his cause: it appeared to me, as to the immense number of Frenchmen, that of liberty, honour, and our country. The laws of Solon declared infamous those, who took no part in civil troubles. I followed their maxims. If the misfortunes of the 20th of March must fall on the heads of the guilty, these guilty, I repeat, will not be in the eye of posterity, the Frenchmen who abandoned the royal standard, to return to the ancient colours of their country; but those imprudent and senseless men, who, by their threats, their acts of injustice, and their outrages, compelled us to choose between insurrection and slavery, between honour and infamy.

During the Hundred Days, there was no person to whom I did an ill turn; frequently I had an opportunity of doing good, and seized it with joy.

Since the return of the regal government, I have lived tranquil and solitary; and, whether from forgetfulness, or from a sense of justice, I escaped in 1815 the persecutions, which the partisans and servants of Napoleon experienced.

This explanation, or this apology, appeared to me necessary: it is right the reader should know, who it is that addresses him.

I could have wished, to abstain from speaking of the royal government in the first part of this work: but it was impossible It was necessary for me, prominently to exhibit the errors and faults of the king's ministers one by one, to render evident this truth, *that they were the sole authors of the 20th of March*. When elsewhere, as here, I say the government, I mean not to designate the King, but his ministers. In a constitutional monarchy, in which the ministers are responsible, we cannot, and ought not to confound them with the King. "It is from the King," said the keeper of the seals, when he proposed to the deputies of the nation the project of a law on the responsibility of ministers, "that every act of equity, protection, and clemency, and every regular employment of power, emanates: it is to the ministers alone, that abuses, injustice, and misconduct, are to be imputed."

MEMOIRS,
&c. &c.

Until the close of the Spanish war, Napoleon, whether as the First Consul of the Republic, or as the Chief of the Empire, had never ceased to be the object of the love, the pride, and the confidence of the people. But the multitude neither judge, nor can judge of the actions of their rulers but from appearances which often mislead them in their judgment; and the loyalty of the nation then became enfeebled. The conduct of Napoleon was stigmatized as a series of hateful aggressions; the war, as an unjustifiable act of violence. Disaffection increased. Napoleon was assailed by the anger of his subjects, and, for the first time, they upbraided him with having spilt their blood, and wasted their riches, in gratifying his vain and culpable ambition.

At this juncture the public mind became absorbed in the contemplation of the invasion of Russia, and the general discontent was withdrawn from the events which had taken place in the peninsula.

Our arms were crowned with good fortune and glory at the commencement of the Russian war; but that conflict was ended by a catastrophe which has no parallel in the annals of the world.

The Emperor, who escaped almost alone from the perils of the campaign, returned to the capital. His countenance was that of a hero who defies adversity. But his firmness was deemed to be the result of heartless insensibility. Instead of inspiring the people with hope, it embittered their feelings. Louder murmurs broke forth; their indignation expressed itself with greater emphasis. Yet such was the enthusiasm which was even then inspired by the proud recollections of the triumphs of Napoleon, that France, blushing for her disgrace, implored him to win new victories. Armies formed themselves as if by enchantment, and Napoleon stood again in the midst of Germany, more terrible than ever.

After we had conquered at Lutzen, at Bautzen, and at Dresden, the battle of Leipsic was fought[1]. Never before that day had we been doomed to witness our national armies flying before the enemy. The scattered wrecks of our battalions, which had been created by the last hope, by the last effort of our country, at length reached our frontiers. But our soldiers were no longer the vigorous and resolute warriors of France; they were bowed down by want, toil, and humiliation. Soon afterwards they were followed by wandering trains of military carriages, loaded with diseased and wounded wretches, who festered beneath the corpses amongst which they were heaped, and who at once absorbed and diffused the germs of pestilence and contagion. Even the firmest minds now yielded to despair; and the grief occasioned by the havoc now made amongst our defenders renewed the sorrows of the mothers and the wives of those who erewhile had perished in Russia and in Spain. Curses upon Napoleon, the author of all these evils, resounded from side to side of the empire.

As long as good fortune waited upon Napoleon, his most ambitious attempts commanded the applauses of the nation. We boasted of his profound political wisdom, we extolled his genius, we worshipped his courage. When his fortune changed, then his political wisdom was called treachery, his genius, ambition, and his courage, fool-hardiness and infatuation.

Napoleon was not to be depressed by ingratitude or misfortune. He re-assembled the feeble fragments of his armies, and proclaimed aloud that he would conquer or die at the head of his soldiery. This resolution only produced a momentary impression. The French, who so lately believed that the happiness and salvation of France depended only upon the life of Napoleon, now coolly considered that his death, the fate which he was prepared to encounter, afforded the only means of putting an end to the calamities of war, for peace otherwise appeared unattainable.

Napoleon departed. He achieved prodigies, but to no effect. National spirit no longer existed, and the nation had gradually sunk into that state of insensibility so fatal to sovereigns, when the public mind has no perception of their dangers, and abandons them to their destiny.

France was thus affected when Napoleon consented to divest himself of his crown[2]. The apathy of the nation drove him to this extremity; for it deprived him of the means either of carrying on the war, or of making peace.

Hostilities ended with the abdication of Napoleon. The people of Paris, who had scarcely recovered from the panic with which they were struck by the marauding hordes of Russia, displayed the most extravagant gladness when they thought that they were delivered from the visitation, which again threatened them in the presence of the allies and the imperial army.

The neighbouring departments, which the enemy prepared to invade, rejoiced on being relieved from impending pillage and devastation.

The departments which had been occupied by the enemy were intoxicated with joy, when they anticipated the termination of their sufferings.

Thus almost all the people of France turned away from their discarded sovereign. And they abandoned themselves to joy when they thought that they were delivered from the scourge of war, and that they could hope to enjoy the blessings of peace.

It was in the midst of this pouring out of the spirit of selfishness, that the senate raised the brother of Louis XVI. to the throne. His election was not in conformity to the expectations of the people, and it disappointed the wishes which had been uttered in favour of the Empress and her son; yet the choice of the senate was but slightly opposed, because the recall of Louis seemed to be necessarily the pledge of peace. And peace was more the object of the public wish than any other thing. Besides which, the Bourbons followed the wise counsels which had been given to them. They lost no time in issuing their proclamations, couched in fair language, in order to calm the fears and diminish the antipathies excited by their recall.

"We will guarantee," said they, "the rank, the honours, and the rewards of the military.

"The magistracy and all public functionaries shall retain their offices and their pre-eminence.

"To the people we promise a total oblivion of their political conduct; and we will maintain them in the full enjoyment of their civil rights, their property, and their social institutions."

The French nation, whose confidence is so easily abused, considered these promises as sacred and inviolable, and they delighted in repeating the happy reply of the Count of Artois[3], "Il n'y aura rien de changé en France, il n'y aura que quelques Français de plus." They, the men, who had banished the imperial dynasty, laboured to foster the growing confidence of the nation. The press was brought into full play, and the country teemed with publications in which they represented the sovereign whom they had brought in, as invested with those attributes which were calculated to conciliate the nation. The public were carefully informed, that the king "opened and read all the dispatches himself. It is he who dictates every answer. Where it becomes necessary to meet the ministers of foreign powers, he transacts business with them; he receives the reports of their missions, which he answers either by word of mouth, or in writing. In short, he alone directs all the concerns of the government, both at home and abroad. If his virtues and goodness are such as to cause the French to know that they will now find a kind and affectionate father in their King, they may also look with confidence to the future fate of the nation, relying on his brilliant information, his strength of character, and his aptitude for business[4]."

Thus the people congratulated themselves, when they were assured that their Chief Magistrate was an enlightened sovereign, a kind sovereign, an equitable sovereign, and one who was determined not to allow the guiding reins of the state to slip from his paternal hands into those of his ministers. Our lively imagination gave us a present enjoyment of the blessings, which, as we anticipated, would hereafter be diffused over the kingdom by his goodness, his prudence, and his acquirements. If this glowing vision of hope and loyalty was slightly dimmed by a few secret doubts, such misgivings were checked and repelled by the name of our native country; nay, by the name of the Emperor himself. For when Napoleon bade farewell to his trusty soldiers, it was in these words: "Be faithful to the new sovereign of France; do not rend asunder our beloved and long-suffering land."

These circumstances (nor must the charm of novelty be excluded) united in favour of the king, and won every head and every heart. He appeared — he was received with acclamations of love and gladness, which resounded until he entered the palace of his forefathers.

No counter revolution ever effected the change of a royal dynasty, under such favourable auspices.

The French nation felt jaded by civil dissensions, by misfortune — even their victories had weaned them. They longed for the happiness of repose. Memorable were the words of the king's brother; "let us forget the past, let us look only towards the future, let us all unite in the good work of labouring to heal the wounds of our common country;" and these honoured precepts had become implanted in every mind. They formed the canon of all our feelings and all our duties.

As long as the machinery of the new government did not begin to work, this loyal harmony subsisted, and no longer. For when it became necessary to settle the organization of the army, the ministry, and the magistracy, then self-love gained an easy victory over patriotism, and the bad passions, pride, ambition, and party-hatred, roused themselves from their slumber.

During a quarter of a century, our emigrants had sojourned in a strange country. Useless and troublesome guests to the strangers by whom they were fed, their lives had been droned away in shameless and cowardly idleness. They could not cheat themselves into a belief that they possessed the talents and experience of the sons of the revolution. But they imagined that nobility, as in the old time, might pass for worth; and that their patents and pedigrees still gave them a right to monopolize all power and all honour.

The citizens, the soldiers, the nation, relied on the lawfulness of their rights no less than on the promises of the king. The members of the old privileged caste, instead of exciting suspicion, were only the objects of harmless mirth. The people laughed at the grotesque appearance of some, and at the decrepit sottishness of others. They never dreamed that these pretended warriors, whose bloodless swords had rusted in their scabbards, would attempt to snatch the staff of command from the veteran generals of France; and that nobles who had grown old in sloth and ignorance would aspire to the direction of public affairs.

But though merit and valour were denied to them, they stood upon a vantage ground, which gave them a direful and incalculable preponderance in the state. They surrounded the throne. Soon did their insolence announce that they had craftily availed themselves of the advantages which they possessed; and we foresaw with affliction that inveterate prejudice, malignant prepossessions, and old habits of familiarity, would, sooner or later, crush the principles of justice and equity, however solemnly proclaimed.

The emigrants, rendered arrogant by the prospects which opened upon them, now treated their rivals with contemptuous disdain. They dared not insult the defenders of our country face to face, because the scars of the warriors scared them. But they were spitefully active in disparaging their birth, their services, and their glory, and these noble retainers of royalty took care to impress the soldiers of Napoleon with a due sense of the width of the gulf which was henceforth to separate a gentleman of good family, from an upstart soldier of the revolution.

The women of the *ancien régime* did not share in the timidity which, to a certain degree, still restrained their husbands. They threw off all decency and all reserve, and indulged in all the fury of their spite and pride. Without attempting to disguise their sentiments, they openly insulted the titled dames belonging to the new nobility, and such of the latter as were compelled to go to court on account of the situations held by their husbands, never entered the saloon without dread, and never quitted it without being bathed in tears.

Uneasy, harassed, and discontented, the people implored the fulfilment of the king's promises: they prayed with confidence; but the government heard them not, and repulsed them harshly. The Doge of Genoa, speaking of Louis XIV, said, "his majesty steals our hearts by his amiability, but his ministers give them back again to us." The apophthegm of the Doge might have been pertinently applied to Louis XVIII. by the people.

Hitherto the government appeared to adhere to the resolution of dealing out impartial justice to both parties, and of performing the covenant which the new monarch had entered into with the nation. But now he was bound by an influence which he could not withstand. Ensnared by the machinations, the threats, and the fears of his emigrant court, and perhaps believing that the new order of things was incompatible with the stability of the Bourbon dynasty, the maxims of his government underwent a total change. He was taught to consider the equality of civil rights as a revolutionary conquest, the liberties of the nation as an usurpation of the authority of the throne, the new constitution as insulting the independence of the sovereign. It was therefore determined that all "dangerous characters[5]" should be led quietly out of all civil and military offices. The old trustworthy nobility of the old kingdom were again to become the sole depositaries of the power of the state: and by slow but sure degrees it was resolved to cancel the royal charter, and either by fair means or by foul, to place the nation again beneath the yoke of absolute power.

The government often appealed to the authority of the King's predecessor on the throne—of Bonaparte. Bonaparte, it was said, had acknowledged that it was dangerous to concede a representative government to the people, and that it was fit and proper to rule them despotically. But Napoleon, he who re-established the authority of royalty, morality, and religion—who had re-organized society—who had given tranquillity to France, at the same time that he rendered her formidable to the world—he had earned his authority by his services and his victories, and, if I may venture to use the expression, he had acquired a legitimate right of despotism, which neither belonged, nor could belong, to a Bourbon. Besides which, in spite of the real or pretended despotism of the imperial government, it was still a national government; a character wholly foreign to the Bourbon government, and which it had no tendency to acquire.

The prognostics of the re-action which the ministers intended to bring about were disclosed in all parts of the body politic. Alarm seized even the Chamber of Deputies: it hastened to become the organ of the uneasiness of the people, and to remind the King of the warranty which he had given to the nation.

In the address, or rather in the protest presented by the chamber on the 15th of June, the national representatives say, "The charter secures to the voice of truth every channel which leads to the throne, since it consecrates the liberty of the press, and the right of petition.

"Amongst the guarantees which it contains, the nation will attend to that which insures the responsibility of any minister who may betray the confidence reposed in him by your Majesty, by trespassing on the public or private rights insured by the constitutional charter.

"By virtue of this charter, nobility in all future times will only command the respect of the people as surrounded by proofs of honour and glory, which the recollections of feudality will not have the power of tarnishing.

"The principles of civil liberty are founded upon the independence of judicial authority, and the retention of trial by jury, that invaluable guarantee of all our rights."

If the King had known the truth, this energetic address would have attained its end. But the truth could not reach him. At first he intended to bestow his personal confidence upon the greater part of the leading "notables" of the revolution; but by means of remonstrances and recriminations, another party contrived to place his good sense again under the yoke of prejudice, and he surrounded himself with old nobility alone, with men who had refused to obey the constitution sanctioned by Louis XVI., because it destroyed their privileges; and who, for the same reason, had refused to acknowledge the new constitution, against which they had even dared to protest. His companions were so blinded, so besotted by their presumption, that they imagined that decrees and ordinances gave them the faculty of overturning the edifice which the nation had erected during five and twenty years of revolution. His confidents were those alone who, instead of wishing to reveal to their sovereign the object of the projects of the ministry, and of the faction which had rendered the ministry their tools, had become the accomplices of ministerial guilt, joint conspirators in the plot which was to destroy the royal charter.

The cabinet contained, however, some able and experienced statesmen. They were convinced that instead of teasing the nation by holding out the probability of the restoration of ancient privileges, it was the duty of government to tranquillize the country by guaranteeing the stability of the new system of polity. These ministers were aware of the impolicy of attempting to re-establish the monarchy on its ancient principles; because by such an attempt it would be deprived of the only advantage which it possessed over the late government—that of being liberal. And, lastly, they felt that if despotism and violence had been the distinguishing characteristics of the government of Napoleon, it was necessary that moderation and justice should be the attributes of the government of a Bourbon.

But they had not sufficient authority or personal influence to enable them to struggle against the emigrants, and the protectors of the emigrant faction. In the council chamber their opinions, cften well concerted, and always benevolent, were sanctioned and approved. Out of the council, each minister acted according to his own plans; and, unfortunately, those departments which ramify most deeply into the nation and its affairs were confided to men who seemed to think that they were bound to irritate and sour the public mind.

General Dupont obtained the important office of minister of the war department, as a reward due to his proscription. According to the government party, the general had been proscribed by the Emperor. An odious name was thus given to the lenient punishment which had been inflicted upon Dupont, he who had shuffled off the allegiance which he owed to his Emperor, and whose cowardice had surrendered into captivity the legions intrusted to his command[6]. Weak, indolent, irresolute, devoid of character and resources, he never had the wish or the ability of becoming any thing else than the pliant functionary of the court and the ruling courtiers.

Another, the Abbé de Montesquiou, received the "porte-feuille" of the home department. When a member of the Constituent Assembly he had been honourably distinguished by his soft and persuasive eloquence. The temperance of his public conduct seemed to be insured by his personal character; he was a servant of the altar, his health was delicate, he had lived long in quiet retirement. But Montesquiou, meek, mild, and timid as long as he was in the background, became scornful, angry, and overbearing the instant that he stepped into power. He detested and despised the revolution—I may almost say, he detested and despised the nation. This sentiment was the principle which guided him. Montesquiou never deigned to inquire whether any given portion of our polity was sound or useful, whether it had been formed with difficulty, whether it could be modified, or ameliorated, or fitted into existing circumstances. He only inquired into the date of its institution—and the date decided the question.

A third, Dambray, the chancellor, and the chief law officer of the nation, had distinguished himself in his youth as a Judge of Parliament. His credit arose from his prudence and his principles no less than from his talents. He had been long since recalled to his country. During the reign of Napoleon he fulfilled the duties of a citizen and a subject with zeal and fidelity. We never doubted but that he would protect those constitutional forms of government under which he had flourished in peace and honour. Scarcely, however, was the Chancellor clothed in his robe, when he became the oppressor of the magistracy, the antagonist of our new system of jurisprudence, and the dull partisan of those slavish forms and barbarous customs and oppressive edicts, which had been long since annihilated by reason, liberty, and knowledge.

The trust reposed in this portion of the cabinet was a source of unhappiness to the nation, but it was not the only one. Louis, according to the promises held out on his restoration, was to reign in person; and the more the French have ever been desirous to obey their sovereign with cheerful alacrity, the greater is the repugnance which they feel to submit to the orders of his minions. Dismay, therefore, prevailed throughout the kingdom when we learnt that Louis, weakened by an obstinate and painful disease, had entirely divested himself of his royal authority in favour of Monsieur de Blacas. And how much more painful did our consternation become, when we were able to understand the views and projects of this Mayor of the palace, and when we ascertained the baneful extent of his ascendancy.

It was impossible that the royal government, including such elements in its composition, could retain its hold on public opinion. It was seen too clearly that the effects of a despicable coterie would tend either to involve our country in a civil war, or overwhelm us again with the wretchedness and slavery from which we had been delivered by the revolution.

The absolute necessity of rising in opposition to these nefarious attempts was felt by the entire country. Not a man would remain neuter.

During the earliest period of the reign of Louis, the emigrant faction comprehended nothing but the party composed of the relics of the ancient privileged cast. The parvenus of the imperial government alone constituted the so called Bonapartists. Considering their private gratification and profit as of greater importance than the public cause, each party had hitherto only wrangled for place and power. Their war was a matter of calculation and selfishness. But soon their disputes involved the fate of the main interests created by the revolution the emigrants directed their attacks not only against individuals but also against principles, and the people, who had hitherto only looked on, now shared the quarrel, and all France was divided into two great hostile parties[7].

The court, the courtiers, and the ministry appeared as the central phalanx of the *pure royalists*. As their auxiliaries, they had the old nobility,— the priesthood,—a certain number of apostates who had skulked away from the imperial government,—and lastly, all those who had been disqualified by their incapacity and disloyalty from obtaining employment under Napoleon. It was the undisguised wish of this party to wash out every stain of the revolution, and to effect a full and unqualified restoration of the *ancien régime* in all its parts, and to all intents and purposes.

On the other side were arrayed the party designated as that of the Bonapartists, led on by our most honourable and most virtuous citizens, and numbering within its ranks the great body of the people; this party strove to withstand the impending resuscitation of the privileges and abuses of the old government, and which was to be effected only by the total subversion of our existing institutions.

The pure royalists endeavoured to annihilate the charter, which their opponents defended, and thus a strange contradiction took place. The royal charter had the royalists for its enemies, whilst its defenders were only found amongst those who were stigmatized as the adherents of Bonaparte.

Abortive attempts were made by the pure royalists to palliate the treachery of the government. They tried to persuade the people that the tranquillity and welfare of the nation depended but on the re-establishment of an absolute monarch, of a feudal aristocracy, and of all the trumpery of superstition. Such was the tendency of the publications which issued from the ministerial press, owing their birth to writers who had either sold themselves to the government, or who had denationalized themselves by their political intolerance. But it must not be supposed that liberty could remain in need of advocates.

Each of the earliest stages of the growth of the young government of royalty had been marked by obscure yet decisive symptoms of bad faith, not the less mischievous because they were restricted to signs, and symbols, and phrases. Instead of the constitution voted by the senate, and which the king had engaged to accept and ratify, he graciously granted and conceded a charter, by which he gave a new form to the government; and which, according to its tenor, emanated from the sovereign in the full and free exercise of his royal authority. The tricoloured cockade worn by Louis XVI. and which our armies had rendered illustrious, was exchanged for the white, though to the mind's eye the latter was seen drenched in the blood of the people. Louis took the title of Louis XVIII. King of France and Navarre, and he dated his proclamations and ordinances in the 19th year of his reign, and thus it was to be inferred, that the nation had been in a state of rebellion during five and twenty years. He had disdained to receive his crown from the will of the people, and rather chose to hold it by divine right and the good offices of the Prince Regent. These ungracious affronts wounded the national feelings, but no notice was taken of them at the time, because it was apprehended that angry recriminations might endanger the profit which had resulted from the important sacrifices to which we had consented for the public good. But when the government unveiled its deformity, the silence of the patriotic party was at end, and they attacked the government most unrelentingly. The editors of the Censeur were most conspicuous. Every abuse of power, every violation of the charter, was proclaimed to France by these young tribunes of the people; and the country was loud in applauding their zeal, their talents, and their courage. Other writers of a more lively class stung the emigrants to the quick by sarcasms and satire, and brought down the chastisement of contempt and ridicule upon those who had been spared by the gravity of the Censeur.

The nation also obtained a clear development of the anti-revolutionary conspiracy of the administration, from the "Memoir" of Carnot, and the pamphlets of Benjamin Constant. The undeniable facts, and the unwelcome truths which were brought forward and stated by these writers, apprized the people that their rights and liberties were in fearful danger.

A judicial blindness had fallen upon the ministers. All warnings, all lessons, all reproaches, were lost upon them. Far from being awed by public opinion, they thought they deserved high honour for defying it. The ministers had made up their mind. Deceived by the opinions which they had formed respecting the preponderance of their faction, they miscalculated the influence and resources of the partizans of the revolution. Confiding in their power, and in the fear inspired by their power, they thought it useless to maintain any further reserve; and that they could charge onwards to the end of the career which they had in view. Intoxicated by their ignorant enthusiasm, they insulted the nation in the person of each individual, whilst they encroached upon the rights which he valued most, and insulted him both in his interests and his feelings. The imperial guard was removed from Paris: the emigrants grudged the renown of these troops, and feared their patriotism. It was given out that the discontent evinced by the guard when the king came in, was the cause of the punishment which they received[8].—But had not the government called forth this discontent? Surely it was ungenerous to compel those heroes to walk as attendants in the triumph of a new master. Their grief and fidelity deserved not to be thus insulted. I then saw these honoured warriors. Haggard looks and sullen silence revealed their feelings. Absorbed by grief, they appeared to be insensible to the outward world. "Vive la Garde Impériale" was the shout of the pitying Parisians, who wished to cheer them. These salutations, which, perhaps, they despised, were unheeded. Submissive to their superiors, they obeyed the word of command which told them that they must march: they marched, and that was all.

Troops of the line replaced the imperial guards, who were drafted out of the capital with great expedition. Little time elapsed before the dissatisfaction of the new troops became manifest. The regiments were wholly disorganized; officers were thrust upon the soldiers, amongst whom they stood as complete strangers. In consequence of these changes the troops were put out of temper; and they became disgusted with service, because they were wearied by endless parades and reviews which took place, not to perfect them in their discipline, but for the instruction of their raw commanders. The government broke their spirit by affronting them: they were compelled to present arms to the king's body guard, whom they detested. The re-establishment of the "Maison du Roi" was opposed by the general feeling of the nation, and it particularly tended to rouse the jealousy and discontent of the garrison of Paris. The troops of the line and the national guards who were on duty at the Tuileries could not submit to acknowledge the "gardes du corps" as their superiors, and refused to present arms to them. The "gardes du corps" complained, and it was ordered that the troops of the line should salute them with military honours, or be punished. After this victory, the young "gardes du corps," who were proud of it, used to walk up and down before the sentinels, in order to force the latter to worship their epaulettes. It may easily be imagined how such childish insults, which were never checked, must have mortified the old soldiers of Napoleon: and we all know that the self-love of a Frenchman is not to be offended with impunity.

Self-love is the medium through which the soldier ascends into glory. When Napoleon earned immortal fame in Italy, he nourished and dignified this passion by addressing his soldiers in language breathing the lofty spirit of the heroic age, he rekindled the courage of his army, and every man became a conqueror. But the royalist officers sought to destroy all warlike sentiment by expressing their contempt for our national victories, by displaying the puffed insolence of birth and rank; and they lost the confidence and the esteem of the army which they were appointed to command.

Widely different, indeed, was the example which was set by the most exalted and most formidable of our enemies. It is needless to name him. This sovereign never tried to undervalue our glory: he was only happy when he could bear testimony again and again to the talents and the courage of the French nation. When he received our officers he did not treat them with that ill-concealed disdain, so often lavished on the conquered, but with the honest esteem inspired by valour; and with that delicacy, I would almost say respect, which is due to honourable misfortune. The subject of his discourse sometimes compelled him to allude to our reverses: but he never failed to allay the smart by lavishing his praises on the efforts which we had made to deprive him of victory. He seemed to be astonished that he had been able to withstand us.

How deeply were our warriors affected when they contrasted his chivalrous magnanimity with the endeavours of their royalist masters, who tried incessantly to poison the fond recollection of their former triumphs, and to deprive them of the only consolation which remained to them in the hour of affliction.

Whatever discontent might prevail amongst the troops, yet the greater part of the staff and regimental officers had transferred themselves to the Bourbons with cordial sincerity. Perhaps a few, who were less confident than the rest, still appeared distrustful and lukewarm; but they might have been easily won over, either by those sugared and alluring phrases which sound so sweetly when pronounced by royalty, or even by merely leaving them quiet until their resentment could cool of itself.

When Henry IV. recovered his throne, the bigoted partisans of the league, whom he had pardoned, continued still to threaten and revile him. It was suggested that he should punish them; but Henry said, "No,—we must wait, they are yet vexed." Those who were constantly invoking the memory of good king Henry, never sought to imitate his conduct. Instead of allowing time to our generals to get over their vexation, they embittered their temper by daily insults. Our officers were treated like ruffian bandits; they were branded as rebels, who were too happy if they obtained a pardon. Praise and favour fell only to the share of the army of Condé, the Vendeans, and the Chouans. The triumphal arches destined to eternize the exploits of our armies were menaced with sacrilegious ruin; and it was solemnly proposed to erect a monument to the memory of the Vendeans and the emigrants who fell at Quiberon.

Certainly our deluded brethren deserved to be regretted and mourned. Yet they had turned their weapons against the sacred bosom of their country. They were either the auxiliaries or the hirelings of our implacable enemies the English, and if honours were paid to them as illustrious victims, it was equivalent to a declaration that their conquerors were their murderers.

Our warriors had been graced with titles of nobility, bought with the blood which they had shed in the defence of the country. Their honours were treated with insolent scorn, and the ghost of Georges Cadoudal, a murderer in effect, and a traitor in intent, was ennobled by the gracious patent which was bestowed upon his father.

Georges in attempting the life of Napoleon had committed an act against all law, whether human or divine. If such a crime was decked out as a virtue, if signal rewards were allotted to the memory of the criminal, the government abetted assassination and regicide. The safety of Louis XVIII. and of every other monarch was compromised, and a sanction was given to the dangerous and antisocial doctrine which teaches that any individual may sit in judgment on the legitimacy of the title of the occupier of the throne, and then determine to murder his sovereign if he doubts the validity of his rights.

Other affronts exactly of the same complexion were offered to France and to the army. Titles, military commissions, and pensions, were showered, in La Vendée, upon the heads of such of the Chouans as were most celebrated for their cruelty[9], and these marks of favour were distributed amongst them in the presence of the victims of their rapine and ferocity.

The members of the ruling faction thought that they had not done enough in endeavouring to honour the French enemies of France at the expense of her defenders, and therefore they compassed the degradation and destruction of the institutions which reminded the people of the praises and the glory of our national armies.

In despite of the most solemn engagements the government robbed the legion of honour of its prerogatives. Then the ministerial papers hinted that henceforward the order of St. Louis was to be the only military order; and that the legion of honour was to be the reward of civil merit. The blow was aimed at the heart; the army shuddered, our marshals burned with indignation. The government was compelled to disclaim and abandon its intent.

Yet one sure method of debasing the legion of honour was completely in the power of government; they could make it cheap, and to this plan they resorted. Under Napoleon the Cross was never granted until it had been long and truly deserved: now it became the prey of meanness. The order was prostituted and cast to favourite underlings and intriguers, to whom it was distributed by caprice or bribery.

Our soldiers, who had purchased this distinction with their blood,— the magistrates, the functionaries, the learned, the manufacturers, who had received it as the reward of the services which they had rendered to the state, to the arts, to useful industry,—all were filled with consternation when they found themselves elbowed by a mean and worthless mob. Yielding to their honest pride, the greater part of our old legionaries refused to wear the insignia, which, instead of conferring distinction, could only confound them with men whom public opinion had branded and proscribed.

Success encouraged the government, and they did not stop. Richly endowed asylums for the daughters of the deceased members of the legion had been founded by the Emperor. Under the pretext of economy, of saving the annual sum of forty thousand francs, the ministers took the King by surprise, and hurried the Sovereign into the signature of an order for turning the orphans out of doors. Marshal Macdonald declared in vain that the old leaders of the army would never abandon the children of their companions, and that they were ready to defray the expense which was falsely assigned as the motive of the expulsion of the girls. Equally fruitless was the generosity of Madame Delchan, the matron of the establishment of Paris, who offered to continue its management without any assistance from the government, and to expend her entire fortune in the support of her pupils. Nor did the ministers pay the least attention to those who stated that the greater part of the children had neither friends nor relations, and that if they were thrown destitute upon the world, they would be inevitably consigned to misery or vice. No consideration could move the pity of the ministry.

But at length the indignation of the public found a voice in the Lower House, and the representatives of the people were about to remonstrate with the Sovereign. Ministers were disconcerted and abashed, and they abandoned their profligate enterprise.

This check, however, did not amend them. A few days afterwards they dissolved the military academies of St. Cyr and St. Germain, alleging that they were superfluous; and at the same moment the "École Royale Militaire" was re-established, "in order that the nobility of the kingdom might enjoy the advantages secured to them by the edict of January 1757."

By this impudent violation of the principles of the charter our representatives were again roused, and the ministers were again obliged to recede.

Irritated by these defeats, they sought revenge and actuated by an ill-judged hope of weakening the resisting obstacles, they dismissed a countless multitude of military officers, who were turned out of the army upon half pay, though their full pay had been formally guarantied. It must be acknowledged that the number of the officers of the imperial army was much greater than was required by the strength of the royal army; but as it was alleged that they were useless and expensive, it was not right to insult them in their misfortunes by ministerial profusion; for, at the same time, they saw the government granting rank and pay to a number of emigrants who were good for nothing in the army. The government raised six thousand "gardes du corps," troops of musketeers and light horse, "gendarmes de la garde," &c. who scandalized Paris, and disgusted the army by their new epaulettes, and their sumptuous and splendid uniforms. Lastly, the government, led on by its innovating madness, did not respect those veterans whom Death had spared on the field of battle. Without pitying age or infirmities, the ministers, using their accustomed pretext of economy, withdrew the benefactions which a grateful nation had bestowed upon two thousand five hundred of these objects of compassion.

Since the ministers did not dread giving public offence to the army, and in matters where the offence would be felt most acutely,—since they refused to recognize both its services and its rights, it may be easily supposed that the military were disgusted and oppressed when they appeared before the ministry as individuals. It is not intended to detail the complaints and accusations which then justly abounded; but one fact may be stated as giving a double illustration of the spirit which prevailed.

General Milhaud had distinguished himself in the course of our national wars, by success and bravery. At the time when France was invaded by the allies, he "covered himself with glory" at the head of a handful of dragoons, who cut a considerable corps of the enemy's troops entirely to pieces. This officer, in consequence of his rank, his standing, and his services, had been appointed a chevalier de St. Louis as a matter of right; but at the moment of his reception, the cross was taken from him with ignominy, because he had been so unfortunate as to vote for the death of the King twenty years before.

Louis XVIII., when he returned to France, had promised that he would not inquire into the votes which had been given against his august brother. This promise, which had been demanded from him, and which he ratified by his charter, could not be otherwise than a painful victory over the feelings of his heart. He must have grieved when he found himself under the necessity of admitting those judges into his court, who had condemned Louis XVI. to the scaffold, and to present them to the daughter of the murdered monarch. But still he had sworn not to avenge his death, and the oaths by which a monarch binds himself to his people should be inviolable.

All resentment was to be repressed. The voters had been pardoned, and therefore the government could not be justified in reviving the memory of their crime, and in bringing down vengeance and death upon their heads. A funeral veil ought to have been drawn over that period of our revolution, during which we were all equally misled or guilty. Besides, we must state plainly and distinctly, that the grief excited by the murder of Louis XVI., was not the true cause of the invectives with which the regicides were assailed by the emigrants. Unfortunately the effect produced at Coblentz by the trial and execution of the king, is too well known. If the errors of some of the men of the revolution were hunted out with so much malignant zeal, it was only for the purpose of coming to this result—that as the revolution was the work of crime, it was necessary to root out every thing which had proceeded from the revolution.

The insult to which General Milhaud was subjected, was therefore rather a political movement, than a punishment inflicted on an individual. In selecting Milhaud as the object of the first assault against the regicides, the government gave a proof of their want of tact; for if they wanted to render the regicides contemptible or odious, they should have avoided attacking an officer who had long since washed away the stains of the blood of his King, by imbruing himself in the blood of our enemies!

But whilst the military, from the highest to the lowest, were exposed to the persecution and tyranny of the prevailing faction, the magistracy, and the civil functionaries of the state, suffered no less from ill treatment and injustice. Commissioners had been despatched into the departments, even at the beginning of the new reign, "in order to consolidate the royal government, and to examine into the conduct of the public functionaries under existing circumstances;" that is to say, at the moment of the restoration of the Bourbons.

Such was the confidence which the nation placed in the promises of the King, that no jealousy was excited by this measure. On the contrary, people expected that great good would result from it, that party heat would be allayed, and public interest and opinion become more speedily united to the throne.

This pleasing illusion was soon dispelled. A great number of emigrants, who had just come in again, were appointed commissioners. Instead of listening to cool and experienced advisers, they gave themselves up to the priests and nobles who beset them, and who were neither moderate nor enlightened.

The middling classes, who, from their habitual intercourse with the lower orders, possess so great an influence over the body of the people, were considered by the commissioners as a rabble multitude of upstart "*roturiers.*" They treated the middling class with disdain and contempt. Deceived by the recollection of the excesses of the revolution, they fancied, that whoever could win the populace, became the ruler of the country. When money is not to be had, the surest way of getting over the multitude, is by appealing to its passions. They therefore announced, that they were sent to do justice to the people, to listen to their complaints, to reform abuses, and to abolish the "*droits réunis,*" and the conscription.

Meetings were announced in the villages and in the country towns. All persons of respectability kept away; but the populace, who are always delighted with uproar and novelty, crowded in. There was no end to the preposterous charges which were preferred against the magistrates, the prefects, the under-prefects, the mayors, the administrators of public affairs, the officers of revenue; in short, none of the depositaries of public authority were spared.

Instead of despising such accusations, or submitting them to an impartial inquiry, the commissioners hailed the popular clamour with transport. They triumphed in the tumult; they were overflowing with happiness at the fancied success of their efforts; they continued exclaiming with increasing joy, "that is right, Good People; the King is your father; these fellows are nothing but *canaille*; upon our word of honour, we will kick them out."

These promises were kept. The public officers and functionaries of all classes were gradually dismissed, and their places given to informers, or to the old nobility. As the common people cooled, they became undeceived, and it was found that they had gained neither in riches nor in loyalty. The commissioners, instead of adding as they expected to the popularity of the government, only helped to cry it down. The cause of royalty was compromised by the scenes of riot which they encouraged, and they degraded it by acts of injustice and oppression. The non-emigrant commissioners acted far otherwise. They knew how to value the lying declamations of the nobles, and of the mob whom the nobles had set on. From the different conduct pursued by each party, effects resulted which exhibited the most striking contrast. In one department the public functionaries retained their situations, in another they were disgraced and vituperated.

These scandalous proceedings excited the general indignation of the country. The government was universally blamed. The important task of instituting inquiries, which were to affect the honour and the civil existence of the most respectable characters, had been entrusted to emigrants who had lived amongst strangers during the best part of their lives. And these men, who knew nothing of the forms, the principles, or even the faults of the imperial government, were consequently wholly unable to appreciate the conduct, whether praiseworthy or blameable, of the depositaries of public authority.

The people discovered that they had been cheated, and that this measure, disguised by specious representations, was in truth adopted only for the purpose of more effectually displacing the old functionaries of the nation. And, lastly, it was evident that this general dismission would carry off those authorities who were the natural guardians of every individual who had taken a part in the revolution. And that all who were thus affected would be placed beneath the sway of their sworn enemies, the nobles, the priests, and their adherents.

Indications were given by the government that a "purification" of the courts of justice was in contemplation; and the public apprehension increased. The independence and immovability of the judges had been guaranteed to the nation, and this guarantee was certainly the most valuable of the rights which we had gained. But on account of its importance, the government were the more desirous of violating it.

When the proposed "purification" became known, our national magistrates trembled in their chairs, and they foresaw that they would be plucked out for the purpose of making way for the antiquated survivors of the courts of parliament.

The nation was alarmed, and protested against the measure. But the "purification" was not to be stopped in its swoop. The process began in the supreme tribunal of the kingdom, the Court of Cassation. And, to remove all doubts respecting the ulterior object of the government, it was officially announced that the *elimination*, disguised under the name of the "installation royale," had been deferred only for the purpose of "obtaining the information which was necessary to direct or decide the choice of the judges, and that it would take place successively in all the courts and tribunals of the kingdom."

The "installation" was felt to be not only a breach of faith, but an open conspiracy against the security of the person and property of the subject. We knew that the tribunals would now be filled with magistrates whose prejudices, principles, and interest, must be in perpetual hostility against our national laws, and that the new men would seek to elude or crush our juridical system. The royal magistrates, as it was but too evident, would be the relations, the friends, or the creatures of the nobility, the emigrants, and of all who claimed to be restored to their rights and privileges. Nor could we hope that judges so constituted would deal out impartial justice between the ci-devant privileged tribes, whom they would naturally consider as the victims of revolutionary principles, and the children of the revolution, who, according to the same mode of reasoning, they could not fail to consider as the oppressors and robbers of the privileged tribes.

The owners of national property were most alarmed by the approaching expulsion of the revolutionary judges. By the charter, the inviolability of their property had been guaranteed to them. But they had not forgotten that a violent debate arose on the "redaction" of this article; and that the ministers had been already accused on account of the obscurity of the clause, which they refused to correct into such words as might prevent all future quibbling and special pleading.

If the emigrants, the priesthood, and the nobility, did not scruple to express their hopes aloud that the sales of the national domains might be declared null and void, it was equally well known to the public that certain Great Personages entertained the same hopes in secret. Doubts respecting the legality, and, consequently, of the validity of the sales, were expressed in the ministerial journals; and various publications were industriously disseminated, in which the purchases were directly impugned. The authors of these works were favoured and protected[10]; and it was whispered that the Great Personages, to whom we have already alluded, had deliberated on the means of realizing their hopes. All these tokens of the times united in giving too reasonable a ground for the apprehensions entertained by the proprietors of the confiscated lands; and the disorganization of the tribunals was considered as a national calamity.

It is calculated that the individuals who are interested directly or indirectly either in the purchases of the national domains, or in the rights and liabilities arising out of them, amount in number to somewhat between nine and ten millions.

An opportunity offered itself when all the uneasiness felt by this integral portion of the population of France might have been removed. It was when the law; by which the emigrants recovered possession of such part of their property as had not been alienated, came under consideration. It was natural to suppose that the administration would take advantage of the capability of the proceeding, in order to revive the confidence of the public, and to renew the guarantee of the charter. Such was not their conduct. On the contrary, M. Ferrand, the government orator, one of the men who did most mischief to the King and the kingdom, abandoned himself—we borrow the expression of the reporter of the committee—to all the acrimony of his passions, and all the profligacy of his principles. His fury could only be equalled by his folly. He did not scruple to maintain, in the midst of the representatives of the nation, that the emigrants had the greatest right to claim the justice and favour of the royal government, because they alone had not wandered from the righteous path. And starting with this position, he represented the forfeiture and sale of their property, not as the justifiable acts of a legislative body, but as revolutionary outrages and robberies which the nation ought to hasten to make good.

The Chamber of Deputies passed their censure upon the inflammatory doctrines and language of the royalist orator, and expunged the word "restitution" from the law. It had not been inserted without design, for "restitution" supposes a previous robbery, and the emigrants had not been robbed of the property: it had been confiscated by virtue of a law sanctioned by the King; and which law was only a new application of the system of confiscation created and followed up by the King's predecessors.

Without travelling into more remote periods, we may ask if it was not with the spoils of the victims who had been sacrificed to the murderous policy of Richelieu, and the religious intolerance of Louis XIV., that the first families had been enriched? And who can tell whether the lands which the emigrants reclaimed with so much pride and bitterness, were not the same which their ancestors had received without a blush from the bloody hands of Richelieu and Louis?

It must be confessed that the unalterable fidelity of a certain number amongst the emigrants bound the royal government to reward their fidelity and to alleviate their misfortunes. But all had not an equal right to the affection and gratitude of the King. If some had generously sacrificed their fortunes and their country in the cause of royalty, yet others only fled from France because they wished to escape their creditors[11], and thought that in strange countries they might find dupes to feed upon, and thus exist upon swindling resources to which they could no longer resort with impunity at home.

It was therefore necessary to separate the first class of emigrants from the last; and after establishing this distinction, the government should have made a fair appeal to the justice and generosity of the nation. Frenchmen, who yield so readily to every dignified sentiment, would not have allowed the faithful and virtuous servants of their King to languish in poverty. We may appeal to the universal assent which was given to the proposal[12] made by the marshal duke of Tarentum, that ten millions of francs should be annually appropriated for the indemnification of the emigrants who had been deprived of their property, and of the soldiers who had lost their "dotations."

But the government party should not have attempted to assist the emigrants by resorting to means offensive to the nation, and derogatory to the charter. And, above all, they should not have puffed up the emigrants with proud and silly hopes. If they had been left to themselves, they would have fallen in with the purchasers of their property, they would have treated for an amicable settlement of their claims, and they would have regained possession of their hereditary estates without jarring and without scandal.

The partiality which was shown towards the emigrants on all occasions produced another evil of still greater extent. It contributed, even more than the efforts of disaffection, in persuading the peasantry that the government wished to chain them again to the soil, and to render them once more the tributaries both of the nobility and of the priesthood.

The revolution has taught the countryman to know that he is somebody in the state. After the revolution the peasants became rich, and they were delivered from the double vassalage of former days, when they crouched before the priest and the lord: therefore they could not think of any alteration without horror. Day after day they heard or they read (in France every body reads now,) that the government intended to restore the *"ancien régime."* And the restoration of the *"ancien régime"* was interpreted by them, as well as by many others, to mean the restoration of tithes, vassalage, and feudal rights. They were confirmed in their dangerous and disquieting opinion by the outrageous claims of the emigrants, and the declamations of the priests. It was to no purpose that the government tried to re-assure them. They had been already deceived and it seldom happens that you can catch a French peasant twice in the same snare. The abolition of the conscription had been promised, and the old code was continued in force with all its harshness, and still the refractory conscripts were sent away in chains, whilst fines were imposed upon their families. The abolition of the *"droits réunis"* had also been promised, and they were not only levied with greater rigour and harshness than before, but even some of these imposts had been greatly increased.

Such was the fatality which influenced all the actions of the government, that all proceedings which in themselves were simple and reasonable, became venomous and corrupted when conducted by the ministry, and only added to the general disorder and discontent, instead of producing the good effects which they might have been justly expected to produce.

The discontent of the people, the inevitable result of the injuries inflicted on the feelings and interests of individuals[13], was increased by the open infringement of the rights of the people, although these rights were secured to the country by a compact which seemed to be inviolable.

Liberty of conscience had been promised by the charter, and this liberty was immediately annihilated. An ordonnance was issued by the police[14], which revived regulations enacted in an age of intolerance, for enforcing the strict and universal observance of the Lord's day, and the festivals of the church. Napoleon, anxious to preserve a strict neutrality between the catholics and the protestants, prohibited the religious processions of the former in all towns containing places of worship belonging to the latter communion. His prohibition was removed, and the catholic priesthood exulted in their processions, in which they marched in triumph. They ought to have tranquillized the apprehensions of their opponents, and to have edified the faithful by humility, or at least by feigning humility; but they disdained to conciliate the public, whom they scandalized by their pride and irritated by their violence[15].

The imagination of the priests became fired by the victory which they supposed they had gained. They dreamt that they were in full possession of their ancient power; and they wished immediately to revive it according to their ancient fashion. An actress belonging to the Theatre Français died without being absolved, and without suspecting that it was necessary to be absolved, from the excommunication which had been formerly fulminated against stage players; and which, as every body knows, deprived Moliere of Christian burial.

Following the same precedents, the clergy would not allow the rites of sepulture to the actress in question. The populace, who followed the funeral out of curiosity, learnt the affront which was thus offered to her remains. Transported by sudden indignation, they rushed to the hearse, and dragged it onwards. The doors of the interdicted church were burst open in a moment. They called for a priest; no priest appeared. The tumult augmented. The church and the neighbouring streets resounded with the groans and threats of ten thousand persons. Their agitation became more violent, and there was no possibility of foreseeing where the effervescence of popular feeling would stop, when a messenger arrived from the court, who ordered, in the name of the King, that the funeral should proceed.

The accounts of this event, and the comments to which it gave rise, excited the most lively interest in Paris and throughout France: nor did it fail to give the greatest pleasure to the enemies of religion. The friends of public decency and good order accused the government of encouraging the alarming progress of sacerdotal despotism. It was particularly in the smaller towns, and in the country, that the priests behaved with the most blamable audacity, abusing the privilege of speech which had been restored to them[16]. The pulpit became a tribunal from whence they pronounced sentence of present infamy, with the reversion of eternal damnation, upon all who refused to participate in their opinions and bigotry. Making common cause with the emigrants, they employed hints, inuendoes, insinuations, arguments, promises, and threats of every species, for the purpose of compelling the owners of the national property to yield up their lands, and of leading the wretched peasantry again beneath the tyrant yokes of feudality and superstition.

During the revolution, the priesthood had betrayed its real character. Contempt had fallen on the clergy, and it was out of the power of the government to invest them suddenly with the salutary influence which they had lost. This influence ought to be gained by wise and prudent conduct, by active and impartial benevolence, by the practice of sacerdotal virtues. It cannot be gained by ordonnances of police, by abuse, by violence, by mumming processions, which, in our times, are out of character and ridiculous.

By the charter the liberty of the press had been guarantied as well as the liberty of public worship; yet every day innumerable publications were seized or suppressed contrary to the laws. M. Durbach, a deputy who never equivocated with his conscience or yielded to danger, complained on this subject in the chamber: the opinion of the house went along with him; and the government, pretending to yield to the feeling of the deputies, presented a bill to the chambers through the medium of M. de Montesquiou, which, instead of delivering the press from its slavery, gave full establishment to the censorship, and legalized the tyranny which had been exercised over the press by mere force under the former government.

Benjamin Constant attacked the bill with vigour: the same side was taken by the public journals, and by all public writers; but there was no possibility of putting M. de Montesquiou out of countenance. It was demonstrated to him that his law would wholly destroy the liberty of the press. By holding the charter before his eyes, the advocates of public rights proved that the charter only declared that the licence of the press was to be restrained, and that his bill was therefore radically unconstitutional, because the preliminary censorship was not intended to restrain abuses, but to prevent their taking place. Montesquiou answered gravely, that the persons with whom such objections originated did not understand French; that the words *"prévenir"* and *"réprimer"* were perfectly synonymous: and that the bill, instead of being offensive or unconstitutional, contained a most complete and a most liberal development of the clause in the charter.

This unparalleled endeavour of Montesquiou, who persuaded himself that he could convince an assembly of Frenchmen that they did not understand their own language, was justly considered by the chamber as a matchless specimen of impudence and folly. Lexicographical subtleties were employed with bitter mockery for the purpose of destroying a public right, consecrated by the constitutional compact. Never had insolence and bad faith been displayed so prominently: Raynouard, the reporter of the committee, exclaimed in the language of grief and indignation, "Minister of our King, confess, at least, that your law is contrary to the constitution, since you cannot refute the evidence adduced against it: your obstinacy in contesting such an indisputable truth would not then inspire us with such just alarms."

The law was ultimately adopted by both chambers; ministerial influence triumphed over reason, and rased the most important bulwark of the rights guarantied to the nation. The result of the conflict produced the most lively sensation. No man who was capable of forethought and reasoning could remain undisturbed. Notwithstanding the patriotism of Dupont (of the department of the Eure), of Raynouard, of Durbach, of Bedoch, of Flaugergues, it was seen too clearly that the chamber of deputies could not oppose any effectual obstacle to the despotic and anti-constitutional plans of the government; and that the ministers would have full power, whenever they thought proper, to interpret the clauses of the charter according to their own way, and to rob the French nation of the few rights which it yet might promise to them. "By means of such interpretations," the people said, "the senate sacrificed the independence of the nation to Napoleon. But at least the imperial despotism assumed a character by which it was justified and ennobled. It tended to render our nation the greatest nation in the world; but the despotism which awaits us has no other accompaniment but bad faith, and no other end except the degradation and slavery of France."

By such reflections, the suspicion and disgust and aversion inspired by the government, were excited to the utmost pitch. The public feeling did not stop there: the French people are naturally inconstant in their opinions and sentiments; and their former prejudices against Napoleon were changed into transports of admiration. France, under the royal government, was humiliated, disorganized, and degenerate; and they contrasted the present state of the country with the influence, the strength, the compactness, which it enjoyed under the reign of Napoleon; and He, who had lately been cursed as the root of all evil, now appeared to be the greatest of men, and the greatest of heroes, though in misfortune.

The government knew that Napoleon was again admired by the people, and that they regretted his loss. To counteract these sentiments, coarse and vulgar caricatures were exposed to the eyes of the populace; and his person and his character became the theme of false and scandalous libels published under the direction of the ministry. No effect was produced. The mob looked at the caricatures with a smile of contempt; and the actions of Napoleon, which, under his reign, excited the greatest censure and disapprobation, now found the most zealous apologists and defenders.

If Napoleon was accused of having overthrown the republican government, and enslaved the country by the revolution of the 18th Brumaire, they answered[17]:—"At that era, anarchy, emboldened by the misfortunes of the country, could only be repressed by victory. Civil war had been organized in twenty departments; insurrections had taken place in many, rapine infected them all; robbery and murder took place with impunity on many of the principal high roads. Two dreadful laws, the law of the hostages, and that of the forced loans, occasioned greater evils than they could cure. No nation had ever existed in which the finances of the state were in equal confusion; and a succession of partial bankruptcies prolonged the opprobrium of the general bankruptcy of the country. The money of the public was robbed whilst in transit on the high roads. Robbers even carried it off from the houses of the receivers, and the deficiency could not be made good by the most violent exactions. The jacobins were on the point of recommencing their reign of terror. The royalists had recourse without scruple to all the measures which might enable them to satiate their revenge; and the peaceable friends of the law were placed between the conflicting parties in a state of disgraceful weakness and neutrality. Such was the desperate situation of France when Napoleon seized the helm of the state. Instead of imputing the slavery of the country to him, he ought to have been blessed; for he delivered us from the spoliations, the murders, and the tyranny which were consequent upon the reign of anarchy and terror."

Was it maintained that Napoleon had reigned despotically? They held that this accusation was unjust; and they had recourse to the following reasoning. "Anarchy was silenced by Napoleon." It became necessary, that order should take the place of disorder; that the authority of one should be substituted for the authority of all. Parties were to be restrained within the bound of moderation; traitors were to be annihilated. It was necessary to curb the prejudices of the nobility, and the revolutionary habits and manners of the jacobins. This great work could not be accomplished, without engaging in a conflict against individual interests and opinions. Napoleon was considered as a despot; this was inevitable. Whenever the existing polity of a state has been totally subverted, he who first raises the edifice of society from its ruins, is necessarily accused of despotism, because apparently he has no other rule except his own will. Nor must we forget that Napoleon had been accustomed to command implicit obedience in the camp. He retained his military attitude on the throne. He usually addressed his courtiers, his connexions, and his ministers, in the tone which he had formerly adopted when speaking to his soldiers or their generals[18]. An appearance of despotism was certainly given to his way of reigning and commanding, by such language which is seldom heard in civil society. And in almost all cases, appearance is taken for reality.

At first the imperious tone adopted by Napoleon was blamed, next it was admired. He soon employed it in his intercourse with foreign ambassadors, with foreign sovereigns. The wily forms of ancient diplomacy were discarded. Napoleon did not negociate; he issued his orders. With one hand he brandished his victorious sword; in the other he held crowns and sceptres. He bade the sovereigns of Europe make their choice; he offered his friendship or his hatred, kingdoms or blows. The monarchs who stood before his throne were taught wisdom by experience. They knew that Napoleon could reward and punish; they crowded into the ranks of his allies; and they consoled themselves for their weakness, by crying out upon his tyranny[19].

When these causes were united, they aided in persuading the world that Napoleon was really a despot. For, as Montesquieu observes, there are some things which we believe at last, merely because we hear them continually repeated. But if the government of Napoleon is considered impartially, we shall feel convinced, that the despotism attributed to him existed rather in words and forms, than in deeds. Let the acts of his reign be scrutinized, and none will be found impressed with the character of real despotism; that is to say, of despotism founded on the mere arbitrary will and pleasure of the prince. On the contrary, they all prove that the interest and aggrandizement of France entered alone into the views of Napoleon, and that instead of being under a tyrannical government, the people never enjoyed the benefits of distributive justice with greater equality, and were never protected more completely against the oppressions of public functionaries, and of the higher ranks. He may, perhaps, be censured for having violated certain laws, for violations in which the senate and the representatives of the people were his accomplices. But laws are only binding upon sovereigns in the ordinary course of things, and the most rigid writers on the law of nations acknowledge this principle. When extraordinary and unforeseen circumstances take place, it is the duty of the sovereign to be above the law. In order to judge fairly of the actions of a monarch, we must not consider them separately. Many an action which, if taken singly, appears unjustifiable or hateful, loses that character when viewed as one of the series of events from which it arose, as a connecting link in the political chain of which it forms a part. Neither should the conduct of a sovereign be judged according to the principles of natural equity. In the estimation of those, upon whom the task of ruling nations has devolved, necessity and the public safety ought to know no law. Every apprehension of injuring private interest vanishes, and must ever vanish, before state considerations.

"After all," continued they, "the real point at issue is, not whether the government of Napoleon was more or less despotic; but whether it was such as was required by the character of his people and of his times,—such as it needed to be, in order that France might become tranquil, happy, and powerful." Now it is impossible to deny but that, during the reign of Napoleon, the interior of France enjoyed an unruffled calm, and that the ascendancy of his genius bestowed upon the country a degree of power and prosperity, which it never attained before, and which probably it will never possess again.

Was the emperor taxed with boundless ambition? Were the calamities of Spain and Russia laid to his charge?—his indefatigable apologists found a ready answer.—The Spanish war, instead of being an unjust aggression, was an enterprise guided by the soundest political talent. It had been provoked by the wavering treachery of that allied government, which, in spite of its engagements, was secretly negociating with the English; and which, yielding to their instigations, had endeavoured to take advantage of our difficulties and of the absence of our armies, in order to invade our territory, and to become a sharer in the plots of our enemies.

The detention of Ferdinand ceased to be an odious breach of faith. It resulted necessarily from his duplicity, his parricidal projects, and his English connexions. The nomination of Joseph as King of Spain and the Indies, had been universally attributed to the excessive vanity of Napoleon, who, as it was supposed, was determined to crop a crown upon the head of every member of the imperial family. But now opinion changed. King Joseph's promotion was felt to have been caused by the necessity of placing Spain for ever out of the reach of English influence. Had not Napoleon allowed the Cortes of Spain to elect their monarch of their own uncontrolled authority? Had he not said to them in public, "Dispose of the throne. Little do I care whether the king of Spain is called Ferdinand, or whether he is called Joseph; let him only be the ally of France, and the enemy of England[20]?"

It was still more easy to justify the Russian war. A Quixotic love of the marvellous was no longer supposed to be the passion which excited it. In making war against Russia, he was actuated by the desire of avenging the injuries which that power had occasioned to France, at the moment when the Russian government again opened its ports to the English, thus snatching from the nation the reward of the sacrifices which we had made for the establishment and consolidation of the continental blockade, — of that universal barrier which made England and her thousand vessels tremble!

The invasion of Germany was no longer the effect of Napoleon's insatiate thirst of power and glory[21]. It was seen, that there was no other sure method, by which the English, the irreconcilable enemies of France, could be deprived of their fatal continental influence, by which they could be compelled to abandon the empire of the seas. In short, Napoleon was only inflicting a salutary and equitable punishment, deserved by those sovereigns of all sizes. After having implored or obtained the alliance of Napoleon, and after having ratified the bond by engagements and promises upon which he generously relied, they compelled him to take up arms, in order to prevent them from receiving the agents of England into their cabinets, and her merchandizes into their ports.

Thus the partisans of Napoleon invented arguments by which they palliated his faults and justified his errors. No objection, no reproach was left without its answer. After defending him against his accusers they became his advocates; and, turning to the fairer pages of his history, their praises knew no bounds; these eulogiums were certainly more just, and, perhaps, more sincere.

"Napoleon," said they, "had all the great qualities of the greatest monarchs, whilst he was exempted from their vices. Napoleon was not stained by the lechery of Cæsar, nor by the drunkenness of Alexander, nor by the cruelty of Charlemagne."

At an age when others scarcely start in life, his years were outnumbered by his victories; and the kings of Europe, conquered by his sword or subjugated by his genius, cowered before the imperial eagle.

In France, when aggrandized by the conquests of Napoleon, the empire of ancient Rome was re-produced before the astonished world. The French name, tarnished by the crimes of the revolution, regained its ancient honour and its mastery. The nation was feared, admired, and respected by the entire universe.

Philosophy graced Napoleon no less than warlike prowess. After he had covered the nation with glory by his victories, he was willing to insure our welfare by his laws. He bestowed upon us that immortal code of jurisprudence which invested him with the title of the legislator of France, a title to which our former kings had aspired in vain. He organised that admirable system of finance and administration, which their subjects, groaning under misrule, implored but without effect.

Still he had not accomplished enough to satisfy his noble and beneficent ardour. Arts, sciences, and industry were to flourish in our country. The munificent aids[22] which were granted by Napoleon, created the thousands and thousands of manufactories from whence proceeded those finished works of skill and labour which became the pride of the French, and the despair and ruin of foreign nations. The sons of Apollo[23], on whom he lavished his gifts and favours, seized the crayon, the compass, and the chisel. Paris became a second Athens, when adorned by the wonders of art to which his munificence gave birth. We then saw the venerable Louvre rise, as by enchantment, from its deserted ruins; the palaces of our Kings became more gorgeous; the temples of the arts were enriched by productions which rivalled the relics of antiquity; our native land brought forth those establishments so proudly useful to the public, and those monuments destined to transmit the recollections of our fame and glory to the most distant posterity.

At the same moment his sovereign will guided the hands which curbed the waves of the ocean, and caused them to roll over a new abyss. He directed those labours which substituted wide harbours, superb dock-yards, and fertilizing canals, in the place of desert shores and pestilential marshes, restoring commerce and existence to the innumerable inhabitants of the sea coast, and of the banks of the Scheld and the Somme. At the same moment his voice created those Roman highways, branching through all parts of France, and Germany, and Italy, equally useful and majestic, and which afforded to the inhabitants of those countries means equally speedy and secure of communicating with each other, and of exchanging the products of their industry: and never will the friend or even the enemy of Napoleon cross the summits of the Alps, or ascend their craggy sides, without venerating the magnanimous sovereign, who, anxious to guide the steps and protect the life of the traveller, has enclosed the precipice, chained the torrent, and linked the great mountains of the earth, which during so many ages have braved the might of man and time. When future ages shall gather up in memory the glorious and transcendent deeds of Napoleon; when they shall number the blessings which he dispensed, and the victories which he gained, never will they believe that one man can have worked such miracles in so short a period. They will rather fancy that the historian was playing with the credulity of posterity, that he culled out all the great deeds performed by successive generations of the greatest men during an infinite series of ages, and that he has attributed them all to his ideal hero.

The soldiers who had bled beneath the banners of Napoleon would not listen in silence to the praises which others bestowed upon his name. His foreign conquests, which even they had lately considered as the causes of our misfortunes, became again the sources of inexhaustible admiration.

They recollected that Napoleon had ruled as the master of Madrid, of Lisbon, of Munich, of Warsaw, of Hamburgh, of Berlin, of Vienna, of Milan, of Amsterdam, of Rome, of Moscow, of Cairo.

Some recalled the memory of the day of Lodi. They saw him standing on the bridge re-animating his dispirited followers, defying danger and death whilst he waved the national flag, and drove the enemy from their entrenchments, and blasted their glory. Others pointed him out whilst crossing the perpetual snows and yawning chasms of Mount St. Bernard, and then victorious on the plains of Marengo, where he won that battle which insured the peace and glory of the country.

Austerlitz had its chroniclers, who described Napoleon as he fell with the rapidity and violence of the thunderbolt on the battalions of the Austrian and the Russian, and when he afforded to those trembling monarchs an example of magnanimity which they knew not how to imitate when generosity became their duty. Nor did his enthusiastic advocates omit the field of Jena, where his victorious ensigns chased the flying troops of Frederic, who, deceived by their recollections, yet held themselves to be the paragons of military worth. They retraced his paths amidst the burning sands of Egypt, amidst the icy wastes of Muscovy; and in either region Napoleon supported fire and frost without ostentation, and taught resignation and endurance to his soldiers by his unshaken constancy.

More recent and more painful victories contributed equally to endear him. They saw Napoleon in Champagne, when his veteran army scarcely equalled one of the numerous divisions of the enemy. At the head of his scanty troops he watched, and avoided, and surprised the Austrians, the Russians, and the Prussians: wounding them on all sides by his victorious weapons, and with such promptitude, that he seemed to have bestowed wings upon iron and death. They placed him at Arcis sur Aube, advancing before his squadrons, and rushing forward to meet the balls and bullets of the enemy; for he sought to sacrifice on the field of battle that life, which he foresaw he could no longer dedicate on the throne, to the glory and prosperity of the nation.

In short, generals, officers, and soldiers, all vied with each other in calling to mind the marches, the sieges, the conflicts, the attacks, the days, which had immortalized their general[24]; and is there a heart amongst us which does not beat higher at these recollections?

The sentiments thus awakening in favour of Napoleon were cherished by his friends, and by all those who, wearied of the Bourbons or discontented with their government, now wished for his return. His name, which lately we had scarcely dared to utter, was now in every mouth, his image in every mind. The nation began to regret the Emperor, then they longed for him; and every one was impressed by a secret presentiment that these expectations would soon be realized.

Whilst this formidable revulsion of opinion was increasing and appearing throughout the kingdom, it was scarcely heeded by the ministry, the court, and the emigrants, who reposed with complacent security on the volcano which they had kindled, and without entertaining the slightest apprehension of the approaching explosion.

"If they wish to go out of the kingdom," said M. de Chateaubriand, when alluding to the partisans of the Emperor, "if they wish to return again, to receive or despatch letters, to send expresses, to make proposals, to circulate false intelligence, and even to distribute bribes, to assemble in secret or in public, to menace, to disseminate libels, in short, to conspire against the government,—they are at liberty to do their worst. The royal government, which began but eight months ago, now rests upon so sure a basis, that, were it now to be obstinate in repeating folly after folly, it would hold good in spite of all its errors."

This infatuation, however, soon diminished. Without understanding the full extent of the evil, the government ascertained that the army and the nation were agitated and discontented, and they deliberated on the methods which it would be proper to employ, not for the purpose of conciliation, but for enforcing silence.

Acquainted with the uneasiness of the government, certain frantic Chouans gave out that it was full time to despatch the Bonapartists. One chieftain, celebrated in the annals of La Vendée, was even so audacious as to declare to general Ex..... that he only waited for the arrival of his faithful Vendeans, and then he would fall upon the Jacobins.

The news of this massacre soon reached the ears of the intended victims. Some quitted Paris, others armed themselves, and prepared to sell their lives as dearly as they could. It is said that the government became acquainted with the bloody conspiracy of the Chouans, and that they relieved France and the world from the spectacle of another St. Bartholomew's day.

This intended massacre (I have never been able to believe in it,) persuaded the revolutionists that they could expect neither respite nor mercy from the royalists, and that one of the two parties would be compelled to destroy the other. The soldiers of Napoleon began to unite, and to make themselves ready. The ministers were anxious to disperse these assemblages, which gave them uneasiness, orders were issued, by which all officers, whether of the staff or regimental, were prohibited from residing at Paris without permission; and all who were not Parisians by birth were ordered to return to their native provinces. This measure increased the exasperation of the military, and it did not diminish the danger. The reduced officers, instead of conforming to the order, encouraged each other in disobedience. According to the regulations of the war department, their contumacious residence at Paris would subject them to the loss of their half-pay; and many of them, though in poverty, preferred independence to submission. The ministers were irritated by this resistance, and they determined to make an example. It happened that a letter of congratulation which General Excelmans addressed to his former sovereign, the king of Naples, was intercepted. This opportunity was gladly seized by the new Minister at war[25]. He put the General on the half-pay list, and ordered him to retire immediately, and until further orders, to the distance of sixty leagues from Paris. Excelmans maintained that the Minister at war had no right to remove an officer, not being in active service, from his domicile; and he would not go: upon this he was immediately taken into custody. It was pretended that he had been guilty of a traitorous intercourse with the enemies of the King, and that he was also guilty of disobedience to his Majesty's orders. The government expected that this blow would produce the best possible effect; but it recoiled against them: Excelmans was known to all France; he was valued as one of her bravest and most estimable children. The spite and hatred of the ministers had loaded him with accusations; but his alleged treasons, far from depriving him of public esteem and public affection, only endeared him to his companions in arms, and to the nation at large.

Excelmans was brought to trial, and the court acquitted him[26]. The council of war, by sanctioning the disobedience of the General, declared that the government did not possess that authority over reduced officers which they had assumed; and from this moment the government was ruined. The decision by which the half-pay military were enfranchised, and which left them at liberty to brave the commands of the government, was a shock which beat the royal authority to the ground.

Here I shall stop. It would be of no further use to lengthen the history and the investigation of the absurd tyranny of the government. If we trace the progress of the principles successively enounced by the ministry, and the actions of which they were the authors, we shall see that they had formed and executed the project of re-establishing the old monarchy, and of overturning the constitutional government either by artifice or by main force. The royal charter was spurned by them, and they trampled without scruple on the civil and political rights which it consecrated. Every guarantee given to the army, the magistracy, the public functionaries, or the nation, was forgotten, attacked, or violated. Our national glory was insulted; public feeling was wounded. The manners and customs and opinions of the new era were all treated with harshness: all ranks and classes of citizens experienced those vexations which filled them with discontent. By injustice and bad faith the government deprived the King of our confidence and love, and caused the restoration of the Emperor to become the hope of the nation. In spite of the obstacles experienced by the ministry, in spite of the affronts to which they had been subjected, in spite of the retrograde steps which they had been compelled to take, they still clung to the baneful system which they had fostered; and, bigoted to these plans, they continued to persevere in those errors which recalled Napoleon from his exile, just as Napoleon persevered in the errors which recalled the Bourbons back from theirs.

But whilst the storm was gathering in France, how was Napoleon employed? Ambition had taken flight, and he was seen to prefer a life of unostentatious retirement to all his former grandeurs. Repose had greater charms for him than the noble turmoil of war; and his genius, no longer teeming with meditation, yielded to the pleasures of retirement. The study of botany, the cares of his household, the plantations which he had made, and those which he was still planning, beguiled his hours[27]; and, like the Roman Diocletian, he might have said to those who suspected that he longed in secret after the throne, "Come and see me in my retirement: I will show you the gardens which I have planted, and you will talk no more to me about the empire."

Napoleon, during the early part of his retirement in Elba, felt only a vague desire of reigning. Grieved by the miseries of France, the country which he loved so truly, wearied by the vicissitudes of fortune, disgusted with mankind, he feared that, if he attempted to seize the sceptre again, he should involve France and himself in new troubles; and, without abandoning his expectation of re-ascending the throne, he resolved to allow his resolutions to be guided by futurity.

The turn taken by public affairs soon roused the Emperor from this state of indifference and hesitation. At first he hoped, and I have heard him say so, that the Bourbons, instructed by adversity, would confer liberty and happiness upon the nation. But when he witnessed the power which was bestowed upon the priesthood, the emigrants, and the courtiers, he foresaw that the very same causes which had produced the first revolution, would soon occasion a second. From that period he watched the continent; nor did he lose sight, even for a moment, of the congress, or of France, or of the Bourbons. He could tell the talents[28], the principles, the vices, and the virtues of all those who had acquired the confidence of Louis XVIII, either by intrusion or by favour. He could measure the degrees of influence which each was capable of acquiring and exercising, and he calculated beforehand on the errors which they would inevitably induce his docile successor to commit.

Napoleon now employed himself again in reading the public journals of France and of foreign countries; he read assiduously all periodical works of a political tendency; he studied these productions; he investigated them with acuteness, and he could well divine the meaning of a writer who was compelled to be silent and conjecture the nature of intelligence which an editor was forced to suppress.

Strangers of distinction, and particularly the English, were received by Napoleon with affability and kindness, and he used to talk freely with his visitors on public affairs. He knew how to draw them out, and to lead them to expatiate on points which he wished to penetrate; and he seldom failed to obtain much useful information from those interviews. By these simple methods Napoleon obtained a correct idea of the events which were taking place on the continent: he was too well acquainted with revolutions not to be sensible that the sway of events would open the gates of France, and admit him; and he was too wary to enter into a private correspondence with his partisans, when any accident might have revealed his secret wishes, and have afforded a pretext to his enemies for attacking his independence and his liberty.

Napoleon thus waited in silence till the fated time of his re-appearance in France should arrive, when a French Officer[29], disguised as a sailor, disembarked at Porto Ferrajo.

Some few days before this Officer set out to join the army in the year 1815, he gave over to me the manuscript narrative of his voyage to the Isle of Elba. "To you," added he, "I deliver my history, which is also that of the revolution of the 20th of March. As the Emperor, when regaining his throne, did not think fit to speak of me, I was therefore bound to be silent; but I am as eager to live in the memory of after-ages as he can possibly be[30]. It is my wish that posterity may learn, that I too shared in the glorious enterprise of subverting the Bourbon government, and of bringing back the Emperor. My mind misgives me. I have a presentiment that I shall die in this campaign. Keep my manuscript, and promise to publish it when the time shall arrive." I gave my word accordingly; and the forebodings of my friend were realised, for he was killed at Waterloo.

I now fulfil my promise. I have not dared to make any alterations in the narrative: if I had, I should have felt that I was betraying the wishes of my friend. But I have suppressed the names of the parties concerned, and I have expunged some passages, in which the Bourbon family were treated with disrespect.

HISTORY OF THE REVOLUTION
OF THE 20th OF MARCH.

When Napoleon resigned his crown, I broke my sword. I swore that I never more would use it in the service of France, or of the new Sovereign of the nation. But the generous farewell of the Emperor could not fail to affect me; and, conquered by the irresistible influence which the love of glory and of our native land exercises upon a French soldier, I soon awoke to more praiseworthy and more tempered feelings. My recollections faded, my regrets were softened, and I aspired most sincerely to the honour of being again useful to my country, and to my country's King.

At first the character which I had earned, procured for me the most gratifying reception. Dazzling prospects were held out to me. I believed that I was treated with sincerity. This error was of short duration. Deceived and baffled, I now understood that they were cheating the army and myself. They affected to honour us in the aggregate, because they were afraid of us; and they insulted us individually, in conformity to their systematic hated. My character was too proud to allow me to bear with the insults and the contempt which they wished to pour out upon me. I resigned my commission. France and her government sickened me; but my military enthusiasm had not abated. I thought that I should be recollected by the Emperor, who had distinguished me in the field of battle; and that he would deign to grant that boon which was dearest to my heart; that he would allow me to live and die in his service. I therefore made up my mind to visit the isle of Elba.

Just, however, as I was on the point of departing, I was stopped by a sudden thought. Abandoned, betrayed, and denied, by men whom he has heaped with rewards and honours, will the Emperor really believe that I am really attached to him? Perhaps he will even suspect that I am a spy, and that the Bourbons have sent me to watch his words and actions. I was still in relation with those persons who had formerly enjoyed the confidence of the Emperor. Since the restoration, their conduct had been marked by frankness and honesty. Their feelings led them to be faithful to the person of Napoleon; their patriotism and their principles led them to be devoted to his cause; and they had not sought to conceal either their fidelity or their devotion. Many efforts had been made to gain them over to the royal party, but they had continued immoveable. I therefore thought, that whatever recommendation I could obtain from any one of the persons in question, would protect me from the suspicions of the Emperor; and to them I therefore confided my plans and the causes of my uneasiness, without hesitation or reserve.

The first, and the second, to whom I thus applied, severally assured me that they took the most lively interest in the undertaking, and they betrayed the most tender anxiety for its result. They desired me to express to the Emperor the grief which his loss had occasioned to them, and their hopes of seeing him once more; but both were afraid to compromise themselves by writing to him, and I quitted them without having obtained my wishes. Then I proceeded to the third, whom I shall call Monsieur X. We had known each other in those eventful periods when men are put to the test, and he had kindly formed and retained a favourable opinion of my character and courage. I unveiled my projects and my fears. "Your fears," answered he, "are well founded. The Emperor will distrust you, and probably he will not allow you to continue with him. My recommendation would, without doubt, be of great utility to you, but I cannot give it without danger. Not that I should be in danger, for my affection towards the Emperor is well known to all the world, but we might put the Emperor himself in jeopardy; for, if they were to take my letter from you, they might give it over to a spy, nay, even to an assassin."

This argument appeared conclusive to me, but I answered, "A lucky thought flashes across my mind. You have acted so long and so often in connexion with the Emperor, that surely you must be able to recollect some circumstances, some disclosures known only to yourselves, which, if I relate them to his Majesty, will prove to him that you trust me, and that I am worthy of his trust." — "Your idea is excellent; yet," added he, "I must either give you insignificant details, and then the Emperor will have forgotten them, or I must reveal important secrets to you, and I am forbidden by my duty to do so; yet I will turn the matter over in my mind. Call here again to-morrow morning."

I called again. "I have ransacked my memory," said M. X*** as he accosted me, "and here is the very thing which you want." He then delivered a note to me. "I had only considered your expedition to Elba," continued M. X***, "in relation to your own concerns; but it is of much greater importance than you imagine, or than I myself thought it would be. It may produce tremendous consequences. It is impossible that the Emperor can be indifferent to what is going on in France. If he was to put any questions to you on that head, how would you answer him? You must be fully aware how very dangerous it might be if you were to give him an erroneous idea of our political situation." — "Though I am a soldier by profession, yet I am not an utter novice in politics. I have often reflected on the present position of France. I really think that I understand enough of the matter to be able to satisfy the curiosity of Napoleon." —"I don't doubt it: but, come, what is your opinion of affairs?"

In answer to this interrogatory, I entered into an illustrative analysis of the faults of government, and of the consequences ensuing therefrom. Our conversation became warmer, and when, after having discussed the time present, we began to contemplate futurity, our thoughts were evolved with so much rapidity; we were carried so much further than we intended, that we ourselves were astonished, and we then both continued during a short interval in a kind of reverie. I was the first who broke silence. "Well," said I, "suppose the Emperor, after having questioned me, were to ask, Do you think the time of my re-appearance in France is arrived, what must I answer?" —"You will tell his Majesty that I could not dare to decide so important a question; but that he may consider it as a positive and incontestible fact that our present government (as you have well observed) has wholly lost the confidence of the people and of the army; that discontent has increased to the highest pitch; and that it is impossible to believe that the government can stand much longer against the universal dislike. You will add, that the Emperor is the only object of the regret and hope of the nation. He, in his wisdom, will decide what he ought to do." —"If he asks me whether this opinion is only yours, or whether Messrs. ******* all share in it, what shall I answer?" —"Tell him that since his abdication those persons have ceased to be in communication with each other, but that my opinion is conformable to the general opinion." —"I am now able to answer all the questions which the Emperor may ask. Adieu."

We embraced each other repeatedly, and we parted.

As soon as I had quitted M. X*** all that had passed between us filled my mind again. I now contemplated at leisure the mission which I was called upon to fulfil. I measured its extent, and weighed its consequences, and I could not help feeling astonished, and in some measure alarmed, by the result of this self-examination. So long as I merely intended to go to Elba for the sole purpose of offering my services to the Emperor, my journey appeared to be nothing out of the common course of things, and I thought that I should not have hesitated to declare to the government that I was going to rejoin my former benefactor, the Sovereign of my choice; but since the object of my journey had become so much more important; since, to use the words of M. X***, it might produce tremendous consequences, it seemed that the government would not fail to watch me; that it would dog me in my path, and endeavour to spy out all my words and actions.

Hence I became suspicious and uneasy. The note of M. X*** appeared an immense burthen. I got it by heart, and then I threw it in the fire. Instead of asking at once for a passport to Genoa or Leghorn, as I had at first intended, I asked for a passport to Milan. There was a General officer then residing in that city whom I knew; and I thought that if the Police were to question me, I might then declare that I was going to Milan in order to settle my accounts with my friend the General, he being in my debt for money which I had advanced to him.

Having thus settled my plan, I went on to the "prefecture de police." Whilst I was stepping across the threshold of the door, my heart began to beat so violently that I could hardly move or breathe. If at that instant any body had cried out to me, "Rascal, what are you about?" I think I should have dropped, and that I should have let out the whole secret. It must not be thought that my confusion arose from cowardly fear; no, it was the impression which every honest man ought to feel, when, for the first time in his life, he commits an action which he is under the necessity of concealing.

In a few minutes I came to myself again. In I went, and presented myself boldly to Monsieur Rivière, the Prefect of Police. He cross-questioned me at full length, but my answers were clear and firm. My countenance was unabashed, and appeared to preclude all suspicion, and he granted my passport. Yet, at all events, I thought it prudent to ascertain whether I was watched, and to my great surprise I found that during two days I was closely followed. I did not give any token by which my spy could ascertain that I was aware of his company, and, in order to mislead him, I went to the *messageries*, where I took and paid for a place in the Lyons diligence. But when night came I hired post-horses under a feigned name, and set off as fast as possible, and in a few days I was at Milan.

My friend the General was absent: I wrote to him, and he hastened to meet me. I confessed that I intended to try to obtain employment under Napoleon.—"You won't get it," said he; "Napoleon has not ready money enough to pay his body guard. A good many of my old officers have joined him, and for themselves and their families they only receive fifty, or perhaps sixty francs a month. They are in a state of starvation and despair."—"No matter; I love the Emperor, and come what may, I will join him. Do tell me how I can soonest put to sea."—"The thing is not easy; there is no place from whence you can sail, except only from Leghorn or from Genoa; and those two points are under such close inspection, that you will be sure to be taken up, if you are known to be a Bonapartist. You might slip through with greater ease if you could pass for a tradesman of this town. I will try to get you a passport, but I am afraid it will be a difficult job."—"Besides, there is another difficulty, which is still greater; *ma foi!* I can't speak a dozen words of Italian." — "Is it possible?" — "Yes, I am in earnest." — "And you would venture on such a scheme! are you crazy?" — "Crazy or not, I will venture; but can I really embark no where but at Leghorn or Genoa?" — "There are very many small ports on the coast of Tuscany, but if you go to any of them you must stop till there is an opportunity of getting out; and in the mean time you would be under the *surveillance* of the authorities, who are, one and all, exceedingly ill-disposed towards the Emperor and his people. Perhaps you might be able to embark immediately in the gulf of Spezzia at Lerici; but, in order to get there, you must go through Genoa, and along the shore; and then there is great reason to fear that you may be snapped either by the Piedmontese carabineers, or by the new consul at Genoa, who, according to what I hear, is quite outrageous. There is another road through the mountains of Spezzia, but it has not been used for a long time, and you would run the risk either of breaking your neck, or of being knocked on the head." — "No matter, if there is no danger in the victory there is no glory in the triumph. That road suits me; and to-morrow I will set out on my expedition." — "Is your passport all right?" — "I will go and get it marked for Lerici." — "Another piece of stupidity; don't you know that here you have to deal with our implacable enemies, the Austrians, who will raise all kinds of difficulties; but I know a Tedesco Colonel (in Italy an Austrian is called a Tedesco), who will probably be able to do the needful for us: we will ask him to come and dine with us. Business or quarrels can all be settled with these gentry when they are feeding."

Our Tedesco Colonel really got my passport through the office. I left my "calèche" and my baggage at Milan, and the next day I started in a "seggiola," a kind of a little cabriolet, in which you drive along at an infernal rate. I travelled through cross roads till I came to the foot of the mountains. As it was impossible to ascend them in a wheeled carriage, I was compelled, though reluctantly, to separate myself from my 'conducteur." I bought two horses, one for myself and the other for my new guide; this new guide could not speak a word of French. I had taken care to provide myself with a pocket dictionary, French and Italian; but I was completely ignorant, or at least very nearly so, of the way either of pronouncing Italian words, or of arranging them; and thus our conversation was reduced on both sides to a few detached phrases, which were often mutually unintelligible.

We set out at break of day. About noon the snow began to fall, and we had the greatest difficulty imaginable in reaching a hamlet, the name whereof I have forgotten. The next day the weather became still more wretched; my guide's horse foundered in the snow, and we lost two hours in hauling him out again. My guide was an Italian, and, like all Italians, he was full of superstition, and easily discouraged. He considered this accident as a bad omen, and he wanted to turn back; I could only conquer his repugnance by means of a double Napoleon d'or. Scarcely had I given it to him when I felt the extent of my imprudence; I was exciting his avarice, and perhaps exposing myself to become his victim. As we advanced, the road became worse and worse; at every step we encountered pits and holes, or the road was stopped by rocks which had fallen in, and which forced us to scramble through new paths. So much snow had fallen in the north of Italy, and particularly in the district which we were then crossing, that even the muleteers had deserted the mountains: and my guide, unable to discern the beaten road, was compelled to make a survey at every step, lest we should either lose ourselves, or else tumble down the precipices which bordered our road of danger. The next day we arrived at Borcetto; the perils which I had escaped taught me caution: I hired two more horses, and another guide; and for this addition to my train, I paid out of all reason. I then met with a custom-house officer, who either out of kindness, or for the purpose of alarming me, I know not which, warned me to be particularly on my guard in crossing "la Size," a very lofty and dangerous mountain, for he told me that it swarmed with robbers. I put fresh priming in my pistols; I turned up my eyes toward Heaven to implore its protection, and I set out. When we had proceeded half way up the mountain, I was accosted by a soldier, who compelled me to enter the guard-house, and to produce my passport. This post, which had been lately established for the security of travellers, was occupied by a subaltern and by six soldiers, who had all served in the imperial army. They guessed by my looks that I had seen some service, and, after a short conversation, they asked me to come in and warm myself by drinking the health of the Emperor Napoleon. I refused at first, lest I should be entrapped, but they insisted so frankly that I was compelled to yield. On taking leave I gave them a twenty-franc piece, in order to drink the health of Napoleon, and mine too; and I begged them to recommend my guides to take care of me. The commandant called the guides, and at the same time that he fired a volley of oaths and curses, he declared that if any accident happened to me, he would shoot them both on their return. My worthy military friends also escorted me during a considerable distance, and we separated with feelings which no one but a soldier can appreciate or understand.

We were to sleep at Pontremoli. Our halt retarded us, and night overtook us. In order to shorten the distance, my guides led me by a broad path which wound round the side of the mountain. The descent was so steep that our horses came down every moment, and we ourselves were obliged to slide along. I found myself at the foot of the mountain in a spot which was so dark and dreary, that I fancied my guides had conducted me thither in order to dispatch me. After having groped along for some time, my guides stopped. The darkness and the snow concealed the face of the country to such a degree, that they did not know where they were, nor which way they ought to turn: their fear became excessive; they prayed to all the Saints in heaven in their turn: they shook each other by the hand, and embraced each other like sailors on the point of being shipwrecked. My *sang froid* did not desert me; I took one of the horses which looked like an old roadster; I dropped the bridle on his neck, and gave him a sound cut with my whip; he started, I followed, and a few minutes afterwards, to the inexpressible surprise, and also to the inexpressible satisfaction of my guides, we found ourselves in the right road, and within half an hour's ride of Pontremoli, where we arrived towards midnight.

From Pontremoli to Spezzia there was yet a journey of four-and-twenty hours; and four-and-twenty hours on such roads as I had gone over are equal to four-and-twenty centuries. But how great was my delight on quitting Pontremoli, when, instead of the frozen rocks and deserts, which I had crossed the eve before, I saw nothing as I looked around, but valleys clothed with verdure, and enamelled with flowers; and hills surrounded and crowned by evergreens and olive-trees. On the day before, winter reigned with all his severity; the day after exhibited spring with all her charms. This pleasing transition beguiled my impatience; and the agitations which had become habitual to my soul were succeeded by that happy tranquillity, which is inspired by the contemplation of the beauties and the gifts of nature.

A few leagues beyond Pontremoli the road is interrupted by a deep and rapid stream. There is a ford across this torrent. It had scarcely been indicated to me by my guides, beyond whom I had advanced, when I dashed into the water; but instead of guiding my horse to the right (as I ought to have done), I took the opposite direction. My guides, who saw my mistake, screamed out in Italian, "fermate, fermate!" which means, "stop, stop!" I thought it meant "firm, firm!" so I whipped and spurred my horse with all my might; he lost his footing, and I narrowly escaped drowning. When I reached the opposite shore my guides treated me with a sermon, which I dare say was very energetic, and in which the "Devil and the Frenchman" appeared to be the leading actors.

I arrived on the ***** at Lerici. I rejoiced when I saw the sea before me, when I saw the last obstacle which was interposed between the fulfilment of my hopes and the termination of my labours. But unhappily my joy was of short duration; in the course of the night I was attacked by an oppression on my chest, accompanied by a burning fever: this was the result of the cold bath which I had taken in the river. My mental sufferings were severe:

I thought to myself, if I should be so unlucky as to get an inflammation on my lungs, what will become of me here without help, without friends, and in a strange land? Ah, my beloved country! ah, my dear mother! have I left you both, in order to perish in the arms of hirelings and of strangers! Have I only reached the long wished-for shores of Spezzia but to experience the grief of not being able to sail from them! Ah, if I could but have reached the Emperor, if I could but have spoken to him, if I could but have expired at his feet, then I should not have regretted life! My devoted attachment would have been known; my memory honoured; my name, linked to the destiny of the Emperor, would, perhaps, have descended with his unto posterity.... I sent for a doctor: by singular good fortune, the medical man who came to attend me was a retired army surgeon, a worthy man, and a great admirer of the French. When I was quite out of danger, he expressed a wish to know the motives which had induced me to cross the mountains to Lerici: and he gave me to understand that he guessed my views. A man who speaks is always liable to less suspicion than a man who says nothing; I therefore thought it right to allay the doctor's curiosity. After exhorting him to secrecy, and making a great mystery of the matter, I confessed that I was a Colonel in the French army, and that an officer who held a high rank in the service of Napoleon had married my sister. My sister, I proceeded to state, was so afflicted and broken down by the expatriation of her husband, that her medical attendants had declared her life to be in the greatest danger. My sister's illness, and the care of her four small children, prevented her from rejoining her husband; and therefore, in order to restore health and happiness to my poor dear sister, I had determined to go to Elba, for the purpose of reminding my brother-in-law of the duty which he owed to his wife and children, and that I hoped to be able to induce him to return to France, at least for a short time.

I took care to diversify my romance with sighs and sentimental reflections, and it appeared to affect him exceedingly. He condoled with me, he tried to console me; he gave me the most flattering hopes, and he promised to serve me to the utmost of his power, and with all his heart and soul.

As soon as I was in a state of convalescence, I became more ardent than before, in search of an immediate opportunity of embarking. My complaisant doctor introduced me to the captain of a running felucca, and I hired his vessel for a fortnight.

The captain asked me for my passport, in order that he might receive his *"feuille de bord"* and his *"boletta"* from the port officer. This was in consequence of regulations of which I was wholly ignorant. The fact is, that no vessel can clear out of one port, or enter another, without a *"feuille de bord*," stating the complement of the crew, and the number of passengers; and a "*boletta*," or certificate, delivered by the health officers to each of the passengers and crew individually, stating that the bearer has not been attacked by any infectious disorder. These papers are only delivered on the production of the passports, to which they must correspond exactly. I did not expect this proceeding; my plans were all disorganized: my passport did not authorize me to embark; and I was afraid if I produced it, (for in such situations we are afraid of every thing), that difficulties might arise, and that they would refer to the Consul or his agents.

The Captain guessed the cause of my uneasiness, and he offered to procure a passport and a *boletta* under a feigned name. I refused: I thought it more advisable to run the risk of being punished as a Bonapartist than as an impostor. "Since you will not do so," said the captain, "there is but one course which you can pursue: you must get on board a boat, and pass for a common sailor. I will manage the business for you."—Some hours afterwards the captain came to me with a Gallo-Genoese sailor, who offered to take me, without any papers, wherever I wished to go. He added, that he had a relation who was a gunner on board the Inconstant, a brig belonging to Napoleon, and that he should be very glad to see him again. I judged that my design of going to Elba had got wind: I therefore determined, if possible, to depart that very night. It was therefore agreed that Salviti, so the sailor was called, should fetch me, and that we should put out to sea, however bad the weather might prove.

Whilst these arrangements were going on my doctor paid me a visit. The doctor told me that the commandant of the town, whom he attended, was going to send a file of his carabineers to bring me before him in order to ascertain the reason of my arrival, and of my residence on the shores of the gulf. "I told him," continued the doctor, "that you are unwell, and that you are going to your family in Corsica, and that you intend to begin your voyage as soon as you are able to support the fatigue. I think I have made him easier, yet don't trust him: be off as quick as you can." —"I shall be off to-night; but as your commandant or his gensdarmes might take a fancy to lay hold of me between this and then, I therefore think it will be more prudent for me to go to him of my own accord, and to confirm the story which you have had the goodness to tell him." Accordingly I went immediately to the Commandant; and as the doctor had let me into the character of the man, I easily succeeded in pleasing and tranquillizing him. However, he made me promise that I would bring my passport to him to-morrow. I gave as many promises as he could wish. At midnight we set sail; and by break of day we had already lost sight of the gulf of Spezzia, and of the majestic scenery which surrounds it. The bark which carried me and all my fortunes was only a common boat with four oars and a lateen sail. The crew consisted of six men; Salviti could speak French, and he was a good-looking fellow: the countenances of the others displayed want and utter profligacy. They examined me with great curiosity, and they were constantly talking about me. Salviti interpreted their discourse. I gave them civil language. We even seek to please sailors when we are in need of their help[31]. I was sea-sick without intermission; and to complete my misfortunes I had omitted to furnish myself with provisions. I was therefore obliged to mess with my companions; and their food consisted of stinking salt fish, and chiefly of bacalao, or salt cod, which is eaten quite raw.

The wind was against us, therefore we did not come in sight of the lighthouse of Leghorn until the morning of the second day. How can I express my surprise and anger when I saw that our vessel was making the mouth of the harbour! "Salviti, where are you taking me?"—"To Leghorn."—"I won't go to Leghorn," I exclaimed with a great oath. "It is not to Leghorn that you promised to take me."—Salviti answered, with confusion, that he was not the owner of the vessel, but that he hired it in partnership with the rest of the crew, that they were all smugglers, and that they were going to Leghorn for the purpose of arranging an expedition of consequence with other smugglers there. Their business would be soon settled, and then they would take me to Porto Ferrajo; and he declared that he gave his word of honour that he would do so, and that I might trust him.—"I will not agree to all this," I exclaimed, presenting my pistols to his breast: "Let us go straight on to Elba, or I will shoot you."—"Shoot away, if you like, but you will not do yourself much good: my companions will heave you into the sea, or else you will be guillotined at Leghorn." The coolness of the fellow completely disarmed me. "Well, then," said I, "swear that you will take me to-morrow to the isle of Elba."—"I have told you already that I am a scoundrel if I break my word." The sailors did not understand a word of our dialogue, nor could they make out what was the cause of my fury. One of them, who had deserted from the English navy, seized a big knife in the shape of a stiletto. The others seemed to wait the result, in order to throw themselves upon me. When this scene had finished, I endeavoured to bribe Salviti to turn back, but no; he had given his word of honour to go to Leghorn, and his word of honour was inviolable. Thus I was conducted against my will into the trap which I wished to avoid. I was worked up to the highest pitch of fury and vexation; I foamed with rage and despair. Thus, thought I, wringing my hands, these ruffians will deprive me of the reward which I was to obtain for my sufferings. Alas! the Emperor, the Emperor! so near him—under his eyes—at the moment that—"Rascal!" I cried out to Salviti, "I will follow you like your shadow, and sooner than allow myself to be arrested, I will blow out your brains!"—Salviti shrugged up his shoulders, and answered, "Well and good; but, in the mean time, strip, and dress yourself like a sailor."—"Why?"—"Why! why, because you have no passport, and they will lock you up."—I submitted to this new tribulation. One of the wretches pulled off a heavy jacket with a hood attached to it, in which I arrayed myself. A coloured handkerchief, all drenched with sweat and filthiness, was taken from the neck of another of them, and tied round mine. A third gave me his woollen cap; and in spite of my unavoidable disgust, I was compelled to draw it on my head down to my eyes. My beard, by good luck, did not disgrace my unshaved messmates, and in order that the colour of my hands might not betray me, I washed them in the bilge-water which stagnated beneath the flooring of our boat. More remained to be done: our "feuille de bord" stated that our crew consisted of six men: we were seven. It therefore, became necessary to hide one[32]. We chose him who was the shortest, and the most slender. He nestled at the end of the boat, and we covered him with some old mats and sailors' jackets. These preparations being terminated, I was told to seat myself in the place of a rower, and to take an oar in my hand; and at night-fall we came into the road of Leghorn.

Salviti presented his papers. The date was too old[33]. The officers raised objections: he lost his temper; and by way, both of punishment and precaution, we were ordered to submit to the lesser quarantine, that is to say, to remain prisoners in the roads during three days.

Salviti came with a sorrowful visage and announced this fresh misfortune; our vessel tacked about, and we reached our station of exile.

On the morning of the third day Salviti informed me that, according to custom, they intended to put an "inspector of health" on board of our vessel, who would pass the night with us, in order to ascertain whether we were all well. From the person who had brought, or who, rather, had thrown us our provisions (for all contact is prohibited under pain of death), he had ascertained the name of our intended inspector. He was a gamester and a drunkard. Salviti procured cards and wine; and he assured me that he would manage the inspector in such a manner as to prevent his taking any notice of me.

As for me, I was not as easy as Salviti. I was afraid lest the inspector might discover the sailor whom we had hidden, or that he might guess by my manner, my looks, and my awkwardness, that I was not really the character which I seemed to be. Besides, a single question would have ended the matter. I did not understand a single word of Italian, and I should have betrayed myself either by answering him, or by remaining silent. It came into my head to counterfeit deafness: this would excuse me from taking a part in the conversation: and to make believe that I had a wound in my hand: this would account for my inactivity, and prevent his observing how little I knew of my pretended occupation. I drew a few drops of blood, which I smeared upon some dirty rags, in which I wrapped my hand. Salviti explained my stratagem to my companions, and their loud peals of laughter explained to me that they approved of it. The inspector arrived. I kept myself to myself. Salviti acted his part admirably. So did I: and to my great delight the evening closed, and nothing disagreeable had happened. Until this night I had always slept separately from the rest on a tolerable mattress. But the inspector was now accommodated with my birth and my bed; and I was compelled to lie on the floor with the sailors; my head being placed even with the feet of my two next neighbours. The stench and closeness of the atmosphere of my den drove the blood into my head, and I thought I should have been suffocated. Early in the morning my companions began to eat and drink: I kept at a distance. "Come here, and eat," said Salviti.—"I can't."—"The inspector will fancy that you are ill, and that will be enough to give us another quarantine."—I ate. At ten o'clock the health-officers came near us; and as our inspector made a favourable report, we were allowed to enter the harbour. I remained on board with one of the crew, whom I kept as a hostage. The smugglers broke up their cabinet council about two o'clock; and at three o'clock we quitted our anchorage. A fair wind filled the sail, and I forgot all my sufferings and my dangers when I perceived the rock where I was to meet with Napoleon the Great.

We entered the road of Porto Ferrajo[34], without any difficulty, at the moment when the cannon fired, announcing that the harbour was about to close. I heard the French drums sounding the roll: my heart beat high: I passed the night on the deck of the boat. Notwithstanding the joy which I felt at my arrival, I could not help indulging in a certain degree of melancholy, inspired, perhaps, by the silence of the night, and the aspect of the arid and gloomy mountains which surrounded me. Ah, how vain is human grandeur! thought I. The air of that sterile islet is breathed by that incomprehensible man who lately felt that he had not breathing room in Europe. It is in that humble hovel that he now dwells with his scanty train of faithful followers; He whom I have seen in the palace of the Cæsars, receiving the homage and the worship of the most brilliant court in the world; He whom I have seen sitting covered, whilst eight Kings stood before him with their hats in their hands. It is over this little tribe alone, not exceeding the population of a village, that Napoleon the Great is now doomed to reign! Napoleon the Great! He who endowed the thrones of his allies with the leavings of his conquests—He who so long was the master and the terror of the universe!

The sun rose, and put an end to my musings. My joy was inexpressible when I recognized on the ramparts those old grenadiers whom I had so often admired and honoured on the field of battle.

I jumped on shore, and I rushed into the nearest inn for the purpose of putting off my sailor's dress, and then flying to the palace of Napoleon. But I had been watched and followed: and the functionaries despatched by general Cambronne, the Commandant of the town, immediately appeared to secure me. I tranquillized them, and they accompanied me to the town-house, where General Bertrand then lodged. I sent in my name, and the General came out. "Sir, do you come from France?" — "Yes, Monsieur le Maréchal." — "What do you want here?" — "I wish to see the Emperor, and to solicit employment " — "Does the Emperor know you?" — "Yes, Sir, and M. X*** has also given me the means of proving to the Emperor that I am not unworthy of his goodness." — "Do you bring us any news from France?" — "I do, Monsieur le Maréchal; and I think that the intelligence which I bring is good." — "Well, Heaven hears you; as for us, we are so wretched—I am dying with impatience to have a talk with you about France; but I must inform the Emperor of your arrival. Perhaps he may not be able to see you immediately. To-day the English corvette[35] is here, and those people are suspicious of every thing: is it publicly known who you are?" — "It is known that I am a French officer." — "So much the worse; hide your decorations, hold your tongue, and remain within doors and rest yourself at your inn. I will send for you." — Half an hour afterwards the Marshal desired me to proceed as quickly as possible to the Emperor's garden-gate: the Emperor, would come there, and speak to me without appearing to know me. I went accordingly: the Emperor, according to his custom, was walking with his hands behind his back. He passed several times before me without lifting up his eyes; at last he looked at me: he stopped, and asked me in Italian what countryman I was. I answered in French that I was a Parisian; that business had called me to Italy; and that I could not resist the desire of seeing my old sovereign —"Well, Sir, talk to me about Paris and France;" — and as he finished these words he began to walk again. I accompanied him; and after he had put several indifferent questions to me aloud, he desired me to enter his apartments: he then ordered Bertrand and Drouot to retire, and forced me to sit down by his side. Napoleon began in a reserved and absent manner: "The grand Marshal tells me that you have just arrived from France." — "Yes, Sire." — "What do you want here?" — "Sire, I wish to offer my services to you; my conduct in 1814—" Napoleon interrupting me, — "Sir, I do not question but that you are a very good officer, however I have so many officers with me already, that it will be very difficult for me to assist you; yet we will see: it appears that you know M. X***." — "Yes,

Sire."—"Has he sent a letter for me by you?"—"No, Sire."—Napoleon, interrupting me, "I see he forgets me just like the rest; since I have been here, I have not heard a word of him or of any body."—I interrupted the Emperor in my turn, "Sire, he has never ceased to entertain those sentiments of devotion and attachment towards your Majesty which are still cherished by all true Frenchmen; and—" Napoleon, with disdain; "What, do they still think of me in France?"—"Never will they forget you."—"Never! that is a strong expression; the French have another Sovereign, and they are commanded both by their duty and their tranquillity to think on him alone." This answer did not please me: the Emperor, thought I to myself, is out of humour because I have not brought him any letters; he mistrusts me: it was not worth while to come so far for the sake of such an ungracious reception.— Napoleon, continuing, "What do they think about me in France?"—"There, your Majesty is universally deplored and regretted."—"Yes, and there, also, they manufacture all sorts of lies concerning me. Sometimes they say that I am mad, sometimes that I am ill, and you may see (here the Emperor looked at his embonpoint), if I look like an ailing man. It is also given out that they intend to transport me either to St. Helena or to Malta. I would not advise them to try. I have provisions for six months, and brave followers to defend me: but I cannot think that Europe will be so dishonourable as to rise in arms against a single man, who has neither the power nor the inclination of hurting others. The emperor Alexander has too much love for posterity to lend himself to such a crime. They have guaranteed the sovereignty of the isle of Elba to me by a solemn treaty. Here I am in my own home; and as long as I do not go out to pick a quarrel with my neighbours, they have no right to come and disturb me ... have you served in the grand army?"— "Yes, Sire, I had the felicity of distinguishing myself under your Majesty's eyes in the plains of Champagne; your Majesty appeared to take such particular notice of me, that I had dared to hope that your Majesty would recollect me."—"Why, yes; I thought, somehow, that I knew your face when I saw you, but I have only a confused recollection of you."—Poor mortals! thought I to myself, go and expose your lives for the sake of Kings, go and sacrifice your youth, your repose, your happiness for their sake!—"In what affairs have you distinguished yourself?"—"Sire, at *****, and at ***** Marshal Ney there presented me to your majesty, saying, 'Sire, here is the intrepid S.... P..... of whom I have spoken to your Majesty.'"—"Ah! ah! I really do recollect—yes, I was very well pleased indeed, with your behaviour at **** and at ****; you showed much resolution, much strength of character. Did I not 'decorate' you on the field of battle?"—"Yes, Sire."—Napoleon, with greater warmth and confidence, "Eh bien! how are they all treated in France by the Bourbons?"—"Sire, the Bourbons have not realized the expectations of the French, and the number of malcontents increases every day."—Napoleon, sharply; "So much the worse, so much the worse: but how, has not X. sent me any letters?"—"No, Sire; he was afraid lest they might be taken from me; and as he thought that your Majesty, being now compelled to be vigilant, and to distrust all the world, might distrust me also, he has revealed several circumstances to me, which are only known to your Majesty and to himself; thus enabling me to give a proof that I am worthy of your Majesty's confidence."—"Let us hear them." I began my detail, but he exclaimed, without allowing me to finish, "that's enough; why did you not begin by telling me all that? there is half an hour that we have lost." This storm[36] disconcerted me. He perceived my confusion, and resumed his discourse with mildness.—"Come, make yourself easy, and repeat to me, with the greatest minuteness, all that has passed between you and X****." I then related the circumstances which had induced me to have an interview with Monsieur X****. I repeated our conversation word for word. I gave him a complete account of all the faults and excesses of the royal government; and I was going to draw the inferences which had occurred to Monsieur X**** and me. But the Emperor, who, when he was affected, was incapable of listening to any recital without interrupting it, and making his comments at every moment, stopped my mouth. "I thought so, too," said he, "when I abdicated, that the Bourbons, instructed and disciplined by adversity, would not fall again into the errors which ruined them in 1789. I thought that the King would govern you 'en bon homme.' This was the only way by which he could obtain a pardon from you, for having been put upon you by foreigners. But since they have stepped into France, they have done nothing but acts of madness. Their treaty of the twenty-third of April," (raising his voice,) "has made me deeply indignant: with one stroke of the pen they have robbed France of Belgium, and of all the territory acquired since the revolution. They have deprived the nation of its docks, its arsenals, its fleets, its artillery, and the immense materiel which I had collected in the fortresses and the ports which they have ceded. Talleyrand has led them into this infamous business: he must have been bribed. Peace is easy upon such terms. If, like them, I had consented to the ruin of France, they would not now be on my throne:" (with energy,) "I would sooner have cut off my right hand. I preferred renouncing my throne rather than to retain it by staining my glory, and the honour of the French nation.... A degraded crown is an intolerable burthen. My enemies have published everywhere, that I obstinately refused to make peace. They have represented me as a wretched madman, eager only for blood and carnage: this language answered their turn. When you wish to hang your dog, you give out that he is mad: Quand on veut tuer son chien, il faut bien faire accroire qu'il est enragé But Europe shall know the truth: I will let the world know all that was said and done at Chatillon. I will unmask the Austrians, the Russians, and the English with a powerful hand. Europe shall judge: Europe shall say who was the rogue, and who was wishing to shed human blood. If I had been mad for war, I might have retired with my army beyond the Loire, and I might have enjoyed mountain warfare to my heart's content. I would not; I was tired of carnage ... my name, and the brave fellows who remained faithful to me, yet made the allies tremble, even in my capital. They offered Italy to me as the price of my abdication: I refused it. After once reigning over France, one ought not to reign anywhere else. I chose the isle of Elba. They were too happy to give Elba to me. This position suited me. I can watch France and the Bourbons. All that I have done has been only for France. It is for her sake and not for mine that I wished to render her the first nation in the universe. My glory is made for myself[37] *******. If I had only thought of myself, I would have returned to a private station, but it was my duty to retain the imperial title for my family and my son.... Next to France, my son is the dearest object in the world to me."

During the whole of this discourse, the Emperor continued striding up and down, and appeared violently agitated. He paused a little while, and then he began again. "They (i.e. the emigrants) know too well that I am here, and they would like to assassinate me. I discover new plots, new snares every day. They have sent to Corsica one of the assassins of Georges, a wretch whom the English journals themselves have pointed out to Europe as a blood-thirsty assassin; but let us be on the alert. If he misses me, I won't miss him. I shall send my grenadiers after him, and he shall be shot as an example to others."

After a few moments of silence, he said, "Do my generals go to court? they must cut a sad figure there." I waited for the end of this digression, in order to resume the thread of my discourse. As I was convinced that I could not possibly lead the conversation, I resolved to let the Emperor have it according to his own way, and I answered, "Yes, Sire, and they are furious to see themselves superseded in favour by emigrants who have never heard the sound of a cannon." — "The emigrants will never alter. As long as they were only required to dance attendance in my anti-chamber, I had more than enough of them. When it was necessary to show any heart, they slunk away like.... I committed a great error, when I recalled that anti-national race into France. If it had not been for me, they would have died of starvation abroad; but then I had great motives. I wanted to reconcile Europe to us, and to close the revolution.... What do my soldiers say about me?" — "The soldiers, Sire, talk constantly about your immortal victories. They never pronounce your name but with respect, admiration, and grief. When the Princes give money to the soldiers, they drink it out to your health, and when they are forced to cry *Vive le Roi!* they add in a whisper, *de Rome.*" — "And so they still love me?" (smiling.) — "Yes, Sire, and I may even venture to say, more than ever." — "What do they say about our misfortures?" — "They consider them as the effect of treachery; and they constantly repeat, that they never would have been conquered, if they had not been sold to their enemies. They are particularly indignant with respect to the capitulation of Paris." — "They are right: had it not been for the infamous defection of the Duke of Ragusa, the allies would have been lost. I was master of their rear, and of all their resources; not a man would have escaped. They too would have had their twenty-ninth bulletin. Marmont is a wretch; he has ruined his country, and delivered up his sovereign. His convention with Schwartzenburg would alone suffice to dishonour him. If he had not known when he surrendered, that he compromised my person and my army, he would not have found it necessary to make stipulations in favour of my liberty and life. This piece of treachery is not the only one. He has intrigued with Talleyrand to take the regency from the Empress, and the crown from my son. Caulincourt, Macdonald, and the rest of the marshals, have been cheated and gulled by him in the most shameful manner. All his blood would not be sufficient to expiate the harm which he has done to France.... I will devote his name to the execration of posterity. I am glad to learn that my soldiers retain the feeling of their superiority, and that they attribute our great misfortunes to the right authors. I collect with great pleasure, from the intelligence which you have brought, that the opinion which I had formed respecting the situation of France, is correct. The family of the Bourbons is not fit to reign. Their government may be good for priests, nobles, and old fashioned countesses: it is good for nothing for the present generation. The revolution has taught the people to know their rank in the state. They will never consent to fall back into their former nullity, and to be tied up by the nobility and the clergy. The army can never belong to the Bourbons. Our victories and our misfortunes have established an indissoluble tie between the army and myself. It is only through me that the soldiers can earn vengeance, power, and glory. From the Bourbons they can get nothing but insults and blows. Kings can only retain their power by the love of their subjects or by fear. The Bourbons are neither loved nor feared. At last they will throw themselves off their throne; but they may yet retain their position for a long time. Frenchmen do not know how to conspire."

In pronouncing these words, the Emperor continued walking hastily, and using many gestures. He rather appeared to be soliloquizing than addressing any one else; he then continued, looking at me aside, "Does M. X*** think that those people can stand much longer?" — "His opinion on this point is exactly conformable to the general opinion; that is to say, it is now the general impression and conviction, that the government is hastening to its fall. The priests and the emigrants are its only partisans; every man of patriotism or soul is its enemy." — Napoleon (with energy), "Yes, all men in whose veins any national blood is flowing must be its enemies; but how will all this end? Is it thought that there will be a new revolution?" — "Sire, discontent and irritation prevail to such an extent, that the slightest partial effervescence would inevitably cause a general insurrection, and nobody would be surprised if it were to take place to-morrow." — "But what would you do were you to expel the Bourbons: would you re-establish the republic?" — "The republic, Sire! nobody thinks about it; perhaps they would create a regency." — Napoleon (with vehemence and surprise), "A regency! And wherefore? am I dead?" — "But your absence...." — "My absence makes no difference. In a couple of days I would be back again in France, if the nation were to recal me. Do you think it would be well, if I were to return?" The Emperor turned away his eyes, and I could easily remark, that to this question he attached more importance than he cared to manifest, and that he expected my answer with anxiety. "Sire, I dare not personally attempt to answer such a question, but...." — Napoleon (abruptly), "That's not what I am asking you; answer yes or no." — "Why then, Sire, — yes." — Napoleon (with tenderness), "You really think so?" — "Yes, Sire, I am convinced, and so is M. X****, that the people and the army would receive you as their deliverer, and that your cause would be embraced with enthusiasm." — Napoleon (appearing agitated and impatient), "Then X*** advises me to return?" — "We had foreseen that your Majesty would make inquiries on this point, and the following is literally his answer. You will tell his Majesty that I would not dare to decide so important a question, but that he may consider it as a positive and incontrovertible fact, that our present government has wholly lost the confidence of the people and of the army; that discontent has increased to the highest pitch, and that it is impossible to believe that the government can stand much longer against the universal dislike. You will add, that the Emperor is the only object of the regret and hope of the nation. He, in his wisdom, will decide what he ought to do."

The Emperor became silent and pensive; and, after a long meditation, he said, "I will reflect upon it; I will keep you with me. Come here to-morrow at eleven o'clock."

On leaving the Emperor, I met the Grand Marshal, who said, "the Emperor has detained you a long time. I am in terror lest this interview should have been noticed. We are surrounded by English spies. The slightest indiscretion might cost us dear. I do not ask you to relate to me any thing which was reserved for the Emperor; but if, without violating your duty, you could give me any details relating to France, you would be doing me a great favour. We hear nothing of what is going forward, except from the journals and a few commercial travellers; and the intelligence which we thus obtain is so trifling and so contradictory, that we do not know what to make of it." — "I can satisfy you, Monsieur le Maréchal, and without acting indiscreetly: what I have told to the Emperor is known to all France. Discontent is at its greatest height, and the royal government is on its last legs." — "I cannot tell what futurity promises to us; but whatever our fate may be, we cannot be worse off than we are at present. Our resources are dwindling away daily; we are becoming home-sick. If we were not a little upheld by hope, I really do not know what would become of us. Has the Emperor allowed you to remain with us?" — "Yes, Monsieur le Maréchal." — "I give you joy, but I pity you. There is no happiness out of one's own country. I do not regret having followed the Emperor — this step was dictated to me by my duty and my gratitude; but I regret France, like an infant who has lost its mother; like a lover who has lost his mistress." The Grand Marshal's eyes were filled with tears; he pressed my hand affectionately, and then said, "Come and breakfast with us to-morrow morning. I will introduce you to my wife; it will be as good as a fête to her when she has an opportunity of receiving a Frenchman, and above all, a true Frenchman."

It was soon known all over the town, that a Frenchman had arrived from the continent. My inn was besieged by a crowd of officers and grenadiers, who overwhelmed me with inquiries after their friends and relations. They seemed to think that I must be acquainted with every living creature in France. Many inquired respecting the state of public affairs. I evaded their interrogatories, by declaring that I had quitted France five months since.

I waited on the Grand Marshal according to his invitation. He resided in one wing of the building occupied by the municipality. In his apartment, there was hardly any thing to be seen except the four walls. He took notice that I was surveying its appearance. — "You are contemplating our misery," said he: "Perhaps it contrasts itself with the opinion which you may have formed respecting our situation. It is supposed throughout Europe, that the Emperor carried off immense treasures; but his camp-plate, his camp bed, and a few broken down horses, are the only objects which he has preserved, or which he wished to preserve. Like Saladin, he could cause an outcry to be made at his door, whilst he exposes our tatters, — behold all that Napoleon the Great, the conqueror of the universe, has retained from his conquests!"

The General was as good as his word: he introduced me to Madame la Maréchale. I was enchanted by her manners and her amiability. Our conversation turned upon France and the Isle of Elba, the present and the future; and on quitting Madame Bertrand, I did not know what I ought most to admire — the lively graces of her mind, or the dignity and energy of her character.

At eleven o'clock I attended, to present myself to the Emperor. They made me wait in his saloon on the ground floor. The striped silk hangings were half worn out and faded; the carpet was threadbare, and patched in several places; a few shabby arm chairs completed the furniture of the apartment. I thought upon the splendour of the imperial palaces, and I drew a deep and melancholy sigh. The Emperor arrived: he had assumed a degree of calmness in his manner, which was belied by his eyes. It was easy to see that he had been violently agitated. "Sir," said he, "I declared to you yesterday, that I retained you in my service. I repeat the same to you to-day. From this instant you belong to me, and I hope you will fulfil your duties towards me like a good and faithful subject: you swear that you will—is it not so?"—"Yes, Sire, I swear."—"That's right." After a pause, "I had foreseen the crisis to which France would come, but I did not think that things were so ripe. It was my intention not to interfere any longer in political affairs. The intelligence which you have brought to me has changed my resolutions. I have caused the misfortunes of France; therefore I must remove them: but before I commit myself, I wish to have a thorough knowledge of the state of our affairs. Sit down: repeat to me all that you told me yesterday; I like to hear you."

Re-assured by these words, and by a look full of kindness and benignity, I abandoned myself without reserve to all the inspirations of my heart and soul. The picture which I drew of the sufferings and hopes of the nation, which I presented to the Emperor, was so touching and so animated, that he was astonished. "You are a noble young fellow," said he, "you have truly the soul of a Frenchman; but are you not carried away by your imagination?"—"No, Sire; the recital which I have made to your Majesty is quite faithful. I may have expressed myself with warmth, because I cannot express my feelings otherwise; but all that I have told you is exact and true. Under such important circumstances, I should have thought it a crime to substitute the inspirations of my imagination in the place of truth."—"You therefore think that France awaits her redemption from me; that I shall be received as a deliverer."—"Yes, Sire; I will even say more: the royal government is so exceedingly hateful and disgusting to the French, the government weighs so very heavily on the nation and the army, that not only your Majesty, but any body else who would endeavour to liberate the French would find them disposed to second him."—Napoleon (with dignity): "Repeat that to me again."—"Yes, Sire, I do repeat it. The French are so wearied, and degraded, and incensed, by the anti-national yoke of the emigrants and the priests, that they are ready to join any one who will promise to deliver them."—"But if I were to disembark in France, is there not reason to fear that the patriots may be massacred by the emigrants and the chouans?"—"No, Sire, I do not think so; we are the most numerous and the bravest party."—"Yes, but they may heap you in the prisons, and cut your throats."—"Sire, the people will not let them do that."—"I hope you may not be deceived: to be sure, I shall get to Paris so speedily, that they won't have time to consider where they are to hide their heads. I shall be there as soon as the news of my disembarkation.... Yes," the Emperor continued, after taking a few steps, "I have resolved.... It was I who gave the Bourbons to France, and it is I who must rid France of them.... I will set off.... The enterprise is vast, it is difficult, it is dangerous, but it is not beyond me. On great occasions fortune has never abandoned me.... I shall set off, but not alone; I won't run the risk of allowing myself to be collared by the gensdarmes. I will depart with my sword, my Polanders, my grenadiers ... all France is on my side. I belong to France; and for her I will sacrifice my repose, my blood, my life, with the greatest joy." After this speech, the Emperor stopped; his eyes sparkled with hope and genius: his attitude announced energy, confidence, victory; he was grand, he was beautiful, he was adorable!—he resumed his discourse, and said, "Do you think that they will dare to wait for me?"—"No, Sire."—"I don't think so, either: they will quake when they hear the thunder of my name; and they will know that they can only escape me by a speedy flight. But what will be the conduct of the national guards? Do you think they will fight for them?"—"I think, Sire, that the national guards will remain neutral."—'Even that's a great deal; as to their 'gardes du corps,' and their red regiments, I am not afraid of them: they are either old men or boys: they will be frightened by the mustachios of my grenadiers. I will make my grenadiers hoist the national flag;" lifting up his voice and his hand: "I will appeal to my old soldiers; I will speak to them. None of them will refuse to hear the voice of their old general.... It is certain that the soldiers cannot hesitate to choose between the white flag and the tricoloured flag; between me, by whom they have been covered with rewards and glory, and the Bourbons, who wish to dishonour them.... And the Marshals, what will they do?"—"The Marshals, who are full of money and titles, have nothing to wish for but repose. They would fear to compromise their existence by embracing a doubtful party; and perhaps they will continue merely spectators of the crisis. Perhaps even the fear lest your Majesty may possibly punish them for their defection or treason in 1814 may induce them to adhere to the king."—"I will punish no one. Do you take me rightly? Tell M. **** clearly, that I will forget every thing. We have all reason to reproach each other."—"Sire, I will tell him so with the greatest joy. This assurance will completely gain all opinions over to your side; because even amongst your partisans there are men who dread your return; lest you should revenge yourself."—"Yes, I know that it is thought that I am revengeful, and even sanguinary; that I am considered as a kind of ogre, as a man-eater. They are mistaken: I will make every one do his duty, and I will be obeyed; and that's all. A weak sovereign is a calamity to his subjects. If he allows criminals and traitors to fancy that he does not know how to punish, there is no longer any security either for the state or for individuals. More crimes are prevented than repressed by severity. A sovereign must govern by his head, and not by his heart. Yet, tell X*** that I except Talleyrand, Augereau, and the Duke of Ragusa, out of the general pardon. They caused all our misfortunes. The country must be revenged."—"But why exclude them, Sire? Is there not reason to fear that this exclusion may deprive you of the fruits of your clemency, and may even raise doubts as to your sincerity in future?"—"It would be much more exposed to doubt were I to pardon them."—"But, Sire...."—"Don't you trouble your head about it ... what is the strength of the army?"—"Sire, I do not know; I only know that it has been much weakened by desertion and by discharges, and that few of the regiments consist of more than three hundred men."—"So much the better; those who are good for nothing have probably left the army; the good soldiers will have remained. Do you know the names of the officers who command the maritime districts, and the eighth division?"—"No, Sire."—Napoleon (out of temper), "Why did not X*** give you that information?"—"Sire, both M. X*** and myself were far from supposing that your Majesty would immediately embrace the glorious resolution of re-appearing in France; besides which, he might believe, according to the common report, that your agents did not allow you to remain in ignorance of any circumstance which might interest you."—"I do know that the newspapers gave out that I had agents.... It is an idle story. It is true that I sent some of my people to France, in order to learn what was going on; but they stole my money, and only treated me with the gabble of the canaille. C**** has been to see me, but he knew nothing. You are the first person from whom I have ascertained the situation of France and the Bourbons under all its extensive bearings. Had it not been for you, I should never have known that the hour of my return had struck. Had it not been for you, they would have left me here to dig in my garden. I have received—I do not exactly know from what quarter—the description of certain assassins, hired against me; and one or two anonymous letters besides—all from the same hand, in which I was told to remain quiet, that the embroideries were coming into fashion, and other nonsense in the same style; but that's all. It is not upon such data that one is induced to attempt a crash. But how do you think foreigners will like my return: there is the great question?"—"Foreign nations, Sire, have been compelled to confederate against us in order to protect themselves; allow me to say it...."—"Speak out, speak out."—"In order to protect themselves against the effects of your ambition, and the abuse of your strength. Now that Europe has recovered her independence, and that France has ceased to be dangerous, foreign powers will probably be unwilling to run the risk of a new war, which may end by restoring to us that ascendancy which we have lost."—"If the allied sovereigns were at home in their capitals they would certainly consider the matter twice before they would take the field again; but they are yet face to face; and it is to be feared that war may become an affair of vanity. Do you think it is true that they are on ill terms with each other?"—"Yes, Sire, it appears that discord reigns in the congress; that each of the great powers wishes to seize the largest share of the booty."—"It appears, also, that their subjects are discontented: is it not so?"—"Yes, Sire; kings and people, every thing seems to unite in our favour. The Saxons, the Genoese, the Belgians, the inhabitants of the banks of the Rhine, the Polanders, all refuse the new sovereigns to whom they are to be given. Italy, tired of the avarice and the grossness of the Austrians, pants for the moment of withdrawing from their sovereignty. Experience has taught the King of Naples that you are his surest protector, and he will assist the rising of the Italians whenever you wish it. The princes of the confederation of the Rhine, warned by the example of Saxony, will become the allies of your majesty after the first victory. Prussia and Russia will sit quiet, if you will only allow them to retain their new acquisitions. The Emperor of Austria, who has every thing to fear from Russia and Prussia, and nothing to hope for from the King of France, will easily consent, if you only guarantee Italy to him, to allow you to do what you think best with the Bourbons. In short, all the powers of Europe, England only excepted, are more or less interested in not declaring themselves against you; and before England can have corrupted, or raised the continent, your Majesty will be so firmly fixed on the throne, that your Majesty's enemies may try in vain to make you totter."

Napoleon (shaking his head), "All this is very fine; ... however, I consider it as certain, that the Kings who have fought against me are no longer guided by the same unity, the same views, the same interests. The Emperor Alexander must esteem me: he must be able to estimate the difference which exists between Louis XVIII. and myself. If he were to understand his policy rightly, he would rather see the French sceptre in the hands of a powerful sovereign, the relentless enemy of England, than in the hands of a weak sovereign, the friend and vassal of the Prince Regent. I would give him Poland, and a great deal more, if he wished it: he knows that I have been always more inclined to tolerate his ambition than to restrain it. If he had continued my friend and my ally, I would have made him greater than he ever will be now. Prussia, and the petty Kings of the Rhenish confederation, will follow the lot cast by Russia. If I had Russia on my side, she would secure me all the second-rate powers. As to the Austrians, I do not know what they would do: they have never treated me candidly. I suppose I could keep Austria in order by threatening to deprive her of Italy. Italy is yet very grateful to me, and much attached to me: if I were to ask that country for an hundred thousand men, and an hundred millions, I should have the men and the money. If they were to force me to make war, I could easily revolutionize the Italians; I would grant them whatever they might wish, independence or Eugene. Mejean and some others have done him harm, but, in spite of that, he is warmly loved, and highly esteemed: he deserves to be so; he has shown that he possesses a noble mind. Murat is ours. I have had great reason to complain of him. Since I have been here, he has wept for his errors, and has done his utmost to repair the injuries which he has inflicted upon me. He has regained my friendship and my confidence: his assistance, if I were engaged in war, would be very useful to me. He has little brains; he has nothing but hand and heart; but his wife would direct him. The Neapolitans like him tolerably well; and I have yet some good officers amongst them who would keep them in the right way. As to England, we should have shaken hands from Dover to Calais, if Mr. Fox had lived; but as long as that country continues to be governed by the principles and passions of Mr. Pitt, we must always be as hostile as fire and water.... From England I expect no quarter, no truce.... England knows that the instant I place my foot in France, her influence will be driven back across the seas ... as long as I live I will wage a war of extermination against her maritime despotism. If the continental powers had seconded me; if they had not been afraid of me; if they had understood my ambition, their flags would have floated from the mast-head throughout the universe, and the world would have enjoyed peace. All things considered, foreign powers have great reasons to declare war against me; whilst there are also great reasons to induce them to remain at peace with me. It is to be feared, as I have already said to you, that they may turn the war into an affair of vanity, or that they make it a point of honour. On the other hand, it is possible that they may renounce their coalition, which has now no longer any object, in order to watch their subjects; preserving at the same time an armed neutrality, until I shall have given them sufficient guarantees.

"Their determinations, whatever they may be, will not influence mine. France speaks, and that is sufficient for me. In 1814 I had to deal with all the powers in Europe, but they should not have laid down the law to me if France had not left me to wrestle alone, against the entire world. Now the French know my value; and, as they have regained their courage and their patriotism, they will triumph over the enemies who may attack them, just as they triumphed in the good days of the revolution. Experience has shown that armies cannot always save a nation; but a nation defended by the people is always invincible.

"I have not settled the day of my departure: by deferring it I should have the advantage of allowing the Congress to run out; but then, on the other hand, I should run the risk of being kept here as a close prisoner by the vessels of the Bourbons and of the English, if, as every thing appears to indicate, there should be a rupture amongst foreign powers. Murat would lend me his navy if I wanted it; but if we do not succeed he would be compromised. We must not be anxious about all these matters: we must allow some room for destiny to come into play.

"I think we have considered all the points upon which it was important that I should be settled, and that we should understand each other. France is tired of the Bourbons; she demands her former sovereign. The people and the army are for us: foreign powers will be silent. If they speak, we shall be able to reply: this, in short, is the state of the present time and of the future.

"Depart. Tell X*** that you have seen me, and that I have determined to expose myself to every danger for the purpose of yielding to the prayers of France, and of ridding the nation of the Bourbons.... Say also that I shall leave this place with my guard, on the first of April—perhaps sooner. I pardon every thing. I will give to France and to Europe all the guarantees which can be expected or demanded of me. I have renounced all my plans of aggrandizement, and I wish to repair the evils which war has caused to us, by a permanent peace.

"You will also tell X*** and the rest of my friends to nourish and strengthen the good disposition of the people and the army by all possible means. Explain to X*** that if the excesses of the Bourbons should hasten their fall, if the French should drive them out before my disembarkation, then I will not allow of a regency, or any thing in the shape of it; but let them establish a provisional government, composed of ... of ... of ... of ... and of.... Go, Sir, I hope that we shall soon meet again." — "Sire, where shall I land?" — "You must proceed to Naples; here is a passport of the island, and a letter for ****. Pretend to place great trust in him, but do not trust him with any thing. You will give him a loose account of the French news; and you may tell him that I send you there to explore the soundings, and settle some concerns of moment. I have directed **** to furnish you with a passport, in order that you may be able to return to Paris without meeting with any obstacle or danger." — "Your Majesty has then determined to send me back to France?" — "It must absolutely be so." — "Your Majesty knows my attachment, and that I am ready to prove it in any way which may be required. But, Sire, deign to consider, both for your interest and for that of

France, that my departure has been remarked, and that my return will excite still more notice, and that it may give rise to suspicion, and perhaps induce the Bourbons to put themselves on their guard, and cause them to watch the coasts and the island of Elba."—"Bah! do you suppose that fellows of the police know every thing, and can foresee every thing? More is invented than is discovered by the police. The agents of our police were decidedly as good as those of the present people, and yet they frequently knew nothing of what was going on but at the end of a week or a fortnight; and then they found it out only by chance, or incaution, or treason. I don't fear that any disclosures will be obtained from you by any of these means. You are clever and decided, and, if they were to work upon you, you would easily get clear. Besides, when you once arrive at Paris, don't show yourself; creep into a corner, and nobody will think of ferreting you out. I could certainly confide this mission to some of the people who are about me; but I do not wish to make any additional confidant: you are trusted by X***: I trust you; and, in one word, you are exactly the man whom I want. Your return is certainly exposed to objections, but they are as nothing when compared to its advantages. All that we have said about the Bourbons, and about France, and about myself, is mere talk, and talk won't overturn a throne. In order that my enterprise may not be rendered abortive, it must be seconded, and the patriots must prepare to attack the Bourbons on one side, whilst I shall occupy them on the other. And, above all, it is necessary that they should know that they may depend upon me; that they may know my sentiments, my views, and the resolution which I have made of submitting to every sacrifice, and exposing myself to every danger, for the purpose of saving the country."—The Emperor stopped to look at me. He certainly thought that I was one of those men who only appear reluctant to obey, in order to enhance the price of their services; so he said, "Money is always wanted in travelling; I will order them to pay you a thousand Louis, and then you may set off."—"A thousand Louis!" I exclaimed with indignation, "Sire, I must answer your Majesty in the words with which the soldier answered his general, 'These actions are not performed for pay.'"—"That's very right; I like to see pride."—"Sire, I am not proud, but I have a soul; and if I thought that your Majesty could believe that I embraced your Majesty's cause for the sake of filthy lucre, I should request your Majesty to cease to rely on my services."—"If I had believed that to be the case, I should not have trusted you. No person ever received a more honourable and splendid proof of my confidence, than that which I am now bestowing upon you, in deciding, merely on the strength of your word, to quit the isle of Elba, and in directing you, as my precursor, to announce my speedy arrival in France. But do not let us talk any more on that head; and tell me if you recollect fully all that I have told you."—"I have not lost one of your Majesty's expressions.

They are all engraven on my memory." — "Then I have only to wish you a pleasant journey. I have directed that everything should be got ready for your departure.

"This evening, at nine o'clock, you will find a guide and horses at the gate of the town: you will be taken to Porto Longone. The commandant has been authorised to furnish you with the necessary quarantine documents. He knows nothing; say nothing to him. At midnight a felucca will leave the port, by which you will reach Naples. I am sorry to have hurt your feelings by offering money to you, but I thought you might be in want of it. Adieu, Monsieur; be cautious. I hope we shall soon meet again, and I shall acknowledge, in a manner worthy of your merits, your exertions in favour of the country and of myself."

Hardly had I gone down to the town, where he sent for me again. "I have considered," said he, "that it is desirable that I should know what regiments are stationed in the eighth and tenth military divisions, and the names of the commanding officers. You will take care to procure this information during your journey, and transmit it to me without the slightest delay. Write triplicates of your letters. Send one by way of Genoa, the second by Leghorn, and the third by Civita Vecchia. You will take care to write this name legibly, (here he gave me a memorandum containing the name of an inhabitant of the island). Fold your letters in a business-like way. In order that the secret of your correspondence may not be discovered, should any accident happen, you will put your intelligence in the shape of commercial transactions, and you will imitate the usual style of bankers. I will suppose, for example, that between Chambery and Lyon, going by the way of Grenoble, there are five regiments. You will write to me ... in my way I have seen the five merchants whom you mentioned; their views continue the same: your credit is increasing daily. The concern will turn out well ... do you understand me?" — "Yes, Sire; but how am I to send the names of the colonels and the generals in command?" — "Transpose the letters of their names, and nothing will be more easy. There is not a single colonel or general whom I do not know, and I shall soon be able to recompose their names." — "But, Sire, the anagrams which I shall make will perhaps be so uncouth, that it will be seen at the post-office, that the names are disguised on purpose." — "Do you think then, that they amuse themselves at the post-office by opening and reading all the letters of business which pass through? They could not get through them. I have attempted to unravel the correspondence carried on under the disguise of banking transactions, but I could never succeed. The post-office is like the police, only fools are caught; yet think of any other method: I shall have no objection."

After I had considered a little while, I said to the Emperor, "Sire, there is a method which perhaps will do. Your majesty has the imperial calendar." — "Yes, sure." — "Well, Sire, the calendar contains the lists of the general officers and colonels of the army. Now, I will suppose, for example, that the regiment quartered at Chambery is commanded by Colonel Paul. I look into the calendar, and I find that Paul stands forty-seven in the list of colonels. I will also suppose that, between ourselves, 'bill of exchange' means 'colonel' or 'general.' Then I shall write to your Majesty, I have seen your correspondent at Chambery; he has paid me the amount of your bill of exchange, No. 47. Your Majesty will turn to your Majesty's calendar, and then your Majesty will see, that the 47th colonel who commands the regiment of Chambery, is called 'Paul.' And, lastly, in order that your Majesty may be able to tell when I speak of a colonel, a general, or a marshal, I shall take care to indicate the rank of the officer by one, two, or three dots, placed after the 'No.' The colonel will have one dot, No. .; the general two, No. .., &c." — "Very good, very good. Here is a calendar for you. Bertrand has one which I will take."

The calendar given to me by the Emperor was richly bound, and stamped with the imperial arms. I tore off the binding. The Emperor kept walking up and down, and saying, as he laughed, "It is really excellent; they will never be able to see through it." When I had finished, he said, "One thought brings on another. I have asked myself how you would manage to write to me, if you should have any thing of unexpected importance to communicate. For instance, suppose any extraordinary event should make you think that my disembarkation ought to be accelerated or retarded; if the Bourbons were to be on their guard; in short, I know not what." He remained silent, and then began again. "I only know one way to provide for it: the confidence which I place in you ought to be unbounded. I will give you the key to a cipher which was composed for my use, in order that I might employ it in corresponding with my family under the most important circumstances. I need not tell you that you must keep it with care: always carry it about you, lest it should be lost: and if the smallest danger arises, burn it or tear it at the slightest suspicion. With this cipher you may write any thing to me which you like. I would rather that you should use it, than be under the necessity of coming back, or of sending any messenger to me. If they intercept a letter written in my cipher, it will take them three months to read it; whilst the capture of an agent might ruin all in an instant." He then went and looked out his cipher; he made me employ it under his eyes, and delivered it to me, exhorting me not to use it unless all other modes of communication should become insufficient.

The Emperor continued, "I do not suppose that you will have occasion to return here before my departure, unless the sudden overthrow of our projects should force you to seek an asylum here. In such a case, apprise me of your intended return, and I will send for you to any place which you may name. But we must hope that victory will declare for us. She loves France.... You have not spoken to me about the affair of Excelmans: if such a thing had happened in my time, I should have thought myself lost: when the authority of the master is not recognised, all is over. The more I think upon the matter (here he displayed a sudden emotion), the more I am convinced that France is mine, and that the patriots and the army will receive me with open arms." — "Yes, Sire, I swear to you, upon my soul, the people and the army will declare for you as soon as they hear your name, as soon as they see the caps of your grenadiers." — "Provided the people do seek to do themselves justice before my arrival, a popular revolution would alarm foreign powers: they would dread the contagion of example. They know that royalty only hangs by a thread, that it does not agree with the ideas of the age; they would rather see me seize the throne, than allow the people to give it to me. They have re-established the Bourbons in order to convince the people that the rights of sovereigns are sacred and inviolable. They have blundered. They would have done more for the cause of legitimacy by leaving my son there, than by re-establishing Louis XVIII. My dynasty had been recognised by France and by Europe; it had been consecrated by the Pope. They ought to have respected it. By abusing the rights of victory, it was in their power to deprive me of the throne: but it was unjust, odious, impolitic, to punish the son on account of the wrongs of his father, and to deprive him of his inheritance. I was not an usurper: they may say so as long as they like; nobody will believe them. The English, the Italians, the Germans, are now too enlightened to allow themselves to be crammed with old ideas, with antiquated notions. In the eyes of nations, the Sovereign who is chosen by the entirety of the nation, will always be the legitimate Sovereign.... The sovereigns who sent their ambassadors to me with servile solemnity; who placed in my bed a girl of their breed; who called me their brother, and who, after doing all this, have stigmatized me as an usurper, they have spit in their own faces by trying to spit at me. They have degraded the majesty of kings. They have covered majesty with mud. What is the name of an emperor? A word like any other. If I had no better title than that, when I shall present myself to future ages they would scorn me. My institutions, my benefactions, my victories—these are the true titles of my glory. Let them call me a Corsican, a corporal, an usurper.... I don't care.... I shall not be less the object of wonder, perhaps of veneration, in all future time. My name, new as it is, will live from age to age, whilst the names of all these kings, and their royal progeny, will be forgotten before the worms will have had time to consume their carcases." The Emperor stopped, and then continued; "I forget that time is precious; I will not detain you any longer. Adieu, Monsieur; embrace me, and depart; my thoughts and good wishes follow you." — Two hours afterwards I was at sea. My attention, my faculties were wholly absorbed by the Emperor, his words, his disclosures, his plans. I had neither leisure nor opportunity to think of myself. As soon as I was quite out at sea, my ideas were filled by the extraordinary part which chance had assigned to me. I contemplated it with pride, and I returned my thanks to destiny for having selected me as the instrument by which its impenetrable decrees were to be accomplished. Perhaps no man was ever placed in so "imposing" a situation. I was the arbiter of the fate of the Bourbons, and of the Emperor, of France and Europe. With one word I could destroy Napoleon; with one word I could save Louis. But Louis was nothing to me: in him I only saw a sovereign who had been forced upon the throne by foreign hands still imbrued with French blood. In Napoleon I saw the sovereign to whom France had freely offered the crown as the reward of twenty years of danger and of glory. The perspective of the evils which the attempt of Napoleon might bring upon France did not arise before my imagination. I was persuaded that all foreign powers (England excepted), would remain neutral; and that the French would receive Napoleon as a deliverer, and as a father. Still less did I consider myself as engaged in treason or conspiracy against the Bourbons. Since I had taken the oath of allegiance to Napoleon, I considered him as my legitimate sovereign; and I rejoiced to think that the confidence which Napoleon reposed in me had induced him to call upon me to concur in restoring to France the liberty, the power, and the glory of which the country had been unjustly deprived. I enjoyed, by anticipation, the public eulogiums, which, after his success, he would bestow upon my courage, my self-devotion, my patriotism. In short, I abandoned myself with rapture and with pride to all the thoughts, and all the generous resolutions which can be inspired by the love of fame and the love of our country.

The dialogues which had taken place between me and the Emperor continued impressed on my memory; yet, lest I might vary them, or omit any part, I employed my time during the voyage in recalling his own expressions, and in classing his questions and my answers. I afterwards got the whole by heart, just as a scholar learns his lesson, in order that I might be able to affirm to M. X*** that I was making a faithful and literal report to him of all that the Emperor had said, and of all that he had ordered me to tell him.

The weather being tolerably favourable, we soon reached Naples. I went immediately to M. ****: he put a great number of indiscreet questions to me; and I replied by an equal number of unmeaning answers. He probably thought that I knew no better, and therefore my caution did not offend him. When our preliminary conversation was exhausted, I desired him to give me my passport; he did so immediately: it was a Neapolitan passport. "This won't do for me," said I; "I must have a French passport."—"I have not got one."—"The Emperor told me that you could get one."—"That is just like the Emperor; he thinks every thing is possible: where does he suppose that I can procure it? I am doing a great deal in giving you a passport as a subject of his Majesty. It is already known that we are in relation with the isle of Elba. If they were to find out that you are attached to Napoleon, and that you are going back to France by his directions, and with the assistance of the King, all Europe would hear of it, and the King would be committed. Why does not the Emperor keep himself quiet? he will ruin himself, and ruin us all along with him."—"It is not fit that I should examine the conduct of his Majesty, much less that I should censure it. I am in his service; and my duty commands me to obey him. I want a French passport: can you, or can you not get me one?"—"I tell you again that it is impossible: it is doing too much if I give you one as a Neapolitan subject."—"Then I must return to Porto Ferrajo: but I cannot conceal from you that the Emperor is very desirous that I should return to France; and he will certainly be very much displeased, both with you and with the King."—"Then he will act unfairly: the King has done, and will do, every thing in his power for him: but the Emperor should know what the King may do under his present critical situation, and what he may not. But why won't you take the passport which I offer you?"—"Because I do not understand Italian, and consequently your passport would expose me to greater suspicion than my own."—"Then why don't you try to push on as far as Rome? there you will find the family of the Emperor. Louis XVIII. has a legation there; and perhaps money may get you a passport."—"Your idea is excellent: I will go. Inform the Emperor of the delay which I have experienced, in order that he may send another agent, if he thinks it advisable so to do."

When the mind is in perpetual activity, and constantly assailed by new feelings, there is no time for reflection. I thus went to Rome, full of the idea that I should visit the family of the Emperor, and request their help to aid me out of my difficulties. But when the time came, and I was to present myself, it then struck me that the Emperor, though aware that I was to pass through Rome, had not directed me to see them; and I concluded that he had his reasons. I therefore determined to continue my route. From Naples I have proceeded to Rome without any obstacle; and I shall proceed, thought I to myself, from Rome to Milan without any greater obstacle: there I shall meet my friend and his Tedesco; I will get them to legalize my French passport for the second time, and destiny will accomplish the rest.

I therefore presented myself boldly to the police at Rome, in order to have my Elba passport indorsed for Milan. I was introduced to his Eminence the Director-general, who, as I believe, had been shut up at Vincennes under the imperial government. He received me with great rudeness; and he wished to compel me to present myself to the French embassy. I would not consent. I answered, firmly, "The King of France is no longer my sovereign; I am the subject of the Emperor Napoleon: the allied sovereigns have proclaimed and recognized him as the sovereign of the isle of Elba: he therefore reigns at Porto Ferrajo like the Pope at Rome, George at London, and Louis XVIII. at Paris. The Emperor and his Holiness are on good terms with each other. The subjects and the vessels of the Roman states are well received in the isle of Elba[38], and therefore you are bound to afford aid and protection to the Elbese, so long as the holy father shall not become the enemy of Napoleon."

This reasoning produced its effect; and his Eminence ordered, though he continued grumbling, that my demand was to be granted. "What are you going to do at Milan?" said he, and I think he muttered an oath between his teeth: "I am going," I answered, "relative to the dotations which were assigned to us upon the 'Mont Napoléon.'" He was satisfied with my answer, and so was I. I wrote to M. ****, the Neapolitan consul, transmitting my letter; and I requested him to send to the island an account of my new route.

I continued my journey. My passport was headed by the imperial arms. The name of Napoleon, and his title of Emperor, were inscribed in large letters. I was the first Frenchman from the island who had been able or who had dared to traverse Italy. How many things there were which roused curiosity and commanded attention! I was overwhelmed with questions relative to Porto Ferrajo and its illustrious sovereign. I answered as fully as they wished. Whilst they were busying themselves about the Emperor, they did not think of me, and that was what I wanted. In order to avoid troublesome examinations, I took care to pass through the towns at night, and never to stop in them. At length, thanks to my address and good fortune, I arrived safe and sound at Milan; there I found my friend and his colonel, and every thing was settled admirably.

I set off again for Turin with all possible speed. When I arrived on the Place of ... I perceived several numerous groups of persons, who appeared exceedingly animated. How great was my surprise when I found that they were talking of Napoleon, and his escape from the isle of Elba. This piece of intelligence, which had been just received, put me in a violent passion:

I accused the Emperor of perfidiousness. I reproached him with having misled, deceived, and sacrificed me.

When my first fit of ill humour was calmed, I considered the conduct of the Emperor under another aspect. I thought that unexpected considerations might have induced him to embark precipitately. I was ashamed of my suspicions and of my violence, and I only wished to fly to his footsteps; but already orders had been given to prevent communication. I passed eight days, which appeared so many ages, in soliciting permission to return to France; and at last I obtained it. I arrived at Paris on the 25th of March: on the 26th M. X*** presented me to the Emperor: he embraced me, and said, "I have weighty reasons for wishing that you and X*** may both forget whatever passed at the isle of Elba. I alone will not forget it. Rely on my esteem and protection on all occasions[39]."

Here ends the memoir of M. Z****.

This officer had scarcely quitted the island of Elba, when the Emperor (and I had the particulars from his Majesty himself) acknowledged and deplored the imprudence of which he had been guilty, in sending Z*** to the continent. The character and firmness of this faithful servant were sufficiently known to him, to prevent his feeling any anxiety on his account. He was certain (I use his own words), that he would suffer himself to be cut to pieces, before he would open his mouth: but he was afraid, that the inquiries he had directed him to make on the road, the letters he might address to him, or the conferences he might have at Paris with M. X*** and his friends, would excite the suspicions of the police; and that the Bourbons would station cruizers, so as to render an escape from the island of Elba, and a landing on the coast of France, altogether impossible.

Thus the Emperor felt that there was but one way of preventing the danger, that of departing immediately.

On this point he did not hesitate. From that moment every thing assumed a different aspect in the island of Elba.

This island, but the moment before the abode of philosophy and peace, became in an instant the imperial head-quarters. Couriers, orders, and counter-orders, were incessantly going and returning from Porto Ferrajo to Longone, and from Longone to Porto Ferrajo. Napoleon, whose fiery activity had been so long enchained, gave himself up, with infinite delight, to all the cares, that his audacious enterprise demanded. But in whatever mystery he fancied he had shrouded himself, the unusual accounts he had caused to be delivered in, the particular attention he had paid to his old grenadiers, had excited their suspicion; and they scarcely doubted, that he had it in contemplation to quit the island. Every one supposed, that he would land at

Naples, or in some other port of Italy: no one ventured even to imagine, that his plan was to go and expel Louis XVIII. from the throne.

On the 26th of February, at one o'clock, the guard and the officers of his household received orders to hold themselves in readiness to depart. Every thing was in motion: the grenadiers with joy resumed their arms, that so long had lain idle, and spontaneously swore, never to quit them but with life. The whole population of the country, crowds of old men, women, and children, eagerly rushed to the shore; the most affecting scenes were exhibited on all sides. They thronged round the faithful companions of Napoleon in his exile, and contended with each other for the pleasure, the honour, of touching them, seeing them, embracing them for the last time. The younger members of the families of the first distinction in the island solicited as a favour, the danger of sharing in the perils of the Emperor. Joy, glory, hope, sparkled in every eye. They knew not whither they were going, but Napoleon was present, and with him could they doubt of victory?

At eight in the evening a gun gave the signal for departure. A thousand times embraces were immediately lavished and returned. The French rushed into their boats; martial music struck up; and Napoleon and his followers sailed majestically from the shore, amid the shouts of "Long live the Emperor!" a thousand times repeated[40].

Napoleon, when he set foot on board his vessel, exclaimed with Cæsar, "The die is cast!" His countenance was calm, his brow serene: he appeared to think less of the success of his enterprise, than of the means of promptly attaining his object. The eyes of Count Bertrand sparkled with hope and joy: General Drouot was pensive and serious: Cambronne appeared to care little about the future, and to think only of doing his duty well. The old grenadiers had resumed their martial and menacing aspect. The Emperor chatted and joked with them incessantly: he pulled their ears and their mustachios, reminded them of their dangers and their glory, and inspired their minds with that confidence, with which his own was animated.

All were burning to know their destination: respect did not allow any one to ask the question: at length Napoleon broke silence. "Grenadiers," said he, "we are going to France, we are going to Paris." At these words every countenance expanded, their joy ceased to be mingled with anxiety, and stifled cries of "France for ever!" attested to the Emperor, that in the heart of a Frenchman the love of his country is never extinct.

An English sloop of war, commanded by Captain Campbell, appeared to have the charge of watching the island of Elba[41]: she was continually sailing from Porto Ferrajo to Leghorn, and from Leghorn to Porto Ferrajo. At the moment of embarkation she was at Leghorn, and could occasion no alarm; but several vessels were descried in the channel, and their presence gave room for just apprehensions. It was hoped, however, that the night breeze would favour the progress of the flotilla, and that before daybreak it would be out of sight. This hope was frustrated. ""Scarcely had it doubled Cape St. Andrew, in the island of Elba, when the wind fell and the sea became calm. At daybreak it had advanced only six leagues, and was still between the islands of Elba and Capræa.

""The danger appeared imminent: several of the seamen were for returning to Porto Ferrajo. The Emperor ordered them to hold on their course, as, at the worst, he had the chance either of capturing the French cruiser, or of taking refuge in the island of Corsica, where he was assured of being well received. To facilitate their manœuvres, he ordered all the luggage embarked to be thrown overboard, which was cheerfully executed at the instant.""

About noon the wind freshened a little. At four o'clock they were off Leghorn. One frigate was in sight five leagues to leeward, another on the coast of Corsica, and a man-of-war brig, which was perceived to be Le Zéphir, commanded by Captain Andrieux, was coming down upon the imperial flotilla right before the wind. It was first proposed to speak to him, and make him hoist the three-coloured flag. "The Emperor, however, gave orders to the soldiers of the guard to take off their caps and conceal themselves below, choosing rather to pass by the brig without being known, and reserving himself in case of necessity, for the alternative of making him change his colours. At six o'clock the two brigs passed alongside of each other, and their commanders, who were acquainted, spoke together. The captain of Le Zéphir inquired after the Emperor, and was answered through a speaking trumpet by the Emperor himself, that he was extremely well.

""The two brigs, steering opposite courses, were soon out of sight of each other, without Captain Andrieux having any suspicion of the valuable prize, that he had allowed to escape.

""In the night of the 27th the wind continued to freshen. At day-break a seventy-four was descried, which appeared steering for San Fiorenzo or Sardinia, and it was soon perceived, that she took no notice of the brig[42].""

The Emperor, before he quitted the island of Elba, had prepared with his own hand two proclamations, one addressed to the French people, the other to the army; and he was desirous of having them copied out fairly. His secretary and General Bertrand, being neither of them able to decipher them, carried them to Napoleon, who, despairing of doing it himself, threw them into the sea from vexation. Then, after meditating for a few moments, he dictated to his secretary the two following proclamations on the spot.

Proclamation.

Gulf of Juan, March the 1st, 1815.

Napoleon, by the grace of God and constitution of the empire, Emperor of the French, &c. &c. &c.

To the Army.

Soldiers!

We have not been vanquished: two men, who issued from our ranks, betrayed our laurels, their country, their prince, their benefactor.

Shall they, whom we have seen for five and twenty years traversing all Europe, to stir up enemies against us—who have spent their lives in fighting against us in the ranks of foreign armies, and cursing our lovely France—now pretend to command us, and to enchain our eagles, the looks of which they could never withstand? Shall we suffer them to inherit the fruits of our glorious toils? to seize upon our honours, and our property, and calumniate our fame? Should their reign continue, all would be lost, even the remembrance of our memorable victories.

With what virulence do they distort them! They endeavour to poison what is the admiration of the world; and if any defenders of our glory still remain, it is among those very enemies whom we combated in the field.

Soldiers! in my exile I heard your voice: I am arrived through every obstacle, through every danger.

Your general, called to the throne by the voice of the people, and raised on your shields, is restored to you. Come and join him.

Tear down those colours, which the nation has proscribed, and which for five and twenty years served as a signal to rally all the enemies of France. Mount that tricoloured cockade, which you wore in our great victories. We must forget, that we have been the masters of other nations; but we must not suffer any to interfere in our affairs. Who shall pretend to be our master? Who is able to be so? Resume the eagles you bore at Ulm, at Austerlitz, at Jena, at Eylau, at Wagram, at Friedland, at Tudela, at Eckmuhl, at Essling, at Smolensko, at Moscow, at Lutzen, at Wurtchen, at Montmirail. Think you that handful of Frenchmen, now so arrogant, can support their sight? They will return whence they came; and there, if they please, they may reign, as they pretend to have reigned for nineteen years.

Your property, your rank, your glory—the property, the rank, the glory of your children—have no greater enemies than those princes, who have been imposed on us by foreigners. They are the enemies of our glory; since the recital of so many glorious actions, which have rendered illustrious the

French people, fighting against them to emancipate themselves from their yoke, is their condemnation.

The veterans of the armies of the Sambre and Meuse, of the Rhine, of Italy, of Egypt, of the west, of the grand army, are humiliated; their honourable scars are disgraced; their successes would be crimes, the valiant would be rebels, if, as the enemies of the people assert, legitimate sovereigns were among the foreign armies. Their honours, rewards, affections, are for those who have served them, against us and against our country.

Soldiers, come and arrange yourselves under the standards of your chief: his existence consists only of yours; his rights are only those of the people and of you; his interest, his honour, his glory, are no other than your glory. Victory will march forward with the charge step: the eagle, with the national colours, will fly from steeple to steeple till it reaches the towers of Notre Dame. You may then display your scars with honour, you may then boast of what you have done: you will be the deliverers of your country.

In your old age, surrounded and respected by your fellow citizens, they will listen with veneration to the recital of your noble deeds: you may proudly say, I too was in that grand army which twice entered the walls of Vienna, and those of Rome, of Berlin, of Madrid, and of Moscow, and which cleansed Paris from the stain inflicted on it by treason and the presence of the enemy. Honour to those brave soldiers, the glory of their country! and eternal shame to those guilty Frenchmen, in whatever rank it was their fortune to be born, who fought for five and twenty years in company with foreigners, to wound the bosom of their country.

Signed, Napoleon.

By the Emperor.

The grand marshal, executing the functions of major-general of the grand army.

Signed, Bertrand.

Proclamation.

Gulf of Juan, March 1, 1815.

Napoleon, by the grace of God and the constitution of the empire, Emperor of the French, &c. &c. &c.

To the French People.

Frenchmen!

The defection of the Duke of Castiglione gave up Lyons without defence to our enemies. The army, the command of which I had entrusted to him, was capable, from the bravery and patriotism of the troops of which it was formed, of beating the Austrian army opposed to it, and taking in the rear the left flank of the enemy's army, that threatened Paris.

The victories of Champ Aubert, of Montmirail, of Château Thierry, of Vauchamp, of Mormane, of Montereau, of Craone, of Rheims, of Arcy-sur-Aube, and of St. Dizier; the insurrection of the brave peasantry of Lorraine, of Champagne, of Alsace, of Franche Comté, and of Burgundy; and the position I had taken in the rear of the enemy's army, cutting it off from its magazines, its parks of reserve, and convoys, and all its waggons, had placed it in a desperate situation. The French were on the point of being more powerful than ever, and the flower of the enemy's army was lost without resource; it would have found its grave in those vast countries, which it had so pitilessly ravaged, when the treachery of the Duke of Ragusa delivered up the capital, and disorganized the army. The unsuspected conduct of these two generals, who betrayed at once their country, their prince, and their benefactor, changed the fate of the war: the situation of the enemy was such, that, after the affair that took place before Paris, he was without ammunition, in consequence of being separated from his parks of reserve[43].

Under these new and important circumstances, my heart was torn, but my mind remained unshaken: I consulted only the interests of our country, and banished myself to a rock surrounded by the seas: my life was useful to you, and was destined still to be so. I would not permit the great number of citizens, who were desirous of accompanying me, to share my fate: I deemed their presence advantageous to France, and I took with me only the handful of brave fellows necessary for my guard.

Raised to the throne by your choice, every thing that has been done without you is illegal. Within these five and twenty years France has acquired new interests, new institutions, new glory, to be guarantied only by a national government, and a dynasty born under these new circumstances. A prince who should reign over you, who should be seated on my throne by the power of the same armies, that have ravaged our territories, would seek in vain to support himself by the principles of feudal right; he could secure the honour and the rights only of a small number of individuals, enemies to the people, who have condemned them in all our national assemblies for five and twenty years. Your tranquillity at home, and estimation abroad, would be lost for ever.

Frenchmen! in my exile I heard your complaints and wishes: you called for that government of your own choice, which alone is legitimate; you blamed my long slumber; you reproached me with sacrificing the great interests of the country to my own repose.

I have crossed the seas amid perils of every kind: I arrive among you to resume my rights, which are also yours. Every thing that individuals have done, written, or said, since the taking of Paris, I shall consign to everlasting oblivion; it shall have no influence on the remembrance I retain of the important services they have rendered, for there are events of such a nature, that they are above the frame of man.

Frenchmen! there is no nation, however small, that has not possessed the right of withdrawing, and that has not withdrawn itself, from the disgrace of obeying a prince imposed upon it by an enemy temporarily victorious. When Charles VII. re-entered Paris, and overturned the ephemeral throne of Henry VI., he acknowledged, that he held his crown from the valour of his brave people, and not from the Prince Regent of England.

It is to you only, and to the brave men of the army, that I make, and shall always make it my glory, to owe every thing.

Signed, Napoleon.

By the Emperor.

The grand marshal, executing the functions of major-general of the grand army.

Signed, Bertrand.

The Emperor, while he dictated these proclamations, appeared to be animated with the most profound indignation. He seemed to have before his eyes, both the generals, whom he accused of having given up France, and the enemies, who had subjugated it. He incessantly repeated the names of Marmont and Augereau, and they were always accompanied with threats and with epithets, suited to the idea he had conceived of their treachery.

When the proclamations were transcribed, the Emperor directed them to be read aloud, and invited all those who could write a good hand to copy them. In an instant, benches and drums were converted into tables; and soldiers, sailors, and officers, set themselves gayly to work.

After a certain time, his Majesty said to the officers around him, "Now, gentlemen, it is your turn, to speak to the army: you must tell it what France expects of it under the important circumstances in which we shall soon find ourselves. Come, Bertrand, take your pen." The grand marshal excused himself. The Emperor then resumed his discourse, and dictated, without stopping, an address to the generals, officers, and soldiers of the army, in which the imperial guard conjured them, in the name of honour and their country, to shake off the yoke of the Bourbons.

"Soldiers," said they to them, "the drum beats the general, and we march: run to arms, come and join us, join your Emperor, and our eagles.

"And if these men, now so arrogant, who have always fled at the sight of our weapons, dare wait for us, where can we find a fairer occasion of shedding our blood, and chanting the hymn of victory?

"Soldiers of the seventh, eighth, and nineteenth military divisions, garrisons of Antibes, Toulon, and Marseilles, retired officers, veterans of our army, you are called to the honour of setting the first example: come with us to conquer that throne, which is the palladium of your rights; and let posterity some day tell, 'Foreigners, seconded by traitors, had imposed a disgraceful yoke on France; the brave arose, and the enemies of the people, of the army, disappeared, and returned to their original nothingness.'"

This address was scarcely finished, when the coast of Antibes was descried at a distance. Immediately on this, the Emperor and his brave fellows saluted the land of their country with shouts of "France for ever! Success to the French!" and at the same instant resumed the tricoloured cockade[44].

On the 1st of March, at three o'clock, they entered the Gulf of Juan. General Drouot, and a certain number of officers and soldiers, who were on board the felucca Caroline, landed before the Emperor, who was still at a considerable distance from the shore. At this moment they perceived to the right a large vessel, which appeared to them (though they were mistaken in this) to be steering with all sails towards the brig. Suddenly they were seized with the greatest disquiet; they walked backward and forward, testifying by their gestures and their hurried steps, the emotion and fear with which they were agitated. General Drouot ordered the Caroline to be unloaded, and to hasten to meet the brig. In an instant cannons, carriages, chests, baggage, every thing was thrown out upon the sand, and already the grenadiers and brave sea officers of the guard were rowing away with all their strength, when acclamations from the brig saluted their ears and their affrighted eyes. It was the Emperor: whether from prudential motives or impatience, he had got into a simple boat. Their alarms ceased; and the grenadiers, stretching out their arms to him, received him with the most affecting demonstrations of devotedness and joy. At five o'clock he landed. I have heard him say, that he never felt an emotion so profound.

""His quarters for the night were taken up in a field surrounded by olive-trees. This, he exclaimed, is a happy omen: may it be realized!""

A few peasants were seen: the Emperor ordered them to be called, and interrogated them. One of them had formerly served under him: he knew his old general, and would not quit him. Napoleon, turning to the grand marshal, said to him, with a smile, "Well, Bertrand, you see we have a reinforcement already." He spent the evening chatting and laughing familiarly with his generals and the officers of his household. "I see from this spot," said he, "the fright I shall give the Bourbons, and the embarrassment of all those who have turned their backs upon me." Then, continuing to joke on the same subject, he defined, with his wonted sagacity, the characters of the marshals and great personages, who had formerly served him; and was much amused with the endeavours they would make ""to save appearances, and prudently await the moment for declaring themselves for the strongest party.""

The success of his enterprise appeared less to employ his thoughts, than the dangers to which his friends and partisans, whom he no longer called by any other name than that of patriots, were going to be exposed. "What will become of the patriots before my arrival at Paris?" he frequently exclaimed: "I tremble lest the Vendeans and emigrants should massacre them. Wo betide those who touch them! I will have no mercy on them."

Immediately after he landed, the Emperor had despatched a captain of the guard with five and twenty men to Antibes: their instructions were, to present themselves as deserters from the island of Elba; to sound the disposition of the garrison; and, if this appeared favourable, to seduce it: but, led away by their imprudent ardour, they entered the city, shouting, "Long live the Emperor!" and the commandant caused the drawbridge instantly to be raised, and detained them as prisoners. Napoleon, finding they did not return, sent for a civil officer of the guard, and said to him, ""You will immediately repair to the walls of Antibes: you will deliver this despatch, or cause it to be delivered to General Corsin: you will not enter the place, as you might be detained: you will draw together the soldiers, you will read to them my proclamations, and you will harangue them. Do you not know, you will say to them, that your Emperor is here? that the garrisons of Grenoble and Lyons have marched to join him with the charge step? What do you wait for? Will you leave to others the honour of joining him before you? the honour of marching at the head of his advanced guard? Come, and salute our eagles and our tricoloured flags. The Emperor and your country command it; then come.""

This officer, on his return, said, that the gates of the town and harbour were closed, and that it was not possible for him to see General Corsin, or to speak to the soldiers. Napoleon appeared disappointed, though but little disturbed by the disappointment. At eleven in the evening he began his march, with four small pieces of artillery in his train. The Poles, though unable to embark their horses, had brought with them their accoutrements, and gayly marched in the advanced guard, bending beneath the weight of their enormous luggage. Napoleon purchased for them every horse he met with, and thus remounted his handful of cavalry one by one.

He proceeded to Cannes, thence to Grasses, and, in the evening of the 2d, arrived at the village of Cerenon, having marched twenty leagues this first day. Every where he was received with sentiments, that presaged the success of the enterprise.

On the 3d the Emperor slept at Bareme, and on the 4th at Digne. The report of his landing, which preceded him from place to place, excited every where a mingled feeling of joy, surprise, and anxiety. The peasants blessed his return, and expressed their good wishes to him in their simple language; but when they saw his little troop, they looked on him with tender pity, and had no hope of his being triumphant with such feeble means.

On the 5th Napoleon slept at Gap, and retained with him only six horsemen, and forty grenadiers.

In this city he printed, for the first time, his proclamations: they were diffused with the rapidity of lightning, and inflamed every head and every heart with such violent and prompt devotedness, that the whole population of the country was desirous of rising in a body, and marching as his advanced guard.

In these proclamations he did not borrow, as has been asserted, the title of general in chief, or of lieutenant general of his son. Before he quitted the island of Elba, he had determined to resume the style of Emperor of the French as soon as he landed.

He was aware, that any other title would diminish his strength, and his ascendancy over the people and the army; would render his intentions doubtful; would give rise to scruples and hesitation; and besides, would place him in a state of hostility against France. In short, he was aware, that it would always be in his power to give legitimacy to his title of Emperor of the French, should the suffrages of the nation prove necessary, to restore to him in the eyes of Europe, and even of France, those rights, which might have been temporarily lost by his abdication.

The superior authorities of Gap had retired at his approach: he had to receive the congratulations only of the mayor, the municipal council, and the half-pay officers. He discoursed with them on the benefits of the revolution, the sovereignty of the people, liberty, equality, and particularly of the emigrants and the Bourbons. Before he left them, he addressed his public thanks to the inhabitants of the Upper and Lower Alps, in the following words:

Citizens,

I have been strongly touched by all the sentiments that you have testified towards me: your prayers will be heard; the cause of the nation will still triumph. You have reason to call me your father; I live only for the honour and happiness of France. My return dissipates your disquietudes; it guarantees the preservation of every one's property, the equality of all classes; and those rights, which you have enjoyed for twenty-five years, and for which our forefathers so frequently sighed, now form a part of your existence.

In whatever circumstances I may be placed, I shall always remember, with a lively interest, what I have seen in traversing your country.

[45]""On the 6th, at two o'clock in the afternoon, the Emperor left Gap, and the whole city went out to see him set off.

""At St. Bonnel the inhabitants, seeing the small number of his soldiers, were full of fears, and proposed to him to sound the alarm-bell, in order to collect the neighbouring villagers, and accompany him in a body. 'No,' said the Emperor, 'your sentiments convince me, that I have not deceived myself; they are a sure guarantee of the sentiments of my soldiers; those whom I meet will range themselves on my side; and the more they are, the more certain will be my success. Remain, therefore, tranquil at home.'""

The same day the Emperor came to sleep at Gorp; General Cambronne and forty men, forming the advanced guard, pushed on as far as Mure.

Cambronne most commonly proceeded alone before his grenadiers to explore the road, and cause quarters and subsistence to be provided for them. Scarcely had he pronounced the name of the Emperor, when every one was eager to testify to him the most lively and tender solicitude. One mayor alone, the Marquis de ***, mayor of Sisteron, tried to raise the inhabitants of that commune, describing to them the soldiers of Napoleon as robbers and incendiaries. Confounded by the sudden appearance of General Cambronne alone, and with no other weapon than his sword, he changed his language, and pretended to have had no fear but that of being paid[46]. Cambronne coolly threw him his purse, and said, "Pay yourself!" The indignant people were eager to furnish more provision than was demanded; and when the battalion of Elba appeared, they offered it a tricoloured flag, as a sign of their esteem and devotedness.

On quitting the mayor, General Cambronne and his forty grenadiers met a battalion sent from Grenoble to block up their passage. Cambronne wished to parley with them, but they would not listen to him. The Emperor, informed of this resistance, immediately went forward: his guard, exhausted by a long march through the snow and rough roads, had not all been able to follow him; but when it heard of the affront offered to Cambronne, and the dangers the Emperor might run, it forgot its fatigues, and hastened after him. Those soldiers, who could no longer support themselves on their galled or wounded feet, were assisted by their comrades, or carried by them on litters formed with their musquets: all swore, like the soldiers of Fabius, not to conquer or die, but to be victors. When the Emperor perceived them, he held out his hand to them, and said, "With you, my brave soldiers, I should not be afraid of ten thousand men."

Meantime the troops come from Grenoble had retreated, and taken a position three leagues from Gorp, between the lakes, and near a village. The Emperor went to reconnoitre them. He found in the line opposed to him a battalion of the fifth regiment, a company of sappers, and a company of miners; in all seven or eight hundred men. He sent to them *chef d'escadron* Roul: they refused to listen to him. On this, Napoleon, turning to Marshal Bertrand, said, "*Z. has deceived me; no matter, forwards!*" Immediately, alighting from his horse, he marched straight to the detachment, followed by his guard, with arms secured (*l'arme baissée*): "What, my friends!" said he to them, "do you not know me? I am your Emperor: if there be a soldier among you, who is willing to kill his general, his Emperor, he may do it: here I am!" and he placed his hand upon his breast....

The unanimous shout of "Long live the Emperor!" was the answer.

""Immediately they requested permission, to be the first to march against the division, that covered Grenoble. The march commenced amid a crowd of the inhabitants, which increased every instant. Vizille distinguished itself by its enthusiasm: "It is here the revolution is born," said these brave fellows: "we are the first who have dared to claim the privileges of men: it is here, too, that French liberty revives, and that France recovers its honour and independence."

""Between Vizille and Grenoble, an adjutant-major of the seventh of the line came to announce, that Colonel Labedoyère, deeply wounded by the dishonour that affected all France, and governed by the noblest sentiments, had separated from the division of Grenoble, and with his regiment was hastening with all speed to meet the Emperor.""

Soon after, numerous acclamations were heard at a distance: they were from Labedoyère, and the seventh. The two troops, impatient to join, broke their ranks: embraces, and shouts a thousand times repeated, of "The guard for ever! the seventh for ever! long live the Emperor!" became the pledge of their union, and of their sentiments.

Napoleon, who saw his forces and the public enthusiasm increase at every step, resolved to enter Grenoble that very evening.

Before he reached the city he was stopped by a young merchant, an officer of the national guard. "Sire," said he, "I come to offer your Majesty a hundred thousand francs, and my sword." — "I accept both: remain with us." Farther on he was joined by a party of officers, who confirmed to him what he had learned from Labedoyère, that General Marchand and the prefect had declared against him, and that neither the garrison, nor the national guard, had yet displayed any favourable disposition.

""In fact, General Marchand had caused the troops to re-enter Grenoble, and closed the gates: the ramparts were covered by the third regiment of engineers, composed of two thousand sappers, all veterans, covered with honourable scars; by the fourth of artillery of the line, the very regiment in which the Emperor had been made a captain five and twenty years before; then the two battalions of the fifth of the line, and the faithful hussars of the fourth.""

Never did a besieged town exhibit a similar spectacle; the besiegers, with arms reversed, and marching in joyful irregularity, approached the walls singing. No noise of arms, no warlike shouts from the soldiers, rose to affright the air: nothing was heard but repeated acclamations of "Grenoble for ever! France for ever! Napoleon for ever!" no cries but those of the most unrestrained gaiety, and the purest enthusiasm. The garrison, the national guard, the town's-people, spread over the ramparts, beheld at first with surprise, with emotion, these transports of joy and attachment. It was not long before they shared them; and the besiegers and besieged, united by the same thoughts, the same sentiments, uttered at once the rallying words, "Long live the Emperor!" The people and the soldiers repaired to the gates, which were in an instant beaten down, and Napoleon, surrounded, thronged by an idolizing crowd, made his triumphant entry into Grenoble. A few moments after, the people came and brought him the fragments of the gates with trumpets sounding, and said, "For want of the keys of the good town of Grenoble, here are the gates for you."

The possession of this place was of the highest importance to Napoleon: it afforded him a point of support, ammunition, arms, and artillery. He could not conceal his extreme satisfaction, and said repeatedly to his officers, "All is now decided; we are sure of getting to Paris." He questioned Labedoyère at large on the state of Paris, and the situation of France in general. This young colonel, full of the noblest sentiments, expressed himself with a frankness that sometimes staggered Napoleon. "Sire," he said, "the French will do every thing for your Majesty; but then your Majesty must do every thing for them: *no more ambition, no more despotism: we are determined to be free and happy.* It is necessary, Sire, to renounce that system of conquest and power which occasioned the misfortunes of France, and of yourself." — "If I succeed," answered Napoleon, "I will do every thing requisite to fulfil the expectations of the nation: its happiness is dearer to me than my own: it is to render it free and happy, that I have embarked in an undertaking, which might not succeed, and might cost me my life; but we shall have the consolation of dying in our native land." — "And of dying," added Labedoyère, "for its honour and its liberty."

The Emperor gave orders to have his proclamations printed in the course of the night, and despatched emissaries in every direction to announce his having entered Grenoble; that Austria was for him; that the king of Naples was following him with eighty thousand men; ... and, in short, to discourage, intimidate, and curb, by false alarms and false confidences, the partisans and agents of the regal government.

The proclamations, posted up in abundance, produced the most lively sensation, as at Gap. In fact, never had the national pride, patriotism, and the noblest passions of the mind, been addressed with more fascination, strength, and eloquence. The soldiers and citizens were never tired of reading and admiring them. Every person was desirous of having them. Travellers, and the inhabitants of the neighbouring country, received an immense quantity, which they took upon themselves to spread abroad on their road, and to send to all parts.

The next day, the 8th, the clergy, the staff-officers, the imperial court, the tribunals, and the civil and military authorities, came to acknowledge Napoleon, and to offer him their congratulations. He conversed familiarly with the judges on the administration of justice; with the clergy on what was necessary to public worship; with the soldiery on the armies; with the municipal officers on the sufferings of the people, the towns, and the country places; and delighted them all by the variety of his knowledge, and the benevolence of his intentions. He then said to them: "I knew that France was unhappy; I heard its groans and its reproaches; I am come with the faithful companions of my exile, to deliver her from the yoke of the Bourbons ... their throne is illegitimate ... my rights were conferred on me by the nation, by the unanimous will of the French people: they are no other rights than theirs.... I am come to resume them; not to reign, the throne is nothing to me: not to revenge myself, for I shall forget every thing that has been said, done, or written, since the capitulation of Paris; but to restore to you the rights, which the Bourbons have taken from you, and to emancipate you from the subscription to the glebe, the vassalage, and the feudal system, with which you are threatened by them.... I have been too fond of war; I will make war no more: I will leave my neighbours at rest: we must forget, that we have been masters of the world.... I wish to reign, in order to render our lovely France free, happy, and independent; and to place its happiness on foundations not to be shaken; *I wish to be less its sovereign than the first and best of its citizens.* I might have come to attack the Bourbons with ships and numerous fleets; but I would have no assistance from Murat or from Austria. I know my fellow citizens, and the defenders of my country, and I reckon on their patriotism."

The audience ended, the Emperor reviewed the garrison, consisting of five or six thousand men. As soon as he appeared, the sky was darkened by the multitude of sabres, bayonets, grenadier-caps, *chacos,* &c., which the people and the soldiers raised in the air, amid the most lively demonstrations of attachment and love.

He said a few words to the people, which could not be heard, and repaired to the front of the fourth of artillery. "It was among you," said he, "that I began my career in arms. I love you all as old comrades; I have observed you in the field of battle, and I have always been satisfied with your conduct. But I hope, that we shall have no occasion for your guns: France has need of moderation and repose. The army will enjoy, in the bosom of peace, the benefits I have already conferred on it, and those I shall yet bestow. In me the soldiers have found again their father: they may reckon upon the rewards they have deserved."

After this review, the garrison set out on its march to Lyons.

In the evening Napoleon wrote to the Empress and Prince Joseph. He directed him to make known at Rome, at Naples, and at Porto Ferrajo, that his enterprise had every appearance of being crowned with the most speedy and brilliant success. The couriers departed with great noise; and care was taken to make known, that they were carrying to the Empress the news of the Emperor's return, with orders to come immediately, with her son, and join him.

On the 9th the Emperor declared the establishment of the imperial power by three decrees.

The first directed all public acts, and the administration of justice, to be executed in his name from the 15th of March.

The two others organized the national guards of the five departments of the Upper and Lower Alps, la Drôme, Mont Blanc, and the Izère, and entrusted to the honour and patriotism of the inhabitants of the seventh division the fortified towns of Briançon, Grenoble, Fort Barreaux, Colmar, &c.

The moment he set off, he addressed to the inhabitants of the department of the Izère the following proclamation:

Citizens,

When in my exile I learned all the misfortunes, that oppressed the nation; that all the rights of the people were disregarded, and that I was reproached with the state of repose in which I lived: I lost not a moment: I embarked on board a slight vessel, crossed the sea in the midst of ships of war belonging to various nations, landed alone on the shores of our country, and thought of nothing but of arriving with the rapidity of an eagle in this good city of Grenoble, of the patriotism of which, and its personal attachment to me, I was well aware. Men of Dauphiny, you have answered my expectation.

I have endured, not without a wounded heart, but without being dejected, the misfortunes to which for a twelvemonth I have been a prey. The spectacle displayed to my eyes by the people on my journey has inspired me with the most lively emotions. Though a few clouds have altered the high opinion I entertained of the French people, what I have seen has convinced me, that they are still worthy of the name of the Great People, which I gave them twenty years ago.

Men of Dauphiny, about to quit your country, to repair to my good city of Lyons, I could not refrain from expressing to you all the esteem, with which your lofty sentiments have inspired me. My heart is filled with the emotions, that you have excited in it, and I shall never forget them.

The news of the Emperor's landing did not reach Paris till the 5th of March, at night. It transpired on the 6th; and on the 7th a royal proclamation appeared in the Moniteur, convoking the chambers immediately; and a decree, that placed Napoleon, and all who should join or assist him, out of the protection of the law[47]; without any farther particulars.

On the 8th the Moniteur and other newspapers announced, that Bonaparte had landed with eleven hundred men, most of whom had already deserted him; that he was wandering in the mountains, accompanied only by a few individuals; that he had been refused provision, was in want of every thing, and, pursued and on the point of being surrounded by the troops sent against him from Toulon, Marseilles, Valence, and Grenoble, he must speedily expiate his rash and criminal enterprise.

This news struck all parties with astonishment, and made different impressions on them, according to their different sentiments and opinions.

The discontented had no doubt of the success of the Emperor, and the ruin of the Bourbons.

The courtiers regretted that there was not sufficient danger in this mad and audacious enterprise, to give at least some value to their attachment.

The emigrants looked at it with pity, turned it into ridicule; and, if they had wanted nothing more than jests, abuse, and swaggering, to beat Napoleon, there could have been no doubt of their victory.

The government itself participated in their boasting and security.

Fresh despatches soon made known the progress of Napoleon.

The Count d'Artois, the Duke of Orléans, and Marshal Macdonald, set off hastily for Lyons.

The royalists were uneasy, the government removed their fears.

The Count d'Artois, they said, at the head of fifteen thousand national guards, and ten thousand of the troops of the line, must stop him before Lyons.

General Marchand, General Duverney, the Prince of Essling, and the Duke d'Angoulême, were getting into his rear, and would cut off his retreat.

General Le Courbe was manœuvring on his flanks.

Marshal Oudinot was arriving with his faithful royal grenadiers.

The national guards of Marseilles, and the whole population of the south, were marching from all quarters in pursuit of him; and it was impossible for him to escape.

This was the 10th of March.

The next day an officer of the King's household appeared in the balcony of the Tuileries, and, waving his hat, announced, that the King had just received an official account of the Duke of Orléans, at the head of twenty thousand men of the national guard of Lyons, having attacked Bonaparte on the side towards Bourgoing, and completely beaten him.

The same day information was given, that Generals d'Erlon, Lefevre Desnouettes, and Lallemand, who had attempted to seduce the troops under their orders, had completely failed, and taken flight[48].

The malecontents were in doubt: the royalists were intoxicated.

On the 12th, the victory of the Duke of Orléans was contradicted. The official paper announced, that Bonaparte must have slept at Bourgoing; that he was expected to enter Lyons on the evening of the 10th of March; and that it appeared certain, that Grenoble had not yet opened its gates to him.

The Count d'Artois soon arrived, and confirmed by his return the taking of Lyons, and the inutility of his efforts.

The alarm was renewed.

The King, whose countenance was at the same time dignified and affecting, invoked by eloquent proclamations the attachment of the French, and the courage and fidelity of the army.

The army maintained silence. The judicial bodies, the civil authorities, the order of advocates, and a number of individual citizens, answered the King's appeal by addresses testifying their love and fidelity.

The two chambers equally laid at the foot of the throne the expression of their sentiments: but their language differed.

"Sire," said the Chamber of Peers, "hitherto paternal goodness has marked all the acts of your government[49]. If it be necessary that the laws should be rendered more severe, you would no doubt lament it; but the two chambers, animated with the same spirit, would be eager to concur in every measure that the importance of circumstances, and the safety of the people, may require."

"Whatever faults may have been committed," said the Chamber of Deputies, "the present is not the moment for inquiring into them. It is the duty of all of us, to unite against the common enemy, and afterwards endeavour, to render this crisis beneficial to the security of the throne and its public liberty."

The King did not stop at empty proclamations. He decreed,

That a new army should be assembled in front of Paris, under the orders of the Duke of Berri and the command of Marshal Macdonald:

That all the soldiers on furlough, or conditionally discharged, should rejoin their corps:

That all the half-pay officers should be called out:

That the three millions of national guards of the kingdom should take up arms, in order to check the factious and disperse their meetings, *while the army took the field*:

That the young national guards, who were desirous of forming a part of the acting army, should be armed and accoutred, and sent to the parts that were threatened.

That to render useful the services of those brave Frenchmen, who on all sides were demanding to be led against the enemy, battalions of royal volunteers should be formed, and make a part of the army of the Duke of Berri.

Marshal Ney, whose popularity and influence were well known, was appointed to take the command of the troops of the east.

The Duke de Feltre took the place of Marshal Soult.

In short, the King omitted nothing, that could concur in protecting his throne from the dangers, with which it was threatened.

Such measures, sufficient to stop an army of three hundred thousand men, could only attest the success of Napoleon; and yet the ministry daily caused the most encouraging reports to be spread among the people, and confirmed by the newspapers.

M. de Montesquiou, faithful to the system of deception he had adopted, continued to mislead the deputies, cheating them by false intelligence, and lulling them with hopes, which he himself no longer entertained. He knew the intoxication. which was excited in every place by the approach and passage of Napoleon. He knew, that he was master of Grenoble and Lyons; that the troops attempted to be opposed to him had joined his with enthusiasm: and nevertheless he announced to the chamber, "that the population of all the departments invaded by the adventurer of the island of Elba loudly manifested their indignation against this audacious robber; that they may have been surprised, but not subjugated; that all his summonses of places, and the orders he had attempted to issue to the local authorities, had been rejected with firmness; that the Lyonese had displayed the attachment, that was to be expected from their noble character; that the departments of Burgundy, Franche Comté, Lorraine, Champagne, Picardy, &c. &c. rivalled each other in their attachment and energy; that the good disposition of the troops was answerable to that of the citizens; and that all together, generals, officers, soldiers, and citizens, concurred in the defence of their country and of their King."

These political juggleries were not without effect. They satisfied some credulous men, and inflamed the courage and imaginations of a few youths. The enrolments of volunteers were more numerous: a certain number of pupils of the schools of law and physic offered their services, and traversed the streets of Paris, shouting "Long live the King! Down with the Corsican! Down with the tyrant &c."

This effervescent movement could not be durable; and whatever pains were taken to deceive the metropolis, the truths announced by travellers and private letters opposed these ministerial falsehoods.

The defection of Marshal Ney soon came to tear off the veil, and spread affright and consternation among the ministers and their partisans.

The King repaired to the Chamber of Deputies, in the hope of confirming their attachment, and of dissipating by a solemn oath those doubts of his adherence to the charter, and of his intention to maintain it, which his ministers occasioned. Never was a more imposing and pathetic spectacle exhibited. What heart could steel itself against the sorrows of that august and aged man, against the sound of his mournful voice? Those prophetic words, "I fear nothing for myself, but I fear for France: at sixty years of age can I better close my career, than by dying in defence of the state?" These words of the King excited the most lively emotion, and tears in abundance fell from every eye.

The oath pronounced by the King, to maintain the charter, was immediately repeated by the Count d'Artois, who had hitherto refrained from it. "We swear," said he, "on our honour, I and my family, to live and die faithful to our King, and to the constitutional charter, which assures the happiness of France." But these tardy protestations could not repair the mischief, that the disloyal conduct of the government had done to the Bourbons and their cause.

In vain did the words country, liberty, and constitution, recur in every discourse, and in every proclamation.

In vain was it solemnly promised, that France, as soon as it was delivered, should receive all the securities claimed by the public voice, and that the press should recover perfect freedom.

In vain was the lustre and the prerogative, of which the legion of honour had been despoiled, offered to be restored to it.

In vain were pompous eulogies and brilliant promises lavished on the army.

The time was past.

The minister had robbed the King of confidence, which is the prime agent of the ascendancy of princes over the people; and of strength, which can alone supply the place of confidence, and command fear and obedience.

The approach of Napoleon;

The desertion of Marshal Ney;

The declaration made by those generals, who still retained their fidelity, that the troops would not fight against the Emperor, left the government no doubt of the fate that awaited it.

From that moment there was no longer harmony in their designs, or concert in the means of executing them.

Orders and counter-orders were given on the one hand, and revoked on the other. Schemes of every kind, all equally inconsiderate and impracticable, were approved and rejected, resumed and abandoned.

The chambers and the government had ceased to act in unison. The ministers complained of the deputies; the deputies publicly demanded of the King the dismissal of his ministers, and that he would place around himself men, "who have been the constant defenders of justice and liberty, and whose names shall be a guarantee for the interest of all[50]."

The same disorder, the same disunion, manifested themselves every where at the same time: there was only one point in which people agreed; that all was lost.

In fact so it was.

The people, whom the nobles had humbled, vexed, or terrified by haughty and tyrannical pretensions;

They who had acquired national domains, whom they had wished to dispossess;

The protestants, who had been sacrificed;

The magistrates, who had been turned out;

The persons in office, who had been reduced to want;

The soldiers, officers, and generals, who had been despised and ill-treated;

The revolutionists, who had been incessantly insulted and menaced;

The friends of justice, and of liberty, who had been abused;

All the French, whom the government had reduced, as it were, in spite of themselves, to wish for another order of things; eagerly embraced the cause of Napoleon, which had become the national cause through the faults of the government.

Royalty had no defenders left but women *and their handkerchiefs*; priests without influence; nobles without courage; body guards without youth, or without experience.

The legions of the national guard, on which such great reliance had been placed, were reviewed by their colonel-general: he harangued them on the charter, and the tyranny of Bonaparte; he told them, that he would march at their head, and said: "Let those, who love their King, come out from their ranks, and follow me." Scarcely two hundred obeyed the order.

The royal volunteers, who had made so much noise, when they expected to be victors without incurring any peril, had gradually dispersed; and those, whom the approach of danger had neither intimidated nor cooled, were too few to have any weight in the balance.

The government had one sole and last hope remaining: it was, dare I say it? that Napoleon would be assassinated.

The same men who had preached up a civil war, *and declared, that it would be shameful not to have one;* soiled the walls of Paris with provocations to murder, and fanatic praises bestowed beforehand on murderers. Emissaries, mixing in the various groups of the people, endeavoured to put the poniard into the hands of the new Jacques Clements. A public act had proscribed Napoleon; a reward was publicly offered for his head. This call for a crime, which indignant France first heard from the assassins of Coligny, was repeated by men, who, like them, had the sacred words of morality, humanity, and religion, continually in their mouths, and who, like them, thirsted only after vengeance and blood.

But while they were conspiring at Paris to assassinate Napoleon, he peaceably pursued his triumphant march.

Quitting Grenoble on the 9th, he came that night and slept at Burgoing. [51]""The crowd and the enthusiasm continued to increase: "We have long expected you," said all these brave fellows to the Emperor; "at length you are come, to deliver France from the insolence of the nobility, the pretensions of the priests, and the disgrace of a foreign yoke."

""The Emperor, being fatigued[52], was in his calash, the horse walking, surrounded by a crowd of peasants, singing songs, that expressed the noble sentiments of these brave Dauphinese. "Ah!" said the Emperor, "I here find again the sentiments, which twenty years ago led me to hail France by the name of the great nation! Yes, you are still the great nation, and you shall ever be so.""""

They approached Lyons: the Emperor had sent his emissaries before him, who informed him, that the Count d'Artois, the Duke of Orléans, and Marshal Macdonald, had determined to defend the city, and that they were going to break down the bridges de la Guillotière and Moraud. ""The Emperor laughed at these ridiculous preparations: he could not doubt the disposition of the Lyonese, still less those of the soldiers; yet he gave orders to General Bertrand, to collect boats at the Mirbel, intending to cross the river in the night, and cut off the roads to Moulins and Macon for the Prince, who wanted to prevent his passing the Rhone. At four o'clock a reconnoitring party of the fourth hussars arrived at la Guillotière, and were received with shouts of "Long live the Emperor!" by the immense population of the suburb, that has always been distinguished for its attachment to its country.""

The Emperor immediately countermanded the passage at Mirbel, and desirous of availing himself of this first enthusiastic movement, as at Grenoble, galloped forward to the suburb of Guillotière.

The Count d'Artois, less fortunate, could not even succeed in opposing to his adversary a shadow of defence.

He was desirous of destroying the bridges, but the city opposed it.

The troops, whose attachment he fancied he could purchase by the distribution of money, or the bait of rewards, had remained deaf to his words, his entreaties, his promises. Passing before the thirteenth regiment of dragoons, he said to a brave fellow, decorated with three chevrons and with scars: "Come, comrade, shout Long live the King!"—"No, Sir," answered the brave dragoon, "No soldier will fight against his father; I can only answer you by saying Long live the Emperor!" Confused and in despair, he exclaimed in a sorrowful tone, "All is lost!" and these words, instantly spreading from one to another, only strengthened the prevailing ill will or discouragement[53].

Marshal Macdonald, however, who was well known to the troops, had succeeded in barricading the bridge of la Guillotière, and led two battalions of infantry thither in person; when the hussars of Napoleon came out from the suburb, and presented themselves before the bridge, preceded, surrounded, and followed, by all the youth of the place.

The marshal restrained the soldiers a few minutes: but moved, seduced, borne away, by the incitements of the people and the hussars, they rushed to the barricadoes, burst them, and were quickly in the arms and in the ranks of the soldiers of Napoleon.

The Count d'Artois, foreseeing this defection, had quitted Lyons, unaccompanied by a single gendarme, but escorted by a detachment of the thirteenth dragoons, commanded by lieutenant Marchebout. It is due to the troops to say, that they did not cease to respect him, and that he ran no risk[54].

At five in the evening the whole garrison rushed out to meet Napoleon.

An hour after, the imperial army took possession of the city.

At seven Napoleon made his solemn entry, proceeding alone before his troops, but preceded and followed by an immense crowd, expressing, by incessant acclamations, the intoxication, happiness, and pride, they felt at seeing him again. He alighted at the archbishop's palace, and quietly took his rest in the very places, which the Count d'Artois, yielding to despair, had just watered with his tears.

Napoleon immediately entrusted the guarding of his person, and the interior charge of the palace, to the national guard. He would not accept the services of the horse-guards. "Our institutions," said he to them, "know nothing of national guards on horseback; besides, you behaved so ill with the Count d'Artois, that I will have nothing to say to you."

In fact the Emperor, who had always respected misfortune, had made inquiries concerning the Count d'Artois on his arrival; and had learned, that the nobles, of whom the horse-guards were chiefly composed, after having sworn to the prince to die for him, had deserted him; one excepted, who remained faithfully attached to his escort, till the moment he thought his life and liberty out of all danger.

The Emperor did not confine himself to commendation of the conduct of this generous Lyonese. "I never left a noble action," said he, "without reward:" and he appointed him a member of the Legion of Honour.

I was at Lyons the moment when Napoleon arrived. He knew it, and sent for me that very evening. "Well!" said he to me with a smile, "you did not expect to see me again so soon[55]." — "No, Sire; your Majesty alone is capable of occasioning such surprises." — "What do they say of all this at Paris?" — "Why, Sire, there, as here, they are rejoiced, no doubt, at your Majesty's happy return." — "And public opinion, how is that?" — "Sire, it is greatly changed: formerly we thought of nothing but glory, now we think only of liberty. The struggle that has arisen between the Bourbons and the nation has revealed to us our rights; it has engendered in men's minds a number of liberal ideas, that did not exist in your Majesty's time; people feel, people experience, the necessity of being free; and the most certain means of pleasing the French would be to promise, and to give them, laws truly popular." — "I know that the discussions they[56] have suffered to take place, have diminished the respect for power, and enfeebled it. Liberal ideas have resumed all the ground I had gained for it. I shall not attempt to reconquer it: no one should attempt to contend with a nation; it is the earthen pot against the iron pot. The French shall have reason to be satisfied with me. I know, that there is both pleasure and glory in rendering a great people free and happy. I will give pledges to France: I did not stint it in glory, I will not stint it in liberty. I will retain no farther power than is necessary to enable me to govern. Power is not incompatible with liberty: on the contrary, liberty is never more entire, than when power is well established. When it is weak, it is captious: when it is strong, it sleeps in tranquillity, and leaves the reins loose on the neck of liberty. I know what is requisite for the French; we shall settle that point: but no licentiousness, no anarchy; for anarchy would lead us to the despotism of the republicans, the most fertile of all despotisms in tyrannic acts, because every body takes a share in it.... Do they suppose we shall come to a battle?" — "They do not think it: the government have never had confidence in the soldiery; it has made itself detested by the officers; and all the troops that may be opposed to your Majesty's, will be so many reinforcements sent you." — "I think so too: and the marshals?" — "Sire, they cannot but be apprehensive, that your Majesty will remember Fontainbleau; and perhaps it will be well to remove their fears, and to make known to them personally your Majesty's intention of consigning every thing to oblivion." — "No, I will not write to them; they would consider me as under obligations to them; and I will be obliged to no person. The troops are well disposed, the officers are good, and if the marshals wished to restrain them, they would be hurried along by them ... where is my guard?" — "I believe at Metz and at Nancy." — "Of that I am sure, do what they will, they will never corrupt it. What are Augereau and Marmont about?" — "I do not know." — "What is Ney doing? On what terms is he with the king?" — "Sometimes good, sometimes bad: I believe he has had reason to complain of the court on account of his wife." — "His wife is an affected creature; no doubt she has attempted to play the part of a great lady, and the old dowagers have ridiculed her. Has Ney any command?" — "I do not think he has, Sire." — "Is he one of us?" — "The part he took in your abdication"--"Ay, I read that at Porto Ferrajo he boasted of having ill-treated me, of having laid his pistols on my table: it was all false. Had he dared to fail of respect to me, I would have ordered him to be shot. A heap of tales has been spread respecting my abdication. I abdicated, not in consequence of their advice, but because my army was out of its senses: besides, I would not have a civil war. It was never to my taste. It was said, that Augereau, when I met him, loaded me with reproaches ... it was a lie: no one of my generals would have dared, in my presence, to forget what was due to me. Had I known of the proclamation of Augereau, I would have forbidden him my presence[57]: cowards only insult misfortune. His proclamation, which I was reported to have had in my pocket, was unknown to me till after our interview. It was General Koller who showed it me; but let us quit these popular rumours. What has been done at the Tuileries?" — "Nothing has been altered, Sire; even the eagles have not yet been removed." — (Smiling) "They must have thought my arrangement of them admirable." — "So I presume, Sire: it has been said, that the Count d'Artois went through all the apartments immediately after his arrival, and could not cease to admire them." — "I can readily believe it. What have they done with my pictures?" — "Some have been taken away, but that of the battle of Austerlitz is still in the council-chamber." — "And the theatre?" — "It has not been touched: it is no longer used." — "What is Talma doing?" — "Why, Sire, he continues to deserve and obtain public applause." — "I shall see him again with pleasure. Have you been at court?" — "Yes, Sire, I have been presented." — "I am told, they all have the air of upstarts of yesterday; that they know not how to utter a word, or take a single step, with propriety: have you seen them on grand public days?" — "No, Sire, but I can assure your Majesty, that people pay as little regard to ceremony at the Tuileries, as at their own homes: they go thither in dirty boots, common frock-coats, and round hats." — "That must have a very majestic appearance. But how do all those old thicksculls spend their money? for every thing has been restored to them." — "But, probably, Sire, they wish to wear out their old clothes." — "Poor France! into what hands hast thou thrust thyself! And the king, what sort of a countenance has he?" — "He has a tolerably fine head." — "Is his coin handsome?" — "Of this your Majesty may judge: here is a twenty-franc piece." — "What! they have not re-coined louis: I am surprised at this. (Turning the piece over) He does not look as if he would starve himself: but observe, they have taken away Dieu protège la France (God protect France), to restore their Domine, salvum fac regem (Lord, preserve the King). This is as they always were: every thing for themselves, nothing for France. Where is Maret? where is Caulincourt? where is Lavalette? where is Fouché?" — "They are all at Paris." — "And Môlé?" — "He, too, is at Paris; I observed him a short time ago at the Queen's." — "Have we any persons hereabout, who were nearly attached to me?" — "I do not know, Sire." — "You must inquire, and bring them to me. I should be glad to be thoroughly acquainted with the spirit of the times, and know something of the present state of affairs. What does Hortense do?" — "Sire, her house is still the resort of men, who know how to appreciate wit and elegance: and the Queen, though without a throne, is not less an object of the respect and homage of all Paris." — "She did a very foolish thing, in exhibiting herself as a spectacle before the tribunals. They who advised her to it were blockheads. Why, too, did she go and demand the title of duchess?" — "She, Sire, did not demand it, it was the Emperor Alexander...." — "No matter, she ought not to have accepted, any more than demanded it: she should have called herself Madame Bonaparte: this name is full as good as any other. Besides, what right had she to have her son made a duke of St. Leu, and a peer of the Bourbons? Louis was in the right to oppose it: he was sensible, that the name of her son was sufficiently honourable, not to suffer himself to change it. If Josephine had been alive, she would have prevented her from engaging in such a foolish piece of business. Was she much regretted?" — "Yes, Sire, your Majesty knows how much she was beloved and honoured by the French." — "She deserved it. She was an excellent woman: she had a great deal of sense. I greatly regretted her too, and the day when I heard of her death was one of the most unhappy of my life. Was there a public mourning for her?" — "No, Sire. Indeed I think she would have been refused the honours due to her rank, had not the Emperor Alexander insisted on their being paid her." — "So I heard at the time, but I did not believe it. He was no way interested in it." — "The generosity of Alexander was not confined within any limits: he showed himself the protector of the Empress, the Queen, Prince Eugene, the Duke of

Vicenza, and a number of other persons of distinction, who, but for him, would have been persecuted or ill treated." — "You love him, it seems." — "Sire...." — "Is the national guard of Paris well disposed?" — "I cannot positively affirm it; but of this at least I am certain, that if it do not declare for your Majesty, at least it will not act against us." — "I imagine so too. What is it supposed, that the foreigners will think of my return?" — "It is thought, that Austria will connect itself with your Majesty, and that Russia will behold the disgrace of the Bourbons without regret." — "Why so?" — "It is said, Sire, that Alexander was not pleased with the princes while at Paris. That the predilection of the king for England, and his attributing his crown to the Prince Regent, offended him." — "It is well to know that. Has he seen my son?" — "Yes, Sire I have been assured, that he embraced him with a tenderness truly paternal, and exclaimed: He is a charming fellow: how have I been deceived." — "What did he mean by that?" — "They say he had been informed, that the young prince was rickety and imbecile." — "Wretches! he is an admirable child: he gives every indication of becoming a distinguished character. He will be an honour to his age. Is it true, that so much was made of Alexander at Paris?" — "Yes, Sire, nobody else was attended to but he: the other sovereigns appeared as if they were his aides-de-camp." — "In fact, he did a great deal for Paris: but for him the English would have ruined it, and the Prussians would have set it on fire. — He acted his part well ... (with a smile) if I were not Napoleon, perhaps I would be Alexander."

The next day he reviewed the division of Lyons in Bellecour Square. "I shall see that square again with pleasure," said he, to the chiefs of the national guard, who stood round him: "I remember, that I raised it from its ruins, and laid the first stone of it fifteen years ago." He went out merely preceded by a few hussars. A crowd of men, old men, women and children, thronged the bridges, the quays, and the streets. They rushed under the horses' feet to hear him, to see him, to have a closer view of him, to touch his garments ... it was an actual delirium. Scarcely had he proceeded a few steps, when the crowd, that had already seen him, ran to another spot, to see him again. The air rung with uninterrupted acclamations. It was a rolling volley of "The nation for ever! The Emperor for ever! Down with the priests! Down with the royalists!" &c.

The division of Brayer, as soon as reviewed, set out on its march to Paris.

When the Emperor returned to the archiepiscopal palace, the great gallery was crowded with generals, colonels, magistrates, and public officers of all ranks and kinds. You might have thought yourselves in the Tuileries.

The Emperor stopped a few minutes: he embraced Generals Mouton Duvernay, Girard, and other officers, whom Paris supposed to be in pursuit of him; and after having distributed on the right and left a few smiles and many compliments, he proceeded to his saloon, and admitted to be presented to him the imperial court, the municipal body, and the chiefs of the military corps and the national guard.

He conversed a long time with them on the faults of the Bourbons, and the deplorable situation in which he found France. He confessed to them with noble frankness, that he was not altogether inculpable for its misfortunes. "I was hurried on," said he, "by the course of events, into a wrong path. But, taught by experience, I have abjured that love of glory, so natural to the French, which has had such fatal consequences to them and to me.... I was mistaken in supposing, that the time was arrived for rendering France the metropolis of a great empire: I have renounced for ever that grand enterprise; we have enough of glory, we want repose.

"It is not ambition, that has brought me back to France: it is the love of the country. I could have preferred the tranquillity of the island of Elba to the cares of a throne, had I not known, that France was unhappy, and had need of me.

"On setting foot on our dear France," continued he, after a few unimportant answers from his auditors, "I made a vow to render it free and happy: I bring nothing to it but benefits. I am returned to protect and defend those interests, to which our revolution has given birth: I return to concur with the representatives of the nation in a family compact, that shall preserve for ever the liberty and the rights of every Frenchman: henceforward it will be my ambition, and my glory, to effect the happiness of the great people from whom I hold every thing. I will not, like Louis XVIII., grant you a revocable charter; I will give you an inviolable constitution, and it shall be the work of the people, as well as of myself."

Such were his words. He pronounced them with an air of such satisfaction, he appeared so confident of himself and of the future, that a man would have thought himself criminal to suspect the purity of his intentions, or to doubt the happiness he was about to secure to France.

The language he held at Lyons we perceive was not the same, as that he had uttered at Gap and at Grenoble. In the last-mentioned towns he sought principally to excite in men's minds hatred of the Bourbons, and the love of liberty: he had spoken as a citizen, rather than a monarch. No formal declaration, not a single word, revealed his intentions. It might as well have been supposed, that he thought of restoring the republic, or the consulship, as the empire. At Lyons, there was no longer any thing vague, any thing uncertain: he spoke as a sovereign, and promised to give a national constitution. The idea of the Champ de Mai had recurred to him.

Not one of us suspected the sincerity of the promises and resolves of Napoleon.

Time, reflection, misfortune, the grand teacher of mankind, had effected the most favourable changes in the principles of Napoleon.

Formerly, when unforeseen obstacles arose, suddenly to thwart his projects, his passions, accustomed to no restraint, to respect no bridle, burst forth with the fury of a raging sea: he spoke, he ordered, he decided, as if he had been master of the earth and of the elements; nothing appeared to him impossible.

After his reverse of fortune, he had learned in the calm of solitude and meditation, to control the violence of his will, and to subject it to the yoke of reason and prudence. He had read attentively the writings, pamphlets, and even libels, published against him: and amid the revilings, calumnies, and absurdities, which they frequently contained, he had found useful truths, judicious observations, and profound views, of which he knew how to benefit himself.

"Princes," observes the learned author of the Spirit of Laws, "have in their lives periods of ambition to which other passions, and even indolence, succeed." Napoleon's hour of indolence was not yet come: but to the ambition of increasing his power without limit, had succeeded the desire of rendering France happy, and of repairing by a durable peace, and a paternal government, all the evils that had been brought upon it by war.

The Emperor spent the evening of the 11th in his closet: his first thought was for the Empress. He wrote her a very tender letter, which began with these remarkable words. "Madam and dear wife, I have re-ascended my throne."

He informed Prince Joseph[58] also, that he had resumed his crown; and directed him to make known to foreign powers, through their ministers to the Helvetic Confederation, that he intended never more to disturb the tranquillity of Europe, and faithfully to maintain the treaty of Paris. He particularly recommended to him, strongly to impress upon Austria and Russia, how desirous he was of re-establishing his former connexions with them in the most intimate manner.

He appeared to set a particular value on the alliance of Russia. His predilection was founded, no doubt, on political motives not difficult to guess; yet I believe he was equally induced to it by Alexander's generous conduct towards the French. The popularity and renown, which this prince had acquired in France, excited, and could not but excite, the jealousy of Napoleon: but this jealousy, the attribute of great minds, did not render him unjust; he knew how to estimate Alexander.

Hitherto Napoleon has been engaged only in depriving the King of his army; he now thought the time was come, to take from him also the sceptre of civil government. "On this I have resolved," said he to me: "I will now annihilate the royal authority, and dismiss the chambers. Since I have resumed the government, no authority but mine ought to exist. The public must be taught from this moment, that they are to obey me alone." He then dictated to me in succession the following decrees, known by the name of the decrees of Lyons.

Lyons, 13th of March, 1815.

Napoleon, Emperor of the French, &c. &c.

Considering, that the Chamber of Peers is partly composed of persons who have borne arms against France, and who are interested in the re-establishment of feudal rights, in the destruction of the equality of the different classes, in the nullification of the sale of the national domains, and finally in depriving the people of the rights they have acquired by fighting for five and twenty years against the enemies of the national glory:

Considering, that the powers of the deputies of the legislative body have expired, and that from that moment the Chamber of Commons has no longer a national character; that a part of this chamber has rendered itself unworthy the confidence of the nation, by assenting to the re-establishment of the feudal nobility, abolished by the constitution accepted by the people; by making France pay debts contracted with foreign powers for negotiating coalitions, and paying armies, against the French people; by giving to the Bourbons the title of legitimate King, which was declaring the French people and the armies rebels, proclaiming those emigrants, who for five and twenty years have been wounding the vitals of their country, the only good Frenchmen, and violating all the rights of the people, by sanctioning the principle, that the nation is made for the throne, not the throne for the nation:

We have decreed, and do decree, as follows:

Article I.

The Chamber of Peers is dissolved.

Article II.

The Chamber of Commons is dissolved: it is ordered, that every one of the members convened and arrived at Paris since the 7th of March last shall repair to his home without delay.

Article III.

The electoral colleges of the departments of the empire shall assemble at Paris in the course of the month of May next, in order to take proper measures for correcting and modifying our constitutions agreeably to the interests and will of the nation; and at the same time to assist at the coronation of the Empress, our dear and well-beloved wife, and that of our dear and well-beloved son.

Article IV.

Our Grand Marshal, executing the functions of Major-general of the grand army, is appointed to take necessary measures for making public the present decree.

SECOND DECREE.

Napoleon, &c.

Article I.

All the emigrants, whose names have not been erased, amnestied, or eliminated, by us, or by the governments that have preceded us; and who have returned to France since the 1st of January, 1814, shall immediately quit the territory of the empire.

Article II.

Those emigrants, who shall be found in the territory of the empire fifteen days after the promulgation of the present decree, shall be arrested and tried conformably to the laws decreed by our national assemblies: unless however it be proved, that they had no knowledge of the present decree; in which case, they shall merely be arrested, and conducted out of the territory by the gendarmerie.

Article III.

All their property, moveable and immoveable, &c. &c. shall be placed in sequestration.

THIRD DECREE.

Napoleon, &c.

Article I.

The nobility is abolished, and the laws of the Constituent Assembly shall be put in force.

Article II.

Feudal titles are suppressed.

Article III.

Those individuals, who have obtained from us national titles, as national rewards, and whose letters patent have been verified before the council by the seal of state, shall continue to bear them.

Article IV.

We reserve to ourselves the power of giving titles to the descendants of those men, who have rendered the French name illustrious in various ages, whether in the command of armies by land and sea, in the councils of sovereigns, in the administration of justice or of civil authority, or finally in the arts and sciences, commerce, &c.

FOURTH DECREE.

Napoleon, &c.

Article I.

All those generals and officers by land and sea, of whatever rank, who have been introduced into our armies since the 1st of April, 1814, who had emigrated; or who, not having emigrated, had quitted the service at the period of the first coalition, when the country had the greatest need of their services; shall immediately cease their functions, relinquish the marks of their rank, and repair to their homes, &c. &c.

FIFTH DECREE.

Napoleon, &c.

Considering, that by our constitutions the members of the judicial order are not removable, we decree:

Article I.

All the arbitrary changes made in our inferior tribunals and courts are null, and to be considered as having never taken place.

Article II.

The presidents of the court of cassation, our procureur-général (attorney-general), and the members who have been unjustly, and from a spirit of reaction, dismissed from the said court, are restored to their functions, &c. &c.

By four other decrees the Emperor ordered, that the property of the Bourbon family should be placed in sequestration.

That all the property of emigrants, which belonged to the Legion of Honour, hospitals, communes, the sinking fund, or the national domains, should be restored to these different establishments.

That the King's household and the Swiss should be dismissed, and that no foreign corps should be admitted as a guard to the sovereign.

And that the decoration of the lily, and the orders of St. Louis, the Holy Ghost, and St. Michael, should be abolished.

These decrees, which embraced at once every part of the political, civil, and military administration of the state, succeeded each other so rapidly, that Napoleon had scarcely time to interpose a few words between them.

By restoring to their seats those magistrates, who had been expelled from them, he gained with a stroke of the pen all the members of the judicial order; but I know not why he did not extend this beneficial measure to the functionaries of the administrative order, particularly to the prefects and sub-prefects, whom M. de Montesquiou had so cruelly persecuted. Among these functionaries there were unquestionably some, who, from the weakness or incapacity they had shown during the last moments of the imperial government, merited no confidence: but the greater part of them had remained worthy of it; and Napoleon, by placing them at the head of their former offices, would have added to the advantage of publicly repairing an act of royal injustice, that of entrusting the administration to experienced men, and who, already knowing the partisans of the revolution and those of the Bourbons, had only to show themselves, to intimidate the latter, and render effective the patriotism of the former.

With this exception, every thing he did at Lyons appeared to me a master-piece of wisdom and address.

It was necessary, to overturn the Chamber of Peers: he did it at one stroke. "It is composed," said he, "only of men who have borne arms against their country, and who are interested in restoring feudal rights, and annulling the national sales."

The Chamber of Deputies had shown some resistance to the ministers, and attachment to liberal doctrines; it was difficult, therefore, to render it unpopular, yet the Emperor did it by a word: "It has shown itself unworthy of the confidence of the nation, by making the people pay debts contracted with foreigners for the shedding of French blood."

It was necessary, to remove the apprehensions of France respecting the future: he called the electors to the Champ de Mai. It was necessary, to excite the belief, that he had a good understanding with Austria, and that Maria Louisa would be restored to him: he announced the approaching coronation of the Empress and her son.

It was necessary, to seduce the patriots, the republicans: he abolished the feudal nobility; and declared, that the throne was made for the nation, not the nation for the throne. It was necessary, to tranquillize those, who had acquired national domains; he expelled the emigrants not erased from the lists, and resumed their property: to please the peasantry and the poor, he restored to the hospitals the property of which they had been despoiled: to flatter the guard and the army, he expelled from their ranks foreigners and emigrants, dismissed the King's household, and restored to the Legion of Honour its endowments and prerogatives.

Men may censure his conduct at Lyons; may represent it as that of a madman, resolved to alter, to destroy, to overturn every thing: no matter ... they who judge with impartiality, I believe, will find, that he conducted himself with all the skill of a consummate politician. He knew how to inspire confidence, dissipate apprehensions, confirm attachments, and fill the people and the army with enthusiasm: what could he do more?

The steps taken at Paris against him were known to him on the 12th. He appeared delighted, that a command was given to Marshal Ney; not that he held any intelligence with him; but because he knew the weakness and fickleness of his character. He directed the Grand Marshal to write to him. "You will inform him," said he, "of the delirium excited by my return, and of all the forces sent against me having joined my army in succession. You will tell him, that the troops under his command will infallibly follow the example of their brave comrades, sooner or later: and that the efforts he might make would have no farther effect, than at most to retard the fall of the Bourbons a few days. Give him to understand, that he will be responsible to France, and to me, for the civil war and bloodshed, of which he would be the cause. *Flatter him*," added the Emperor, "but do not *caress* him too much; he would think me afraid of him, and require to be entreated."

Letters were written also to all the commanders of corps, that were known to be quartered in the neighbouring departments. None of them were in a supplicatory style: the Emperor already spoke as a master; he did not entreat, he commanded.

Every thing being finished, on the 13th Napoleon departed; and profoundly moved with the affection the Lyonese had shown him, he bade them adieu in the following words:

"Lyonese,

"At the moment of quitting your city to repair to my capital, I feel it necessary, to make known to you the sentiments with which you have inspired me: you have always ranked with the foremost in my affections. On the throne or in exile, you have always displayed the same feelings towards me: the lofty character that distinguishes you, has merited my entire esteem:

in a period of greater tranquillity, I shall return, to consider the welfare of your manufactures, and of your city.

"Lyonese, I love you."

These last words were the ingenuous expression of his feelings: in dictating, he pronounced them with that indefinable charm, that was impressed on his words when they came from the heart.

So much has been said of the hardness of Napoleon's heart, and the harshness of his language, that whatever is at variance with the received opinion must appear fabulous. Yet it is a truth, and they who have been about the Emperor's person will vouch for it, that he was far from being so unfeeling, as he was commonly thought. His military education, and the necessity of commanding fear and respect, had rendered him grave, severe, and inflexible; and had accustomed him, to check and despise the suggestions of his sensibility. But when nature resumed her rights, he felt a delight in yielding to the movements of his soul, and he then expressed the emotions or sentiments, that had overpowered him, in an ardent and impassioned tone, and with a sweetness and grace, as seducing as it was inimitable.

Indeed the Lyonese merited the esteem and love, that Napoleon avowed for them. Though yet young, I have more than once seen popular displays of enthusiasm and infatuation; yet never did I see any thing comparable to the transports of joy and tenderness, that burst from the Lyonese. Not only the quays, and the places near the palace of the Emperor, but even the most distant streets rung with perpetual acclamations[59]. Workmen and their masters, the common people and the citizens, rambled about the city arm in arm, singing, dancing, and giving themselves up to the impulse of the most ardent gaiety. Strangers stopped one another, shook hands, embraced, and congratulated each other on the return of the Emperor, as if he had conferred on them fortune, life, and honour.

The national guard, affected by the confidence he had shown it, by entrusting to it the care of his person, participated with equal ardour the general intoxication; and the day of Napoleon's departure was a day of sorrow and regret to the city of Lyons, as that of his arrival had been a day of real festivity.

We slept at Macon. The Emperor would not alight at the prefect's, but went to lodge at the sign of the Savage. He found it was no longer necessary, to wait at the gates of the towns, as at Grenoble and Lyons: the people and the magistrates ran out to meet him, and disputed the honour of being foremost, to do him homage, and express their good wishes.

The next morning he received the felicitations of the national guard, the municipal body, &c. One of the colleagues of the mayor gave us a long, ridiculous harangue, which amused us much. When he had finished, the Emperor said to him: "You were much astonished, then, at hearing of our having landed?"—"Yes, faith:" answered the orator: "when I knew you had landed, I said to every body, the man must be mad, he will never be able to escape."—Napoleon could not help laughing at this simplicity. "I know," said he, with a sarcastic smile, "that you are all a little inclined to be frightened; you gave me a proof of this last campaign; you should have behaved as the men of Chalons did; you did not maintain the honour of the Burgundians."—"It was not our fault, Sire," said one of the party: "we were badly commanded; you had not given us a good mayor."—"That is very possible; we have all been guilty of foolish actions, and they must be forgotten: the safety and happiness of France are henceforward the only objects, to which we ought to attend." He dismissed them in a friendly manner.

The prefect had taken flight. The Emperor asked me his name. It was one Germain, whom he had made a count, and a gentleman of the bedchamber, without well knowing why. "What!" said he to me, "does that little Germain fancy it necessary to shun me? he must be brought back:" and he thought no more of him.

He directed me, to cause an account of the events at Grenoble and Lyons to be inserted in the newspaper of the department. The editor, a furious royalist, had hidden himself. I entrusted to the new subprefect the business of fulfilling the Emperor's orders; but, whether it were carelessness or incapacity on his part, he had recourse to the printer of the paper, who supplied him with an article far from answering our views.

It began with a very just, but ill-timed eulogy of the goodness of Louis XVIII.; and ended with declaring in substance, that so good a king was not fitted to reign over the French, and that they required a sovereign such as Napoleon, &c.

The Emperor, who would read every thing, asked me for the paper. I pretended I could not lay my hand upon it: but, after a thousand attempts to put him off from seeing it, I was at length obliged to bring it him. I thought he would have given me a severe reprimand, but he contented himself with saying: "Change that man, he is a fool; and desire him for the future, never to attempt a eulogy of me." I sent for him, scolded him, and, like me, he was let off for the fright.

It was at Macon, that we first received official news of what was going on at Paris. It was brought us by M. ***. The unskilful manner in which the royalist party superintended the police of the roads, was truly astonishing. Not one of its emissaries escaped us, while ours went and came without any obstruction. Rage or fear must have turned the brains of all the royalists. M. *** assured the Emperor, that the national guard appeared determined to defend the king, and that the king had declared, he would not quit the Tuileries. "If he choose to wait for me there," said Napoleon, "I have no objection: but I doubt it much. He suffers himself to be lulled by the boastings of the emigrants; and when I get within twenty leagues of Paris, they will abandon him, as the nobles of Lyons abandoned the Count d'Artois. What indeed could he do with the old puppets that are about him? One of our grenadiers would knock down a hundred of them with the butt-end of his musket.... The national guard shouts at a distance; when I am at the barriers it will be silent. Its business is not to raise a civil war, but to maintain peace and order in the country. The majority is sound; there is nothing rotten in it but a few officers; and them I will expel. Return to Paris; tell my friends not to implicate themselves, and within ten days my grenadiers will mount guard at the Tuileries: go."

We arrived at Chalons on the 14th, at an early hour. It was terrible weather, yet the whole population had come out of the city, to see the Emperor a few minutes the sooner. On approaching the walls, he perceived artillery and ammunition waggons, and was surprised at it. "They were intended," said the people, "to act against you; but we have stopped them on their way, and present them to you."—"That's right, my lads; you have always been good citizens."

He was well pleased, to find himself among the Chalonese, and received them with much affection and regard. "I have not forgotten," said he, "that you resisted the enemy for forty days, and valiantly defended the passage of the Saône. Had all the French possessed your courage and patriotism, not a single foreigner would have escaped out of France." He expressed to them his desire of knowing the brave men, who had most distinguished themselves; and on their unanimous testimony, he granted on the spot the decoration of the Legion of Honour to the mayor of St. Jean Delonne. "It was for the brave men like him and you," said he to them, "that I instituted the Legion of Honour, and not for emigrants pensioned by our enemies." When the audience was ended, he said to me: "The mayor of Chalons is not come; yet it was I who appointed him: but he is related to an ancient family, and probably has his scruples. The inhabitants complain of him, and will make him suffer for it. You must go and see him. If he object to you his oath, tell him, that I absolve him from it; and make him sensible, that, if he wait till he is freed from it by Louis XVIII., he will wait a long time. Say to him, in short, what you please; I care little about his visit; it is for his own sake I wish him to come. If he do not come, the people will stone him to death after I am gone. Germain was lucky to escape[60]; let his example be a lesson to him."

I repaired immediately to the municipality, where I found the mayor, and a few municipal counsellors. He appeared to me a man of merit. I informed him, that it was my usual office, to introduce to his Majesty the municipal authorities; that I had observed with surprise, he had not been as eager as the mayors of other cities, to pay his duty to the Emperor; and that I was come to remove his fears, &c. He answered me frankly, that he had great respect and admiration for Napoleon; but, having sworn fealty to Louis XVIII., he thought it his duty to keep his oath, till he was absolved from it. I had my answer ready. "I, like you," said I, "consider perjury as the most degrading act, of which man can be guilty. But it is necessary, to make a distinction between a voluntary oath, and the stipulated oath, which people take to their government. In the eye of reason, this oath is merely an act of local submission; a pure and simple formality, which the monarch, whoever he may be, has a right to require of his subjects; but which cannot, as it ought not, enchain their persons and faith to perpetuity. France, since 1789, has sworn by turns to be faithful to royalty, to the convention, to the republic, to the directory, to the consulship, to the empire, to the charter: if those Frenchmen, who had taken an oath to royalty, had sought to oppose the establishment of a republic, by way of acquitting themselves of their oaths; if those, who had taken an oath to the republic, had opposed the establishment of the empire, &c.; into what a state of anarchy and disorder, into what a deluge of blood and evils, would they not have plunged our unhappy country? On similar occasions, the national will ought to be the sole guide of our conscience and our actions: the moment it is manifested, it is the duty of good citizens, to yield and obey."

"These principles," replied he, "may be very good as a general rule; but our present case is an exception, never before known. When the governments, that have existed since the revolution, were overturned, the new government seized the authority, and it ought to be presumed, that the assent of the nation was on its side: but here it is a different affair; the royal government subsists; the Emperor abdicated voluntarily; and till the king has renounced the crown, I shall consider him as the sovereign of France."

"If you wait for the king's renunciation," rejoined I, "before you acknowledge the Emperor, you will wait a long time. Has not the king pretended, that he has not ceased to reign over France these five-and-twenty years? And if he thought himself sovereign of France at a time, when the imperial government was rendered legitimate by the unanimous suffrages of France, and acknowledged by all Europe, do you think he will renounce the crown at present?

"The time when kings reigned in virtue of right divine is far removed from us: their rights are no longer founded on any thing but the formal or tacit consent of nations: the moment nations reject them, the contract is broken; the conditional oaths taken to them are annulled in law and in fact, without their intervention or consent being necessary; for, as the proclamations of Napoleon say, kings are made for the people, not the people for kings.

"As to the abdication of Napoleon, whether voluntary or compulsive, and the rights newly acquired by Louis XVIII.. it would be requisite, in order to answer this part of your objections, to inquire, whether the chief of a nation have a right to relinquish the authority entrusted to him, without the consent of that nation; and whether a government imposed by foreigners, either through influence or force of arms, unite those characters of legitimacy, which you ascribe to it. I have read in our publicists, that we owe obedience to a government *de facto*: and since the Emperor has in fact resumed the sceptre, I think we cannot do better, than submit to his laws; with the proviso," added I jocularly, "of leaving to posterity the task of deciding the question of right between Napoleon and Louis XVIII.

"However," continued I, "I leave you perfectly at liberty to embrace which side you judge best: it is not my intention to take you by surprise, or to put any violence on your conscience; and I beg you to consider the attempts I have made to convince you, only as a proof of my desire to bring you over to my opinion by the force of reason."

"Well, sir," said he, "I yield to your observations: be so good as to announce me to his Majesty."

The next day he was displaced!

On the 16th we slept at Avalon. Napoleon was received there as he had been every where; that is to say, with demonstrations of joy, that were actually bordering on madness. People crowded, thronged, to see, to hear, to speak to him; his quarters were instantly surrounded, besieged, by such a numerous and obstinate multitude, that it was impossible for us to enter or go out, without walking on the heads of all the population of the country. Those men who made part of the national guard would remain on duty from morning to night. Women of the greatest distinction in the place spent the day and night on the stairs and in the passages, to watch for his going by. Three of them, tired with standing the whole day for want of seats, requested permission to sit down by us: it was in the hall (adjoining the Emperor's chamber), in which some mattresses had been laid on the floor, in order that we might gain a few minutes' rest. It was pleasant enough, to see these three young and elegant Bonapartists timidly huddling together on a little couch in the midst of our dirty guardroom. We endeavoured to keep them company but our eyes closed in spite of us. "Go to sleep," said they to us, "we will watch over the Emperor." In fact, fatigue got the better of gallantry; and, to our shame be it spoken, we were soon asleep at their feet. When we awoke, we found one of these ladies keeping guard at Napoleon's door. We heard of it, and thanked her for her attachment, in very polite and pleasing terms.

I think it was at Avalon[61], that an officer of the staff came and brought us Marshal Ney's submission, and his orders of the day[62]. These orders of the day were printed that night; but the Emperor, after having read them over, directed them to be changed and reprinted. I know not whether his Majesty judged it proper to alter them, or whether the printer had made any mistake.

On the 17th the Emperor arrived at Auxerre, where he was received for the first time by a prefect. He alighted at the prefect's house. On the mantel-piece of the first saloon were the busts of the Empress, and of her son; and in the next was a whole-length portrait of Napoleon, in his imperial robes: it might have been supposed, that the reign of the Emperor had never been interrupted.

Napoleon immediately received the congratulations of all the authorities, and of the tribunals. These congratulations began to be no longer a mark of attachment in our eyes, but the fulfilment of a duty. After having discoursed with them on the grand interests of the state, the Emperor, whose good humour was inexhaustible, began to joke about the court of Louis XVIII. "His court," said he, "has the air of that of King Dagobert: we see nothing in it but antiques; the women are old and frightfully ugly; there were no pretty women in it but mine, and those were so ill-treated, that they were obliged to desert it. All those people are made up of nothing but haughtiness and pride: I have been reproached with being proud; I was so to strangers; but never did any one see me suffer my chancellor to set one knee to the ground to receive my orders, or oblige my prefects and mayors to wait at table on my courtiers and dowagers[63]. They say, that the men about the court are little better than the women; and that, to distinguish them from my generals, whom I had covered with gold lace, they are dressed like beggars. My court, it is true, was superb: I was fond of magnificence; not for myself, a plain soldier's coat was sufficient for me; I was fond of it, because it encourages our manufactures: without magnificence there is no industry. I abolished at Lyons all that parchment nobility; it was never sensible of what it owed me: it was I that exalted it, by making counts and barons of my best generals. Nobility is a chimera; men are too enlightened to believe, that some among them are noble, others not: they all spring from the same stock;

the only distinction is that of talents, and of services rendered the state: our laws know no others."

The Emperor imagined, that he should find Ney at Auxerre on his arrival: "I cannot conceive," said he to General Bertrand, "why Ney is not here: I am surprised at it, and uneasy: has he changed his opinions? I cannot think so; he would never have suffered Gamot[64] to implicate himself. Yet we must know on what we are to depend; see to it." A few hours after, the marshal arrived. It was about eight o'clock, and Count Bertrand came to inform the Emperor of it. "The marshal, before he comes into your Majesty's presence," said he, "is desirous of collecting his ideas, and justifying in writing his conduct both previous and subsequent to the events of Fontainbleau."—"What need is there of any justification to me?" answered Napoleon: "tell him, that I love him still, and that I will embrace him to-morrow." He would not receive him the same day, as a punishment for having had to wait for him.

The next day the Emperor, as soon as he perceived him, said: "Embrace me, my dear marshal; I am glad to see you. I want no explanation or justification: I have honoured and esteemed you as the bravest of the brave."—"Sire, the newspapers have told a heap of lies, which I wish to confute: my conduct has ever been that of a good soldier, and a good Frenchman."—"I know it, and accordingly never doubted your attachment."—"You were right, Sire. Your Majesty may always depend upon me, when my country is concerned.... It is for my country I have shed my blood, and for it I would still spill it to the last drop. I love you, Sire, but my country above all! above all."—(The Emperor interrupting him) "It is patriotism too, that brings me to France. I learned, that our country was unhappy, and I am come to deliver it from the emigrants and the Bourbons. I will confer upon it all that it expects from me."—"Your Majesty may be assured, that we will support you: he who acts with justice, may do what he pleases with the French. The Bourbons have ruined themselves, by having wished to act as they thought proper, and thrown aside the army."—"Princes who never saw a naked sword could not honour the army: its glory humbled them, and they were jealous of it."—"Yes, Sire, they incessantly sought to humiliate us. I am still enraged, when I think, that a marshal of France, an old warrior like me, was obliged to kneel down before that ... of a Duke of B..... to receive the cross of St. Louis. It could not last; and, if you had not come to expel them, we should have driven them out ourselves[55]."—"How are your troops disposed?"—"Very well, Sire; I thought they would have stifled me, when I announced to them, that they were about to march to meet your eagles."—"What generals are with you?"—"Le Courbe and Bourmont."—"Are you sure of them?"—"I will answer for Le Courbe, but I am not so sure of Bourmont." —"Why are they not come hither?" —"They showed some hesitation, and I left them." —"Are you not afraid of Bourmont's bestirring himself, and embarrassing you?" —"No, Sire, he will keep himself quiet: besides, he would find nobody to second him. I have expelled from the ranks all the light infantry of Louis XIV.[66], who had been given to us, and all the country is fired with enthusiasm." —"No matter, I shall not leave him any possibility of disturbing us: you will direct him and the royalist officers to be secured till we enter Paris. I shall be there without doubt by the 20th or 25th, and sooner. If we arrive, as I hope, without any obstacle, do you think they will defend themselves" —"I do not think they will, Sire: you know what the Parisians are, more noise than work." —"I have received despatches from Paris this morning: the patriots expect me with impatience, and are on the point of rising. I am afraid of some quarrel taking place between them and the royalists. I would not for the world, that my return should be stained with a single drop of blood. It is easy for you, to hold communication with Paris: write to your friends, write to Maret, that our affairs go on well, that I shall arrive without firing a single musket; and let them all unite, to prevent the spilling of blood. Our triumph should be as pure, as the cause we serve." Generals Bertrand and Labedoyère, who were present, then mixed in the conversation; and after a few minutes the Emperor left them, and retired into his closet.

He wrote to the Empress for the third time. This letter finished, Napoleon turned his thoughts to the means of embarking a part of his army, harassed by forced marches. He sent for the chief of the boat department, required an account of the number of boats, the means of preventing accidents, &c. He entered so minutely into particulars with him, that the man could scarcely recover from his surprise, or comprehend how an Emperor should know so much as a boatman. Napoleon persisted in the speedy departure of his troops. Several times he ordered me to go and hasten the embarkation: he was in the habit of employing those about him for every thing that came into his head. His genius knowing no bounds, he imagined, that we poor mortals ought equally to know every thing, and do every thing.

The Emperor had given orders to his scouts, to bring him all the mails; and he had appointed me, to examine their contents. I waged implacable war with the correspondence of ministers; and if I frequently found in it threats and abuse, of which I came in for my share, it presented me at least with matters as important as curious. I particularly remarked two secret instructions, the publication of which, even now, would cover their authors with eternal disgrace. The letters *comme il faut* were equally revolting. Most of them, dictated by frantic hatred, might have sanctioned the rigours of the law: but I considered them as the offspring of brains to be pitied for their diseased state, and contented myself with writing on them in large letters, before I returned to the post-boy, a *Seen*; which, like the head of Medusa, no doubt petrified more than one noble reader.

The darksome conspiracies of the enemies of Napoleon were not the only objects, that met my indiscreet eyes. Sometimes I found myself unintentionally initiated into gentler mysteries and my pen, by mistake, traced the fatal *Seen* at the bottom of epistles, which should have charmed the sight only of the happy mortals, for whom love had destined them.

It was from the newspapers, and the private correspondence, we learned, that some Vendeans were set off from Paris, according to their own account, with the design of assassinating the Emperor. A paper, which it is unnecessary to name, even said, that these gentlemen were disguised as soldiers, and as women, and that most assuredly the Corsican could not escape them.

Though Napoleon did not appear to be uneasy about these criminal plots, we were under apprehensions for him. Previously, when travellers were desirous of telling him news, I stepped aside to enjoy a few minutes' liberty: but from that time I never quitted him, and, with my hand on my sword, I never for a moment lost sight of the eyes, attitude, and gesture of the persons I admitted to his presence.

Count Bertrand, General Drouot, and the officers of his household, equally redoubled their care and attention. But it seemed as if the Emperor made a point of setting his murderers at defiance. That very day he reviewed the 14th of the line in the public square, and afterwards mixed with the people and the soldiers. In vain did we endeavour to surround him; we were jostled with so much perseverance and impetuosity, that it was impossible for us to remain close to him for two minutes together. The way in which we were elbowed amused him extremely: he laughed at our efforts, and, in order to brave us, plunged himself still deeper amid the crowd that besieged us.

Our mistrust was nearly fatal to two of the enemy's emissaries.

One of them, a staff officer, came to offer us his services. Being questioned, he scarcely knew what answers to make. His embarrassment had already excited violent suspicions, when it was unfortunately perceived, that he had on green pantaloons. This was sufficient to convince every body, that he was one of the Artois guards in disguise. Interrogated anew, he answered still more awkwardly; and, attainted and convicted of being a highly suspicious person, and of wearing green pantaloons to boot, he was on the point of being thrown out of the window, when fortunately

Count Bertrand happened to pass by, and ordered him merely to be turned out at the door.

This officer of the new batch had not come to kill Napoleon; he had only been sent to spy what passed at his head-quarters.

The same day witnessed another scene. A chef d'escadron of hussars, adorned with a sabre-cut in the face, came also to join us. He met an extraordinarily good reception, and was even invited to breakfast at the table of the great officers of the household. In wine there is truth; and the new comer, forgetting his part, explained himself so clearly, that it was easy to distinguish in him a false brother. He told us, that the national guard of Paris, and all the imperial guard, were for the King: that every soldier, who retained his fidelity, had a gift of a hundred francs, every officer a thousand, and was promoted a step, &c. &c; that Napoleon had been outlawed, and that if he were taken.... At these words Colonel ***, who sat next him, seized him by the collar; every body was for knocking him on the head at once; I alone was against it. "Gentlemen," said I, "the Emperor will not hear of any blood being shed; you have sworn to give no quarter to assassins, but this man is not one; he is no doubt a spy. We are not afraid of them; let them go, and report what they have seen to those who have sent them: let us all drink the health of our Emperor, Long live the Emperor!" He was spitten upon, turned out, and we saw him no more.

Another deserter from the royal army presented himself, to reveal an important secret, as he said, to the Emperor. The Emperor, who knew no secret but strength, would not waste time in listening to him, and sent him to me. He was an officer of hussars, the friend and accomplice of Maubreuil. He did not think me worthy of his secrets, and I introduced him to the grand Marshal. The substance of what he said was, that he, as well as Maubreuil, had been commissioned by the provisional government, and by very great persons, to assassinate the Emperor, at the time of his departure for the island of Elba: that he held in execration such an execrable crime, and would not commit it; and that, after having once saved the life of Napoleon, he came to place himself near his person, to make a rampart for him with his body in case of necessity. He delivered to the grand Marshal a memorial of Maubreuil's, and divers papers, of which the Emperor directed me to give him an account. I examined them all with the greatest care. They proved incontestably, that mysterious rendezvous had been given to Maubreuil in the name of the provisional government; but they contained no clue, that could enable any one to penetrate the object and end of these secret conferences: the names of those illustrious personages, whom some persons have since been desirous of implicating in this odious plot, were not even mentioned in them. This officer reaped no benefit from his disclosures, real or pretended, and disappeared.

From hearing so much of plots against his life, however, a painful impression was at length made on the Emperor. "I cannot conceive," said he to me, "how men liable to fall into my hands can be incessantly urging my assassination, and setting a price upon my head. Had I wished to get rid of them by similar means, they would long ago have been mingled with the dust. Like them, I could have found Georges Brularts, and Maubreuils. Twenty times, if I had wished it, persons would have brought them to me bound hands and feet, dead or alive. I had always the foolish generosity, to despise their rage: I despise it still; but wo betide them, wo to all their infernal gang, if they dare touch one of my people! My blood boils, when I think, that they have dared, in the face of nations, to proscribe without trial the thousands of Frenchmen, who are marching with us: is this known to the army?" — "Yes, sire, some persons have had the imprudence, to spread the report, that we are all proclaimed out of the protection of the laws, and that some of the body guards and Chouans have set out to assassinate you: accordingly, the troops have sworn, to give them no quarter, and already two spies have with difficulty escaped being knocked on the head before my eyes." — "So much the worse, so much the worse; such are not my intentions. I wish not a single drop of French blood to be shed, not a single gun to be fired. Girard[67] must be desired to restrain his soldiers; write: "General Girard, I am informed, that your troops, being acquainted with the decrees of Paris, have resolved, by way of reprisals, to kill all the Royalists they meet: you will meet none but Frenchmen; I forbid you to fire a single musket: calm your soldiers; contradict the reports by which they are exasperated; tell them, that I will not enter Paris at their head, if their weapons be stained with French blood[68].""

Ministers of the King, guilty authors of the parricidal ordinance of the 6th of March, read this and blush!

The moment he was quitting Auxerre, the Emperor heard, that the Marseillese appeared to have an intention of annoying his rear. He gave orders to the general posted in échelon on the road, and set out without fear.

In advance of Fossard, he perceived, drawn up in order of battle, the dragoons of the King's regiment, who had deserted their officers, to come and join him. He alighted, saluted them with that military gravity, which so well became him, and bestowed on them compliments and promotions. No regiment could escape us. When the officers demurred, the soldiers came without them. I am wrong, however: there was one regiment, the third of hussars, that the Emperor could not bring over to him. The brave Moncey, who commanded it, was a man of sound understanding, and his attachment to Napoleon, his ancient benefactor, could not be doubted: but all men do not see with the same eyes; some made their duty consist in running to meet Napoleon, Moncey thought himself obliged to avoid him.

He had conjured his regiment, not to subject him to the disgrace of being deserted. His officers and his hussars, by whom he was adored, followed him, while they made the air ring with shouts of Long live the Emperor! thinking thus to reconcile their respect for their colonel with their devotion to the cause and person of Napoleon.

We were informed on the road, that two thousand of the body guards were posted in the forest of Fontainbleau. Though this account was improbable, it was thought necessary, not to cross the forest without precaution. At our urgent solicitation, the Emperor took about two hundred horse to accompany him. Hitherto his only escort had been the carriage of General Drouot, which preceded his, and mine, which closed the march. Colonels Germanouski and Du Champ, Captain Raoul, and three or four Polanders, galloped by the side of them. Our horses, our postillions, our couriers, with tricoloured ribands, gave our peaceable party an air of festivity and happiness, that formed a singular contrast to the proscription suspended over our heads, and to the mourning and despair of the men who had proscribed us.

We marched almost all night, as the Emperor was desirous of reaching Fontainbleau at break of day. I observed, that I thought it would be imprudent in him, to alight at the castle. "You are a child," answered he; "if any thing be to happen to me, all these precautions would be of no avail. Our fate is written above:" and he pointed with his finger to the sky[69].

I had imagined, that the sight of the palace of Fontainbleau, the place where he had so lately descended from the throne, and where he now re-appeared as conqueror and sovereign, would make some impression on him, and impel him to think of the fragility of human grandeur. I watched him attentively; but he did not appear to me, to experience any emotion. Immediately on his arrival, he rambled over the gardens and the palace with as much pleasure and curiosity, as if he came to take possession of them for the first time. Napoleon occupied the little apartments, and complaisantly made me notice their extreme elegance. He then led me to his library, and in going up, said with an air of satisfaction, "We shall be very well here." — "Yes, sire," answered I, "people are always well at home." He smiled, and I believe was pleased with my well-timed compliment.

At eleven o'clock he dictated to me the orders of the day; and these orders announced, that we should sleep at Essonne. It was not till noon, that the news of the King's departure was brought at once by a courier from M. de Lavalette, by a letter from Madame Hamalin, and by M. de Ség.... He sent for me immediately. "You will set out first," he said, "to get every thing ready."—"It is to Essonne, I presume, your Majesty orders me to repair?"—"No, to Paris. The King and the Princes have fled. I shall be at the Tuileries this evening." He gave me some secret directions, and I quitted Fontainbleau with a heart full of happiness and joy. I had never doubted Napoleon's triumph; but from hope to reality how great the distance!

In fact the King had quitted Paris.

The aspect of affairs had never changed since the royal session of the 17th of March. The minister, persevering in his system of falsehood and dissimulation, still distorted the truth with the same impudence, and did not cease to predict the approaching destruction of Napoleon and his adherents. At length, after a thousand subterfuges, it became necessary to confess, that Napoleon was within a few leagues of Paris. The King, whom the minister had not been afraid to deceive, had scarcely time to think of retreating. In this painful situation, he displayed a strength of mind above all praise. His courage was not that of a warlike prince, who defends his capital inch by inch, and trembles with rage and despair when forced to quit it; but that of a good father, who separates himself with regret from his children, and from the roof under which they were born. The Bonapartists themselves, who made a great distinction between the king and his family, were not insensible to the tears of that august and unfortunate monarch, and sincerely prayed, that his flight might be exempted from danger and trouble.

It was supposed, that Napoleon would make a triumphal entry into his capital. His old grenadiers, who had marched in seventeen days a distance that would commonly require five-and-forty, seemed, as they approached their object, to acquire fresh strength at every step. On the road you might see them in agitation, pressing upon and encouraging one another. They would have marched twenty leagues in an hour, if necessary, not to be deprived of the honour of entering Paris by the side of Napoleon. Their hopes were disappointed: the Emperor, who had witnessed their fatigues, ordered them to take a day's rest at Fontainbleau.

At two o'clock on the 20th of March, Napoleon set out for Paris. Retarded by the crowd, that accumulated on his way, and by the felicitations of the troops and the generals, who had run to meet him, he could not reach it till nine in the evening. As soon as he alighted, the people rushed on him; a thousand arms lifted him up, and carried him along in triumph. Nothing could be more affecting than the confused assembly of the crowd of officers and generals, who had pressed into the apartments of the Tuileries at the heels of Napoleon. Happy to see themselves once more triumphant, after so many vicissitudes, humiliations, and disgusts, they forgot the majesty of the place, to give themselves up without constraint to the desire of expressing their happiness and joy. They ran to one another, and hugged each other again and again. The halls of the palace seemed metamorphosed into a field of battle, where friends, brothers, unexpectedly escaped from death, found and embraced one another after victory.

We had been so spoiled on the road, however, that the Emperor's reception by the Parisians did not answer our expectations. Multiplied shouts of "Long live the Emperor!" saluted him on his way; but they wanted those characters of unanimity and frenzy, which were displayed by the acclamations, that had accompanied him from the gulf of Juan to the gates of Paris. It would be a mistake, however, to infer, that the Parisians did not behold the return of Napoleon with pleasure. We must only conclude, therefore, that the Emperor missed the proper time for his entrance.

The people of great cities are eager for sights: to move their hearts, you must astonish their eyes. If Napoleon, instead of traversing Paris in the evening, and without being announced or expected, had put it off till the next day, and allowed the disquietudes inseparable from such a crisis time to be allayed; if he had given his entrance the pomp and splendour it ought to have had; if he had caused the troops and half-pay officers, who had hastened to his call, to march before him; if he had presented himself at the head of his grenadiers of the island of Elba, with all their decorations; if he had been surrounded by Generals Bertrand, Drouot, Cambronne, and the faithful companions of his exile; this grand and affecting train would have produced the most lively sensation, and the whole population of Paris would have applauded the return and the triumph of Napoleon. Instead of those unanimous transports, he received only the applauses of the populous part of the capital, that he had occasion to traverse; and his detractors did not fail, to compare this reception with that of Louis XVIII., and to publish, that he was obliged to enter Paris by night, in order to escape the maledictions and vengeance of the public. Napoleon, who had just travelled two hundred and fifty leagues amid the acclamations of two millions of Frenchmen, could not be agitated by any such fears; but it is well known with what confidence, what intoxication, he was inspired by the anniversary of a victory or happy event; and as the 20th of March was the birthday of his son, he determined at all events to enter the capital under such fortunate auspices.

The very evening of his arrival, Napoleon had a long conversation with the Duke of Otranto, and the other dignitaries of the state, on the situation of France. They all appeared intoxicated with happiness and hope. The Emperor himself could not disguise his rapture: never did I see him so madly gay, or so prodigal of boxes on the ear.[70] His conversation savoured of the agitation of his heart: the same words incessantly recurred to his tongue; and, it must be confessed, they were not very flattering to the crowd of courtiers and great personages, who already besieged him: he was continually saying: "It was the disinterested persons, who brought me back to Paris; the sub-lieutenants and soldiers did every thing; I owe all to the people and the army."

That night and the following morning the Emperor was busied in the choice and nomination of his ministers.

At their head Prince Cambacérès found himself placed. The system of defamation directed against him had not altered the high consideration, which he had acquired by his great wisdom, and constant moderation. The Emperor offered him the port-folio of the minister of justice, and was obliged to command him to accept it. His sagacity and foresight, no doubt, presaged the fatal issue of the new reign of Napoleon.

The Prince of Eckmuhl was named minister of war. By the harshness of his manners, by acts of severity almost barbarous. he had formerly drawn upon himself universal animadversions; his fidelity to the Emperor, and his defence of Hamburgh, had subsequently conciliated public opinion. The feebleness and versatility of his character indeed excited some apprehensions; but it was hoped, that the Emperor would know how to master him, and that the army would derive happy advantages from his indefatigable zeal, and his strict probity.

The Duke of Vicenza[71] was placed at the helm of foreign affairs. The rectitude of his principles. the firmness, nobleness, and independence of his character, had justly acquired him the esteem of France and of Europe; and his appointment was considered as a pledge of the loyal and pacific intentions of Napoleon.

The Duke of Gaëta and Count Mollien became again ministers of the finances and the treasury. They had obtained the confidence of the public by the ability, prudence, and integrity of their preceding administration; and the choice of them met with general applause.

The Duke of Otranto had the charge of the police. He had been at the helm of the state in circumstances of difficulty and peril; he had learned to form a sound judgment of the public mind, and to foresee, prepare, and guide events. Having belonged to all parties in succession, he knew their tactics, their resources, their pretensions; and the whole nation, convinced of his experience, talents, and patriotism, hoped, that he would successfully concur in the safety of the Emperor and the empire.

The recall of the Duke of Bassano to the ministry, as secretary of state, displeased the court, and also those credulous people, who, having no opinions but what are suggested to them, adopt praise and blame without discernment.

Few men have been so ill treated, as this minister.

Every one has taken pleasure in disfiguring his character and even his features.

The Duke of Bassano had an open countenance, an agreeable manner of conversation, a politeness always uniform, a dignity sometimes affected, but never offensive, with a natural propensity to esteem men, courtesy in obliging them, and perseverance in serving them. The favour he enjoyed was at first the reward of unexampled readiness in business; of indefatigable activity; of pure intentions, lofty views, probity, proof against all temptation, and I will even add an iron constitution; for physical strength also was a quality in the eyes of Napoleon. Subsequently it became the just return for an attachment not to be shaken; an attachment, which, by its force, vivacity, and constancy, seemed to be a compound of love and friendship.

I must own, I believe, that M. de Bassano most frequently shared and approved without exception the opinions of the Emperor; but it was not from interested or base motives: the Emperor was the idol of his heart, the object of his admiration: with such sentiments, how was it possible for him, to perceive the errors and faults of Napoleon? Besides, having continually to express the ideas of the Emperor, and to imbue himself as it were with the emanations of his spirit, he had identified himself with his way of thinking and of viewing things, and saw and thought as he did with the most perfect sincerity. Not but that he sometimes differed from him in opinion; yet whatever efforts he made, he always yielded ultimately to the irresistible ascendancy, that the genius of Napoleon exercised over him, as it did over every other person.

The Duke of Decrès was called anew to the post of minister of the navy, and this unexpected choice was completely disapproved. This minister was not deficient in understanding, talents, or bravery; but from the little importance he appeared to set on acting with justice or injustice, his cynicism, and his brutal contempt for those under him, he had acquired the aversion of all who came near him; and, as evil spreads readily, this aversion, though unjust, had become general.

The discontent this appointment excited was repaired by the good effect, which was produced by that of M. Carnot to the ministry of the home department. The soldiery did not forget, that he had paved the way to victory for many years; and the citizens remembered with what zeal, this courageous patriot had shown himself the defender of public liberty under Napoleon, both when consul and when Emperor, and under Louis XVIII. To be a real patriot, says one of our celebrated writers, it is requisite, to possess greatness of soul; to have knowledge, to have probity, to have virtue. In M. Carnot all these rare and valuable qualities were combined: and, far from acquiring any personal lustre from this great name of patriot, he seemed on the contrary to embellish the name by wearing it so well had he preserved it in its primitive purity, amid the debasement into which it had been plunged by the excesses of the revolution, and the abuses of despotism.

The choice of such a minister was considered as a pledge to the nation. The sovereign, who was not afraid to introduce this illustrious citizen into the government of the state, could not but entertain the generous design of securing the happiness of his subjects, and respecting their rights.

The same day the Emperor gave the chief command of the gendarmerie to the Duke of Rovigo.

The Duke of Rovigo, an old aide-de-camp of Napoleon, had sworn him an eternal attachment, both from feeling and gratitude. This attachment, born in a camp, had retained the character of military obedience: a word, a gesture, was sufficient to call it into action. But however great its strength, or, if you will, its fanaticism, it never affected the rectitude and frankness, which were the base and ornament of the duke's character.

From no other person, except the Duke of Vicenza, did the Emperor hear more bold and useful truths. Twenty times did he venture to say to him, as his ministerial correspondence testifies, that France and Europe were tired of shedding blood; and that, if he did not renounce his system of war, he would be abandoned by the French, and precipitated from the throne by foreigners.

The command of the gendarmerie was taken from Marshal Moncey, not from disgust or dissatisfaction, but because the marshal showed little eagerness to retain it. On this occasion he wrote to the Emperor a letter full of fine sentiments, in which he requested him, to continue to his son the kindness he had formerly conferred on himself: it was difficult to reconcile the gratitude he owed Napoleon with the fidelity he had promised the King: in this he was so happy as to succeed.

All the marshals were not so fortunate.

M. de Montalivet, formerly minister of the home department, became intendant of the civil list, an office that suited him better. In administration, as in many other things, endeavours to do better prevent people from doing so well; and M. de Montalivet, from a desire to neglect no minute particular, and seeking to carry every thing to perfection, lost in empty trifles that time, which he might have employed in promoting the general good on a large scale.

The strangest metamorphosis was that of the Duke de Cadore: he was made a surveyor of buildings.

"Soyez plutôt maçon, si c'est votre métier."[72]

This place, hitherto the modest portion of auditors or masters of request, who had interest at court, was astonished at the honour of belonging to a duke and peer, ex-ambassador, ex-minister, ex-grand chancellor, &c. &c. &c. But so much was his excellency then devoted to the sovereign of the day, that he would readily have accepted the post of a gentleman usher, had there been no other to offer him.

The council of state was re-established on the ancient footing, and composed of nearly the same members.

The Emperor was neither politic nor prudent in ostensibly bestowing his confidence on some of them, who were obnoxious to the public. The usurpations of the imperial power were ascribed to their servile counsels, and their presence near the throne could not but revive recollections and anxieties, which it was of importance to destroy for ever. If their merit and experience rendered them necessary, they should have been consulted in private, but not held up to public view. A government firmly established may sometimes brave opinion, but a rising government ought to respect and submit to it.

All the aides-de-camp of the Emperor, with the exception, I believe, of General Lauriston, whom he would not employ again, were recalled. He could not place around him officers more worthy of his confidence for their noble-mindedness and superior talents. Generals Le Tort and Labedoyère were added to their number. The Emperor, deceived by false appearances[73], had taken from the former the command of the dragoons of the guard, and to compensate for this involuntary injustice, he made him his aide-de-camp. The same favour was conferred on Labedoyère, as a recompense for his conduct at Grenoble; but he answered the kindness of Napoleon by a formal refusal. "I will not allow it to be thought," said he proudly, "that I joined the Emperor for the sake of reward. I espoused his cause, simply because it was that of liberty, and of my country; the honour of having served it is enough for me: I desire nothing more; the Emperor personally owes me nothing."

This noble refusal will not surprise those, who had an opportunity of knowing and esteeming the patriotism and disinterestedness of that brave and unfortunate young man.

Introduced to society at an early age, he conducted himself at first as those generally do, who have a handsome face, elegance of manners, wit, a name, wealth, and no experience. Soon brought to himself, he felt, that he was not born to lead a life of dissipation; and his conduct became as honourable, as it had been irregular. His mind, turned to serious occupation, engaged in political speculations: his soul, naturally proud and independent, matured and enlarged itself, and expanded to those liberal ideas and noble sentiments, that the love of glory and of our country inspires. Nature, in giving him a lofty, firm, and daring character, unquestionably destined him to act an important part in the world; and if death, and what a death! had not struck him in the flower of his years, he would assuredly have fulfilled his shining destiny, and done honour to France.

The Emperor set several persons to speak to him, and after three days negotiations Labedoyère yielded. Napoleon persisted in recompensing him. In ordinary cases, the Emperor looked with indifference on the endeavours made to please him; never was he known to say, I am pleased; and a person conjectured he had given him satisfaction, when he did not show any marks of discontent. If, on the other hand, the services rendered him made a noise, like those of Labedoyère, he was lavish of his praises and rewards: and in this he had two objects; the one, that of appearing not only just, but generous; the other, that of inspiring emulation. But frequently on the very day, on which he had bestowed on you praises, and proofs of his satisfaction, he would treat you with disdain and harshness, to prevent your attaching too much importance to the service you might have rendered him, or believing, that he had contracted a debt of obligation to you.

The Emperor replaced about his person most of the gentlemen of the bedchamber, equerries, and masters of ceremonies, who were with him in 1814. He had retained his unfortunate predilection for the great lords of former times, and must have them at any price: had he not been surrounded by ancient nobles, he would have fancied himself in a republic.

Most of these (for there were some who were most honourably excepted, as the Prince de Beauveau, Messrs. de Turenne, de Montholon, de Lascases, Forbin de Janson, Perregaux, &c. &c.) had meanly renounced him in 1814, and become the common valets of the Bourbons; but he would not believe a word of it. He had the weakness, common to all princes, of considering his most cringing courtiers as his most devoted subjects.

He would also form an establishment for the Empress, and re-appointed Mesdames de Bassano, de Vicenza, de Rovigo, Duchâtel, and Marmier, ladies of the bedchamber. The Duchess of M*** was not recalled. He heard from Prince Joseph, that after the events of Fontainbleau, she had abused the confidence of the Empress, and betrayed the secret of her correspondence.

It was said, but falsely, that the gracefulness and beauty of the Duchess had formerly obtained the homage of Napoleon; and her disgrace did not fail to be urged as a fresh proof of the inconstancy of men; but I have assigned the true and only cause.

The corruption of courts often sanctions a number of lying suppositions, against which few reputations can stand. This justice however must be done Napoleon; no prince was ever a man of purer manners, or took so much pains to avoid and even check scandal: he was never seen, to be followed to the army by his mistresses, like Louis XIV.; or disguised in the dress of a porter, or of a small-coal man, like Henry IV., to carry disgrace and despair into the houses of his most faithful servants.

As a pretty remarkable contrast, Napoleon, at the moment when he resumed with delight his own upper servants, sent about their business without pity the lacqueys, who had served Louis XVIII. and the princes.

"De tout tems les petits ont payé pour les grands."[74]

These poor people were left destitute. It has been said and repeated a hundred times, that Napoleon ill-treated and struck all those who came near him, right or wrong. Nothing can be more false. He had his moments of impatience and warmth; and what honest citizen has not? But in general, the officers and even subalterns of his household were in easy circumstances with him, and he was more frequently in a gay than in a serious humour. He very easily became attached to a person; and when he liked any one, he could not do without him; and treated him with a kindness, that frequently degenerated into weakness. It is true, it would have been very difficult for him to find servants more able, or more devotedly attached to him: every one of them had made it his particular study, to become, not what he did wish, but what he might wish.

Tacitus has observed, that voluntary slaves make more tyrants, than tyrants make slaves. When we recollect the officiousness, the meannesses, and the adulation, of certain nobles, who had become the courtiers of Napoleon, we are astonished, that it never entered his head to follow the example of Alexander, and cause himself to be adored as a god.

Counts Drouot and Bertrand were retained in their posts of grand marshal of the palace, and major-general of the guards. It had been imagined, that the Emperor would have conferred on them the titles of Duke of Porto Ferrajo, and Duke of Porto Longone, as memorials of their fidelity. He did no such thing. They were fully recompensed, however, by the veneration, with which Frenchmen and foreigners were inspired for them both. Still, for what reason, I cannot conceive, a higher value was generally set on the devoted attachment of General Bertrand.

When the Emperor had laid down his crown, Count Drouot did not hesitate an instant, to preserve that fidelity to him in adversity, which he had sworn in his prosperity: and this fidelity was not in his eyes a proof of attachment, still less a sacrifice; it appeared to him only the natural fulfilment of a duty imposed on him by the kindnesses and misfortunes of Napoleon.

To follow him, he abandoned all that is most dear to a well-born mind, his family and his country, as well as the military career, in which he had acquired the most glorious renown.

Transported into the midst of the seas, he frequently cast his looks towards the land of his birth: but no regret, no complaint, escaped from his heart. His conscience was satisfied, how could he be unhappy? As disinterested in the service of the sovereign of the island of Elba, as he had been in that of the Emperor of the French[75], though poor, he would receive no reward from Napoleon: "Give me food and clothing," said he, "I want nothing more." The most seducing offers were lavished on him, to draw him over to the Bourbons. To these he was insensible; and he felt no difficulty in preferring the rock of Napoleon to the lustre of their throne.

Such was General Drouot; and such also was his worthy rival, Count Bertrand; for there existed no difference in the generosity of their conduct, and none ought to exist in the admiration they deserve.

The Emperor himself was not free from this injustice: he seemed to give the preference to Count Bertrand. This difference proceeded, I believe, from that degree of intimacy, which the functions of the grand Marshal established between the Emperor and him, and perhaps from the suitableness of their characters.

Bertrand, amiable, witty, insinuating, united the agreeable and polished manners of a courtier with an air of distinction Feeble, irresolute, in the ordinary conduct of life; he yielded to no one in courage and firmness, on occasions of difficulty and danger. A stranger to intrigue, inaccessible to seduction, he was in the camp, as in the palace, a man of honour, a man of probity.

Drouot, simple in his manners, affectionate in his speech, displayed that rare assemblage of virtues, which compel us to love the sages of antiquity, and the heroes of the days of chivalry. He had the wisdom, the prudence of Aristides, the valour, the modesty, the loyalty of Bayard. The favour he enjoyed, the military power with which he was invested, inspired him with no pride: he was not less humble and timid at court, than he was terrible and daring in the field of honour.

Bertrand, when he was consulted, delivered his opinion with the caution and skill of a courtier; Drouot, with the precision and frankness of a soldier: but neither was false to his conscience. Their language, though different in structure, was the same in substance; it was always that of truth and honour.

The Emperor, though greatly fatigued by nocturnal marches, reviews, perpetual harangues, and his labours in the closet, which for the last thirty-six hours had occupied all his moments, would nevertheless review the troops, that previously composed the army of the Duke of Berri.

He caused them to be assembled in the court of the Tuileries; and, to use his own words, "The whole capital was witness to the sentiments of enthusiasm and attachment, by which those brave troops were animated: they seemed to have reconquered their country, and found again in the national colours the remembrance of all those generous sentiments, which have ever distinguished the French nation."

After having gone through the ranks, he made the troops form square battalions, and said to them:

"Soldiers, I came to France with six hundred men, because I reckoned on the love of the people, and the remembrance of the old soldiers. I have not been deceived in my expectations: soldiers, I thank you. The glory of what we have just done belongs wholly to you and to the people, mine is only that of having known you, and judged you rightly.

"Soldiers, the imperial throne only can guarantie the rights of the people, and more especially the first of our interests, that of our glory. Soldiers, we are going to march, to chase from our territories those princes, who are the auxiliaries of foreigners. The nation will not only second us with its good wishes, but will follow our impulse. The French people and myself depend upon you: we will not interfere with the affairs of foreign nations; and wo to the nation, that shall interfere with ours!"

At this moment General Cambronne, and some officers of the guards of the battalion of the island of Elba, appeared with the ancient eagles of the guard: the Emperor resumed his harangue, and said[76]: "Here are the officers of the battalion, who accompanied me in my adversity: they are all my friends, they were dear to my heart! Whenever I saw them, they reminded me of the different regiments of the army; for among these six hundred brave fellows are men from every regiment. They recalled to my mind those great victories, the remembrance of which is so dear; for they are all well covered with honourable scars received in those memorable battles! In loving them, it was all of you, soldiers, of the whole French army, whom

I loved. They bring back to you these eagles; let them serve you as a rallying point: in giving them to the guards, I give them to the whole army."

"Treason and unfortunate circumstances had covered them with a funereal veil: but, thanks to the French people and to you, they appear again resplendent with all their glory. Swear, that they shall always be found, wherever the interests of our country call them! that traitors, and those who would invade our territories, shall never stand their appearance."

"We swear it," answered all the soldiers with enthusiasm. They then filed off with shouts of "Long live the Emperor!" and to the sound of military music, playing the favourite tunes of the revolution, and the Marseillese march, so celebrated in the annals of our crimes and our victories.

When the review was over, the Emperor returned to his closet, and applied himself immediately to business. His situation rendered it necessary, that he should ascertain without delay the precise state of the country, of the government of which he had resumed the reins. This was so vast an undertaking, that the faculties of any other man would have been overwhelmed by it. He found the writing table covered with mystic authors[77]; and substituted for them plans and maps. "The closet of a French monarch," said he, "should resemble the tent of a general, not an oratory." His eyes rested on the map of France. After having contemplated its recent limits, he exclaimed in a tone of profound sorrow, "Poor France!" He kept silence a few minutes, and then began to hum in a low voice one of his usual burdens of songs:

"S'il est un tems pour la folie,
Il en est un pour la raison[78]."

The Emperor entered his closet habitually before six in the morning, and seldom quitted it till night.

Impatience and vivacity are almost always incompatible with order and precision. Napoleon, destined to be like no other person, added to the fire of genius the methodical habits of cold and little minds. For the most part, he took care to arrange his numerous papers himself. Each of them had its settled place. Here was found whatever related to the war department: there, the budgets. the daily statements of the treasury and finances: farther on, the reports of the police, his secret correspondence with his private agents, &c. He carefully returned every thing to its place, after having used it: compared with him the most methodical clerk would have been but a bungler.

His first business was to read his correspondence, and the despatches that had arrived in the night. He put aside the interesting letters, and threw the rest on the floor: this he called his *answered*.

He afterwards examined the copies of letters opened at the post office, and burnt them immediately. It seemed, as if he wished to annihilate all traces of the abuse of power, of which he had been guilty.

He finished by casting an eye over the newspapers. Sometimes he said, "That's a good article; whose is it?" He must know every thing.

These several readings ended, he set to work; and it may be said without exaggeration, that he was then as extraordinary, as incomparable, as at the head of his armies.

As he would entrust to nobody the supreme care of the government, he saw every thing himself; and it is easy to conceive, on what a multiplicity of objects he had to fix his eyes. Independently of his ministers, the Duke of Bassano, the commandant of the first division of Paris, the prefect of the police, the inspector general of the gendarmerie, the major-general of guards, the grand marshal of the palace, the great officers of the crown, the aides-de-camp, and the orderly officers (*officiers d'ordonnance*) on missions, daily sent him circumstantial reports, which he examined, and answered immediately: it being a maxim with him, to put nothing off till to-morrow. And let it not be supposed, that he satisfied himself with a superficial judgment of affairs: he read every report through, and examined every voucher attentively. Frequently the super-human sagacity, with which he was gifted, enabled him to perceive errors and imperfections, that had escaped the scrutinizing eyes of his ministers; and then he corrected their labours. But still more frequently he fashioned them anew from beginning to end; and what was a fortnight's work to a whole ministry, scarcely cost the genius of Napoleon a few minutes.

The Emperor rarely sat down, but dictated as he walked about. He did not like to repeat his words; and if you asked him a word not clearly understood, he answered impatiently, "*I said,*" and went on.

When he had to treat a subject worthy of himself, his style, habitually nervous and concise, rose to the level of his grand conceptions: it became majestic and sublime.

If the possibility of expressing his ideas was shackled by the want of the proper word; or if the customary terms did not appear to him sufficiently strong, sufficiently animated, he brought together words, that were astonished to find themselves in each other's company, and created a language of his own, a language rich and impressive, that might sometimes infringe established rules, but compensated this happy fault, by giving more loftiness and vigour to his thoughts[79].

Sometimes, hurried away by the impetuosity of his character, and eager to arrive more quickly at his object, he did not take time to weigh his words, his ideas, his desires. When his orders had been dictated to us in such a fit of hastiness, we were careful, as far as possible, not to present them for signing the same day. The next day, they were almost always modified, softened, or torn. Napoleon was never displeased with us, for endeavouring to guard him against the dangers of precipitancy. They who think, that he never corrected a false step, are mistaken: if under certain circumstances his determinations were inflexible, in a number of others he yielded to remonstrance, and relinquished his projects and resolves without difficulty.

The Emperor seldom wrote with his own hand. Words of many syllables were tedious to him; and, not having patience to write them at length, he mutilated them. This habit, added to the defective formation of his letters, rendered his writing altogether illegible. Frequently, too, from carelessness, or absence of mind, he infringed the laws of orthography; and people have not failed thence to infer, that he was completely ignorant.

Most assuredly the ignorance of Napoleon, were it proved, would detract nothing from his glory and renown. Charlemagne could scarcely sign his own name. Louis XIV., and I quote him by choice, though born on a throne, was unacquainted with *the rules of grammar*. Yet Charlemagne and Louis were nevertheless great kings. The imputation, however, is as false as it is absurd. Napoleon, educated at the school of Erienne, was distinguished there by that facility of comprehension, that disdain of pleasure, that fondness for study, that enthusiastic regard for models of greatness, which commonly indicate superior minds. Destined for the profession of arms, he would not aspire to become a man of letters, a man of reading, a learned man: his object, for he had an object in his earliest years, was to become some day a distinguished officer, perhaps even a great captain. It was to the military sciences, therefore, he bent his genius ... the universe knows the rest.

But do I say his genius? the detractors of Napoleon also assert, that his mind was too subject to irregularities, for the possession of genius to be granted him: do they not know, or do they pretend to be ignorant, that such irregularities are on the contrary the proof, the distinguishing characteristics, of this precious gift of nature.

"Genius," says one of our philosophers, "rises and stoops by turns; it is often imperfect, because it does not take the trouble to improve itself. It is great in great things, because they are adapted to excite its sublime instinct, and call it into action. It is negligent in ordinary things, because they are beneath it, and have nothing in them to stir it up: if, however, it do turn its attention to them, it fertilizes them, aggrandizes them, and gives them a new and unexpected appearance, that had escaped vulgar eyes."

And with how vast a genius must he have been endowed! he, who, occupied by the torments of ambition, military calculations, political schemes, and the anxieties inspired by the enemies of his crown and of his life, still found sufficient time, sufficient calmness, sufficient power, to command his numerous armies; to govern twenty foreign nations, and forty millions of subjects; to enter solicitously into all the particulars of the administration of his states; to see every thing; to sift every thing to the bottom; to regulate every thing; in fine, to conceive, create, and realize those unexpected improvements, those bold innovations, those noble institutions, and those immortal codes, that raise the civil glory of France to a degree of superiority, which alone can match its military glory. But I know not why I attempt to combat such adversaries: they who are blind to the genius of Napoleon, have never known genius itself, and I ought to give them no answer, but that of Rousseau: "Silence, ye uninitiated!"

The Emperor, by his decrees issued at Lyons, had in some degree repaired the wrongs imputed to the royal government. One grievance still remained for him; the slavery of the press. The decree of the 24th of March[80], by suppressing the censors, the censorship, and the superintendance of the bookselling trade, completed the imperial restoration.

This last concession was unquestionably the greatest, that Napoleon could make to public opinion. A press in the general interest of the people is the surest protection of their rights. It is the most noble conquest liberty can gain over despotism: to honest men it gives dignity; it inspires them with the love of their country, and of the laws; in fine, according to the English definition, it is the mother of all liberty: but in times of trouble and of revolution, it is a dangerous weapon in the hands of the wicked; and the Emperor foresaw, that the royalists would employ it in the cause of the Bourbons; and the Jacobins, to calumniate his sentiments, and render his designs suspected. But, a declared enemy of half-measures, he resolved, since he had set thought at liberty, that it should circulate unshackled[81].

This decree, and those that preceded it, were undoubtedly sufficient to testify to the nation the liberal disposition of Napoleon: but no speech from the throne had yet declared with solemnity the positive intentions of the Emperor.

At length he fixed on Sunday, the 26th of March, as the day, on which he would make his new profession of faith in the face of the nation[82].

The ministers, the council of state, the court of cassation, the court of accounts, the imperial court, the prefect, and the municipal council of Paris, were admitted to the foot of the throne.

The prince arch-chancellor, speaking in the name of the ministers, said:

"Sire, Providence, that watches over our destiny, has re-opened to your Majesty the road to that throne, to which you had been raised by the free choice of the people, and the national gratitude. Our country raises its majestic brow, and for the second time salutes with the name of deliverer the prince, who destroyed anarchy, and whose existence alone is at present capable of consolidating our liberal institutions.

"The most just of revolutions, that which will restore to men their dignity, and all their political rights, has hurled from the throne the dynasty of the Bourbons. After five and twenty years of war and troubles, all the efforts of foreigners have proved unable, to awaken affections that are extinct, or wholly unknown to the present generation. The struggle of the interests and prejudices of a few against the enlightened state of the age, and the interests of a great nation, is at length terminated.

"Our destinies are accomplished: the only legitimate cause, the cause of the people, has triumphed. Your Majesty has yielded to the wishes of the French; you have seized anew the reins of the state, amid the benedictions of the people and of the army.

"France, Sire, has as a guarantee of it her will, and her dearest interests; she has as a guarantee of it all that your Majesty has said to the population of the different parts of the country, which assembled in crowds on your passage. Your Majesty will keep your word, you will remember only the services rendered your country; you will prove, that in your eyes, and in your heart, whatever the different opinions and exasperations of parties may have been, all citizens are equal, as they are in the eye of the law.

"Your Majesty will also forget, that we have been the masters of the nations around us. Generous idea! that adds another glory to the glory already acquired.

"Already has Your Majesty traced out to your ministers the path they have to pursue: already have you made known to all the people by your proclamations the maxims, by which you would have your empire governed for the future. No war without, unless to repel unjust aggression; no re-action within, no arbitrary proceedings; security of person, security of property, and the free circulation of opinions, are the principles you have sanctioned.

"Happy those, Sire, who are called to cooperate in so many sublime acts! Such benefits will ensure to you from posterity, when the days of adulation are at an end, the name of Father of your country: they will be guarantied to our children by the august heir, whom your Majesty is preparing to crown in the Champ de Mai."

The Emperor answered:

"The sentiments you have expressed to me are mine. 'Every thing agreeably to the sense of the nation, and every thing for France:' such is my motto.

"I and my family, whom this great people has raised to the French throne, and maintained on it in spite of vicissitudes and political tempests, will not, ought not, cannot, ever claim any other title to it."

The Count Défermon, father of the presidents of the council of state, delivered to the Emperor the following declaration, tending to prove the nullity of the abdication of Fontainbleau:

"The council of state, in resuming its functions, thinks it necessary to make known the principles, by which its conduct and opinions are guided.

"The sovereignty resides in the people, who are the only legitimate source of power.

"In 1789 the nation recovered its rights, which had long been usurped, or misunderstood.

"The National Assembly abolished the feudal monarchy, and established a constitutional monarchy, and a representative government.

"The resistance of the Bourbons to the wishes of the people occasioned their downfal, and their banishment from the French territories.

"Twice the people sanctioned by its votes the new form of government established by its representatives.

"In the year 8th, Bonaparte, already crowned by victory, found himself raised to the government by the assent of the nation. A constitution created the consular magistracy.

"The senatus consultum of the 16th of Thermidor, year 10, named Bonaparte consul for life.

"The senatus consultum of the 28th of Floréal, year 12, conferred on Napoleon the imperial dignity, and made it hereditary in his family.

"These three solemn acts were laid for acceptance before the people, who sanctioned them by nearly four millions of votes.

"Accordingly, the Bourbons had ceased to reign in France for two and twenty years; they were forgotten there by their contemporaries; strangers to our laws, our institutions, our manners, our glory; and the present generation knew nothing of them.

"In 1814 France was invaded by the armies of the enemy, and the capital occupied. The foreigners created a pretended provisional government. They assembled a minority of the senators, and compelled them, in opposition to their delegated powers and to their will, to destroy the existing establishments, to overturn the imperial throne, and to recall the family of the Bourbons.

"The senate, which had been instituted solely to maintain the constitution of the empire, acknowledged itself, that it had no power to alter it. It decreed, that the scheme of a constitution, which it had prepared, should be submitted to the people for their acceptance, and that Louis Stanislas Xavier should be proclaimed King of the French, as soon as he had accepted the constitution, and sworn to observe it, and cause it to be observed.

"The abdication of the Emperor Napoleon was solely the result of the unfortunate situation, to which France and the Emperor had been reduced by the events of the war, by treason, and by the occupation of the capital. The only object of the abdication was, to avoid a civil war, and the shedding of French blood. Unsanctioned by the will of the people, this act could not annul the solemn contract, that was established between them and the Emperor. And if Napoleon possessed the power of abdicating the throne in his own person, he had none to sacrifice the rights of his son, appointed to reign after him.

"The Emperor, therefore, by re-ascending the throne, to which the people had elevated him, restored the people to their most sacred rights: he only called into execution the decrees of the Representative Assemblies, sanctioned by the nation: he returns to reign on the only legitimate principle, that France acknowledges and has acknowledged for five and twenty years, and to which all the authorities bound themselves by oaths, that they can be released from by the will of the people alone.

"The Emperor is called upon, to guaranty anew, by institutions, as he has engaged to do in his proclamations to the nation and the army, all the principles of liberty: personal freedom, and equality of rights; the freedom of the press, and abolition of the censorship; freedom of religious worship; the voting of laws and contributions by the representatives of the nation lawfully chosen; national property, from whatever source arising; the independence and stability of our tribunals; the responsibility of ministers, and of all the agents of authority.

"The more perfectly to sanction the rights and obligations of the people and the monarch, the national institutions should be revised in a grand assembly of the representatives already announced by the Emperor.

"Previous to the meeting of this grand representative assembly, the Emperor ought to exercise, and cause to be exercised, conformably to the existing laws and constitution, the authority they have delegated to him, which could not be taken from him, which he could not abdicate without the consent of the nation, and which the wishes and general interest of the French people render it his duty to resume."

The Emperor answered:

"Princes are the first citizens of the state: their authority is more or less extensive according to the interests of the nations they govern: the sovereignty itself is hereditary only because the interest of the people requires it. I know nothing of a legitimacy extraneous to these principles.

"I have renounced the idea of that grand empire, of which in the course of fifteen years I had merely laid the foundations: henceforward the happiness and consolidation of the French empire will be the object of all my thoughts."

The court of cassation expressed the same principles and the same sentiments as the council of state.

To this the Emperor answered:

"In the earliest ages of the French monarchy, rude tribes made themselves masters of Gaul. The sovereignty, of course, was not framed for the benefit of the Gauls, who were slaves, or destitute of political rights; but for the benefit of the conquering tribe. It can never have been said with truth, therefore, in any period of history, in any nation, even in the east, that the people exist for kings. Every where it has been established, that kings exist only for the people. A dynasty created under circumstances, that have created so many new interests, being itself interested in the maintenance of the rights and properties of all, can alone be natural and legitimate, and in possession of strength and confidence, the two leading characters in all government."

The court of accounts, and the imperial court, held the same language as the preceding authorities.

To these the Emperor answered:

"What particularly distinguishes the imperial throne is, that it has been raised by the nation, that it is consequently natural, and that it guaranties the interests of all. This is the true character of legitimacy. It is the interest of this throne, to consolidate all that at present exists, and all that has been done in France during the twenty-five years of revolution. It comprises all interests, and particularly that of the national glory, which is not the least among them.

"Whatever has returned with the foreign armies, whatever has been done without consulting the nation, is null. The courts of Grenoble and Lyons, and all the tribunals of the judicial order, which I met with while the success of events was yet uncertain, have shown me, that these principles are engraved on the heart of every Frenchman."

The reception of these public bodies being over, there was a grand audience in the apartments of the palace. The answers of the Emperor, repeated with embellishments, had produced the most profound sensation. The words national glory, liberty, country, so long unknown and proscribed within these walls, resounded on every side. When the emigrants re-appeared, and the most illustrious servants of the state were expelled, to make room for men, who had become strangers to our manners, our institutions, and our triumphs; you would have said, that France existed no longer, that it had passed under the dominion of foreigners. When Napoleon returned, our country appeared to have returned with him: he seemed to have brought it back from exile, and he might then exclaim with just pride: "I am the nation."

The example set by the magistrates of Paris soon found numerous imitators in the departments. The public functionaries, the judicial and administrative authorities, which but a few days before had offered up prayers to Heaven and to the King for the extermination of the Corsican, the tyrant, and the usurper, were eager to congratulate *the Emperor* on his miraculous return; and to confer on him the titles of hero, deliverer, and more especially of legitimate sovereign.

Napoleon's progress had been so rapid, that many addresses to the King did not reach Paris before the King was gone; and all these were delivered at the same time with the new addresses voted to his successor[83]! I remarked this to the Emperor; who answered me with a smile of pity: "See what men are!"

The favourites of Apollo did not fail to offer up their obsequious incense to the god of the day. We received from the Countess de G*** some very pretty verses in honour of the violet. Another woman, still more celebrated, the Baroness de S***, took occasion from some flattering words said for her to M. B. C., to write an epistle to the Emperor, which would make a curious figure at the head of her last work.

The most rigid writers and lecturers on the common law, who the evening before, with Cujas and Bartholi in their hands, had formally impleaded Napoleon, were eager to testify their admiration of him, and proclaim him the sovereign of sovereigns.

Thus Napoleon was more honoured and lauded than ever; and it must be confessed, that he conducted himself so as to deserve it: on one hand he caressed the nation, and on the other private interests, which it is much more difficult to conciliate than what is called the public interest.

The decrees of Lyons had sequestrated anew the estates restored to emigrants since 1814. Part of these had been sold by those who had recovered them; and it was necessary, to quiet the apprehensions of the purchasers. The Emperor declared irrevocable all the sales, that had been completed; and confirmed those, that had taken place subsequently to the decree, when it could be proved, that they were not collusive.

On the other hand, the emigrants, who had returned, had purchased property, the price of which might not have been entirely paid: and in order to do justice both to the emigrants and to the sellers, he ordered, that estates recently acquired should not be subject to sequestration, on condition of being re-sold within a certain period.

Another decree from Lyons had indiscriminately abolished all promotions in the legion of honour, and in the army, made since the royal restoration. He subjected to revision the nominations, that appeared to him the result of favour, intrigue, and venality; and confirmed all, that had been the reward of real and meritorious services. He would not even allow men's opinions, to constitute a line of demarcation and directed the minister, to pay regard to ancient services rendered by officers since incorporated in the King's household.

He confirmed also the decorations granted to the national guard; and distributed new ones among the brave pupils of the polytechnical school, whose noble conduct had so much excited the admiration of Paris, and of foreigners, at the time of the occurrences of 1814.

The daughters of the members of the legion of honour had claims to his remembrance, and his consolation, too sacred, not to participate in his favours. He went to visit them. His presence excited inexpressible enthusiasm among these young orphans: they threw themselves at his feet, embraced his knees, and watered them with their tears. He had taken a spoon, to taste their food: after he was gone, as every one wished to have it, they broke it to pieces, and shared it amongst them. Most of them had braided rings of hair, on which were traced patriotic devices, or the ingenious expression of their sentiments for Napoleon. The Emperor having condescended to accept some of these, and place them on his fingers, every one of the orphans was desirous of obtaining the same favour: they rushed on him, seized his hands, and in an instant covered them with these innocent pledges of love and gratitude. The Emperor, moved, enchanted, submitted with kind complaisance to the gentle fetters of these amiable infants. They ingeniously intreated him, not to give away the rings they had presented to him; and he promised to keep them, assuring them, that they would be as valuable in his eyes as the jewels of his crown.

The working class, who had surnamed Napoleon le grand entrepreneur[84], also received its share of the imperial favours. The works commenced in his reign, and buried in dust under that of the Bourbons, were resumed with activity. The capital became, as before, a vast workshop: and the Parisians, who had learned from strangers to perceive the beauty of their edifices, saw with a mingled sentiment of gratitude and pride, that new marvels were still more to embellish their majestic city.

In fine, all classes received testimonies of the solicitude and justice of Napoleon. Must it be said? his old companions in the island of Elba alone were forgotten

While Napoleon had no throne but his rock, they had shown themselves as disinterested as faithful: when he had recovered his crown, they flattered themselves, that they should be recompensed with generosity.

Some, whom honour alone had attached to Napoleon, enjoyed in prospect the praises, titles, ribands, that would be bestowed on them: others, inspired with less lofty sentiments, expected benefits more solid. The guard and its worthy chiefs were ambitious only of the favour of retaining the glorious title of grenadiers of the island of Elba. Vain illusions! the Emperor's thoughts, entirely absorbed by other cares, were no longer turned to those brave fellows, who had shared his exile and his misfortunes. The moment of forgetfulness, however, had not time to degenerate into ingratitude: it was repaired: promotions, endowments, indemnifications, were bestowed on them; and, if they did not feel themselves completely satisfied with the conduct of Napoleon, they had at least no reason to complain.

The Emperor would have wished from feeling, and perhaps too from ostentation, to have had it in his power, to acknowledge in a manner more worthy of himself their services and attachment: but he was deterred by the fear of being charged with imitating the Bourbons. and of preferring those Frenchmen, who had gone into exile with him, to those who had retained their fidelity in their mother country.

These scruples appear to me unfounded.

The emigrants had sullied their native land with blood, shed either by their own weapons, or in the civil wars they had fomented and cherished;

and the indignant nation had long combated them, and pursued them with its maledictions, as the enemies of its happiness and tranquillity.

The Frenchmen who returned from the island of Elba with Napoleon, on the contrary, had spilt their blood in the defence of their country. They were beloved, honoured, respected and the recompenses the Emperor might have bestowed upon them, instead of tending to alienate France, would have fulfilled her wishes. She would have enjoyed it with that feeling of pride and pleasure, which a mother experiences, when she hears the triumphs of her children proclaimed in the lists opened for youth, and sees their heads adorned with the rewards of their success.

Policy, no less than justice, required, that Napoleon should confer, even with prodigality, his favours and benefits on men, who had sacrificed themselves for him. In his situation it would have been better, to have been deemed prodigal than ungrateful: but fortune favoured him so highly, that he might be allowed, in some degree, to neglect the means of securing the feeble support of men.

The re-establishment of the imperial government, which appeared as if it would experience some obstacles, took place on all sides with a promptitude and facility truly extraordinary. Marshal Augereau, who had endeavoured in his proclamation of 1814 to disgrace the Emperor, was eager to make his public recantation in a fresh proclamation.

The Duke of Belluno, and Count Gouvion St. Cyr, after attempting in vain to curb their insurgent troops, were forced to shun their resentment by flight.

The troubles excited in La Vendée and Calvados by a few royal volunteers had been appeased, and the perturbators disarmed.

The military household of the King had submitted to their discharge, and readily surrendered their horses and arms.

In fine, the royal family had evacuated the imperial territory.

The Emperor thought proper, to acquaint his army in person with these happy results. "Thanks to the French people and you," said he, on reviewing the troops on the 27th of March, "the imperial throne is re-established. It is acknowledged throughout the empire, and not a single drop of blood has been spilt. The Count de Lille, the Count d'Artois, the Duke de Berri, the Duke of Orléans, have passed our northern frontier, and sought an asylum among foreigners. The tricoloured flag waves on the towers of Calais, Dunkirk, Lille, Valenciennes, Condé, &c. A few bands of Chouans had attempted to form themselves in Poitou and La Vendée: popular opinion, and the march of a few battalions, were sufficient to disperse them. The

Duke of Bourbon, who came to excite disturbances in the provinces, has embarked at Nantes.

"How senseless were they," continued the Emperor, "and how little did they know of the nation, who imagined, that the French would consent to receive a prince from those very hands, that had ravaged our territory, and, aided by treason, had for a moment obscured our laurels!"

The King, who at first took refuge at Lille, had in fact just retired to Ghent. His Majesty had given orders to his household and the princes, to join him in the former city, where it had been apparently his intention, to take up his residence, and convene the chambers. But marshal the Duke of Treviso, governor of that division, declared to him, that he would no longer answer for his troops, if the musketeers, the body guards, &c., entered the place; and advised him to repair to Dunkirk, which, from its geographical position, and the attachment of its inhabitants, afforded him an opportunity of awaiting the issue of events without danger. M. de Blacas and the emigrants with the King remonstrated with him strongly, that he would not be out of danger there; and that he could no longer be safe from the pursuit of Napoleon, except in a foreign country. The Duke of Treviso still insisted on the contrary: and the King, in spite of the alarm and entreaties of the Count de Blacas and the other courtiers, had resolved to follow the advice of the marshal, when some despatches from the Count d'Artois, received in the course of the night, determined him to pass the frontier.

The Emperor thought at first, that the design of Louis XVIII. was to return to England. He was glad of this: and it was not without extreme vexation, that he learned the intention of this Prince, to remain on the Belgic frontiers, observing the course of affairs. But if this resolution, to which perhaps the King was indebted for the recovery of his throne, was displeasing to Napoleon, it never inspired him with the criminal desire, as some wicked writers have pretended, of making any attempts against the lives or liberty of the Bourbons.

The orders given to General Excelmans merely were, to drive the King and the Princes out of France step by step. He was never commanded, "either to secure their persons, or to kill them in case of resistance."

The instructions given at the same time to Marshal Ney, sent on a mission to the frontiers of the North and East, directed him also in express words, "to cause the royal family to be respected, and facilitate its procuring the means of quitting France freely and quietly[85]."

It has been asserted, that the Duke of Bassano, who had the temporary charge of the port-folio of the home department, had sent orders to M. Siméon, then royal prefect at Lille, to arrest the King. The Duke of Bassano, indignant at such an odious charge, would not quit France, without having refuted it. He proposed, to summon M. Siméon to declare the truth; and his declaration would have been made public through the means of the newspapers and the press, if the police had not opposed it.

The King quitted Lille on the 23d of March. The Duke of Orléans, who had attended his Majesty, and whom the King on his departure had invested with the command of that place, did not quit it till twenty-four hours after; when he addressed the following letter to Marshal Mortier.

"I commit entirely to your hands, my dear Marshal, the command which I was so happy as to exercise with you in the department of the North. I am too good a Frenchman, to sacrifice the interests of France, because fresh misfortunes compel me to quit it. I go to bury myself in retirement and oblivion. The King being no longer in France, I cannot issue orders in his name: and nothing remains for me, but to absolve you from all obedience to the orders I have already transmitted to you; requesting you, to do whatever your own excellent judgment, and pure patriotism, shall suggest to you as most conducive to the interests of France, and most agreeable to the duties you have to fulfil."

The Emperor, after having read this letter, turned to the Duke of Bassano, and said: "See what the Duke of Orléans writes to Mortier; this letter does him honour. *His heart was always French.*"

I then informed him, that I had been assured, that the Duke of Orléans, when he parted from his officers, said to one of them, Colonel Athalin: "Go, sir, resume the national cockade: I take a pride in having worn it, and I wish I could wear it still." The Emperor appeared struck with these words, and made no reply. A few minutes after he asked me, if I had not a letter from Madame the Duchess of Orléans. I delivered it to him: he read it, and said: "Let his mother *be treated with the regard he merits.*" And he ordered, that the duchess, whose property had just been sequestrated, should receive annually from the public treasury three hundred thousand francs as an indemnification. At the same time another indemnification of a hundred and fifty thousand francs was granted to the Duchess of Bourbon.

The Duke of Bourbon, though the Emperor had announced his embarkation, did not sail however till several days afterward. His presence and his proclamation had produced a partial rising in the circle of Beaupréau; but convinced by his own eyes, and by the reports of his principal officers, that the great body of the Vendeans would not stir, he yielded to the wishes of Colonel Noirot, commandant of the gendarmerie, expressed in the following letter:

"Monseigneur,

"It will not be in vain, I am persuaded, that I make an appeal to your magnanimity. It is in your power, with a single word, to calm an effervescence, the first results of which may once more stain with blood the fields of the too unhappy Vendée: this word your Highness will pronounce, and every thing will be restored to order. You will be aware likewise, Monseigneur, that a longer stay in the circle of Beaupréau, while it endangers the internal security of the country, will also endanger the personal safety of your Highness.

"Deign then, I conjure you, Monseigneur, to yield to the wishes I entertain for your happiness, and for that of my country. For all the means of safety, which your Highness may desire, to repair to the place of destination you may choose, I will engage."

This letter, which I take a pleasure in quoting, to prove what was the language of the men of the 20th of March, was not without effect. The Duke of Bourbon directed his aide-de-camp to have an interview with Colonel Noirot and it was determined, that his Highness should quit la Vendée, and embark at Nantes for England.

For reasons with which I am unacquainted, the prince did not fulfil his engagements. In fact, he quitted Beaupréau, but still roamed about the coast some time with a fictitious passport, and under a borrowed name. General—[86] recognised him, but respected his disguise. The Emperor approved this deference, and gave orders, that he should merely be obliged to depart: the father of the Duke of Enghien was become sacred to him, and to France.

Of all the family of the Bourbons the Duke and Duchess of Angoulême alone persisted in struggling against their ill-fortune.

She was at Bordeaux at the time of the landing. The entrance of Napoleon into Paris, the flight of the King, and the general defection of the army, did not abate her courage. She made the national guard take up arms: she hastened to the barracks, to harangue the soldiers, and remind them of what they owed to their oaths and to their King. Numerous battalions of volunteers were instantly formed, and directed by her orders, to defend the avenues to the city, intercept all communication, and prevent popular commotions.

General Clausel, however, appointed by the Emperor head commandant of the 11th division, had advanced as far as St. André de Cubsac, six leagues from Bordeaux, at the head of about five and twenty gendarmes collected on the road, and of a hundred and fifty men from the garrison of Blayes, who, informed of his arrival by his emissaries, had come to meet him.

On his approach, a battalion of volunteers, posted at Cubsac with two pieces of cannon, retreated hastily to St. Vincent, and there joined some other volunteers, to defend with them the passage of the Dordogne.

The soldiers of General Clausel attempted to seize the flying bridge, and were saluted with several discharges of artillery and small arms, which they received without returning. Their chief, desirous of avoiding a civil war, requested, that some person might be sent, to hold a parley with him. The Bordelese having deputed their commandant, M. de Martignac, for this purpose, he charged this officer, to make known to them, that he had no design of making any attempts against their persons or property; and that he conjured them, in the name of their country, not to spill the blood of Frenchmen to no purpose.

Nevertheless some hostile appearances were continued on both sides; but the royal volunteers were alarmed at the sight of three boats, which they supposed to be filled with troops, and took flight.

General Clausel, thus become master of the Dordogne, was preparing to cross it, when M. de Martignac returned to inform him, that Madame the Duchess of Angoulême consented to retire, and that the city should be delivered up to him in twenty-four hours.

Madame, instead of fulfilling this double promise, allowed herself to yield to the desire and hope of prolonging the defence. She assembled the national guard, and made fresh attempts to bring over the troops of the garrison to the royal party.

General Clausel perceived her at a distance reviewing the national guards and volunteers: he ordered M. de Martignac to be called back, and complained of the promises made him not being fulfilled. He urged in excuse, that the national guard and the garrison were no longer disposed to surrender the city. The general, perceiving that the Bordelese flattered themselves with being seconded by the troops of the line, assured M. de Martignac, that, on the contrary, they only waited for a concerted signal, to declare themselves in favour of the imperial cause. M. de Martignac appearing to doubt this, the general ordered a flag to be waved in the air, and immediately the tricoloured standard was hoisted on Trompette castle[87].

The Bordelese, astonished and affrighted, requested a capitulation. General Clausel was eager to grant all their proposals, and the next day they opened the gates of the city to him.

The Emperor was well pleased with the happy issue of this affair. He gave orders, to publish the report of General Clausel immediately: but as this report was a mere military statement, he added to it himself the supplementary particulars below, which he directed to be inserted in the Moniteur under the head of Bordeaux.

"The firm and courageous conduct of General Clausel has prevented great evils: the passage of the Dordogne made a strong impression here. Before he reached la Bastide, the Duchess of Angoulême, feeling an alarm she was unable to conceal, sent him a promise, that she would quit Bordeaux in the morning of the 1st of April; which induced General Clausel, to halt at la Bastide, in front of Bordeaux, on the right bank of the Garonne, where he arrived on the 31st of March in the evening. The Duchess of Angoulême thought proper, to avail herself of this delay, and break her promise: she went to the barracks, caused the troops to be assembled, and endeavoured to persuade them, to oppose the entrance of General Clausel into Bordeaux. The officers of all ranks told her plainly, that they would pay her all the respect due to her unfortunate situation, and to her sex, but that, being Frenchmen themselves, no motive could induce them, to take up arms against Frenchmen. The Duchess shed abundance of tears: she requested, that the troops would at least remain neutral, if the national guards should be willing to fight for her. The officers answered, that they would not fire on the national guard; but they would not suffer the national guard, to fire on the troops of General Clausel: they would not allow a single drop of French blood to be spilt. The soldiers joined with one voice in the sentiments of their officers: the Duchess retired with alarm in her heart, and threats in her mouth: she was all trembling. When she reached the quay, where the national guard was under arms, she was received in profound silence. A murmur pervaded the ranks of "No fighting! no civil war!" The Duchess hastened to retire to the imperial palace, where she gave orders for her departure[88]. At eight o'clock she had quitted Bordeaux. The fire she had kindled was not extinguished in every bosom. The national guard, which had just conducted itself so prudently, had in company with it some unruly persons. These were the dregs of the people, forming the bulk of the companies of royal volunteers, who had been bribed to enlist, and reckoned upon plunder. Their hopes were already disappointed by the firmness of the national guard. A small number of the most outrageous fired on the company of M. Troplong, who was reputed to be of the soundest principles. The national guard returned the fire. The volunteers fled, but Captain Troplong had received a mortal wound. He has just been interred with military honours. More than ten thousand persons attended the funeral of this excellent citizen; the regret occasioned by his death suspended for a moment the gaiety of the people, happy in being at length freed from the evils, with which they were threatened."

The energy and intrepidity, which the granddaughter of Maria Theresa displayed on this occasion, excited the praise of the Emperor, and drew from him the well known phrase: "She is the only man in the family."

He no less admired the firm and respectful demeanour maintained by the regiments of the garrison, amid the provocations and reproaches of the Duchess. "Every thing that passed at Bordeaux," said he, "is truly extraordinary; and I know not which most demands our astonishment, the noble boldness of Madame d'Angoulême, or the magnanimous patience of my soldiers."

The effervescence of the Bordelese having subsided, Provence and Languedoc, where the Duke of Angoulême had excited and maintained the flames of insurrection, still remained to be pacified.

This prince, having heard at Toulouse, that the Emperor had landed in the gulf of Juan, repaired immediately to the principal towns in the South, and made the partisans of the Bourbons and of royalty take up arms.

Three thousand two hundred Marseillese, and three thousand five hundred volunteers from Nismes, Avignon, and Montpelier, ranged themselves under his standards.

The 10th, 53d, and 83d, regiments of the line, containing about nine hundred men each;

The depôts of the 9th and 87th of foot, about five hundred and fifty strong;

Two hundred and fifty chasseurs à cheval of the 14th regiment, a hundred and fifty artillerymen, and three hundred soldiers of the royal regiment of foreigners, were drawn from their respective garrisons; and formed, with the royal volunteers, an army of twelve thousand men; which must necessarily be increased by the levies daily made in the provinces, that continued subject to the royal government, and by the succours, which the Prince had hastened to demand from the King of Sardinia, and from Switzerland, and which he hoped to obtain from them.

The Duke of Angoulême divided his army into two corps.

The first, commanded by General Ernouf, under whose orders were Major-Generals Gardanne and Loverdo, proceeded through Sisteron for Grenoble.

The second, commanded by the Prince in person, and under his orders by Lieutenant-general Monnier, Baron Damas, and Viscount Descars, took the road of Valence.

These two corps, after having reduced the country to submission, and rallied the royalists, were to join at Grenoble, and march together to Lyons.

The advanced guard of the second corps, conducted by M. Descars, met no serious resistance, till it came to pass the Drôme.

General De Belle, at the head of a few hussars of the 4th, a battalion of the 39th, and about eight hundred national guards, had suffered himself to be driven from Loriol, and retired as well as he could behind the Drôme.

The volunteers of Vaucluse, covered by the royal artillery, forded the river, and came and took post on the left flank of the national guards. At the same moment the Prince directed the 10th of the line, to attack the bridge. This manœuvre did not intimidate the national guards; they stood firm; and the 10th, notwithstanding the ardour, with which it was inspired by the example of the Duke of Angoulême, was on the point of giving way; when several of the light infantry, who were at their head, discovered among their antagonists some of their ancient comrades. They began with a mutual cessation of firing, and finished with embracing amid shouts of Long live the Emperor.

During this conversation and embracing, the rest of the 10th regiment recovered ground. The imperials, supposing they were coming to join them, advanced without distrust: a volley undeceived them: the troops of General De Belle were thrown into disorder, he made no attempt to rally them, and the rout became complete. Part of the imperials were made prisoners by the royalists; others took refuge in the mountains, or went to carry the news of their defeat to Grenoble or Valence.

The next day, the 3d of April, the Duke of Angoulême and his victorious army entered Valence, and proceeded without loss of time to Romans on the Isère.

The first corps, after having occupied Sisteron, separated into two columns: one, with General Loverdo at its head, proceeded to Lamure; the other, commanded by General Gardanne, having taken Gap in its way, advanced as far as Travers; where the garrison of Grenoble, and the national guards of Vizille, Lamure, and the surrounding communes, had just taken up a position.

Hitherto every thing had proved favourable to the wishes of the royal army: it marched from one success to another; and the noise of its victories, swelled by fear and rumour, had spread consternation and dismay as far as Grenoble and Lyons.

The Emperor himself was uneasy. On leaving Lyons he had foreseen the possibility of a partial rising in the south; and, relying on the energy and patriotism of the Dauphinese, he had entrusted to them the care of defending their territory and their capital. But, if they were strong enough to repel the aggressions of the royalists, they were not in a condition to resist four thousand soldiers, who had embraced their cause, and fought in their ranks.

General Grouchy had orders, to hasten to Lyons, and raise in mass the national guards of Dauphiny, the Lyonnais, and Burgundy.

At the name of the Emperor and of their country all were in motion: the patriots of la Drôme and the Isère descended from their mountains; the Lyonese quitted their workshops; the Burgundians spontaneously began their march with half-pay officers at their head.

This patriotic burst was so unanimous, that the roads were instantly covered with national guards; and General Corbineau, whom the Emperor had despatched to accelerate their march, was obliged, on the contrary, to retard it. But all these arrangements, sad presages of a civil war, were happily unnecessary.

The troops of General Gardanne, during their stay at Gap, became acquainted with the Emperor's proclamations. These had awakened their remembrances, electrified their minds, and the 58th mounted the tricoloured cockade.

The defection of this regiment was soon known to the division of General Loverdo; and, in spite of this general's efforts, a part of the 14th chasseurs, and the whole of the 83d, equally embraced the imperial cause. On the other soldiers, though faithful in appearance, the generals could no longer confide: "they could not speak to a single inhabitant of the country, without receiving impressions absolutely inimical to the party of the King[89]," and they expected every moment, to see them go over to the enemy.

General Loverdo, impatient to give battle, and imagining, that he could dispense with their assistance, attempted to force the defile of Saulces, in advance of Gap, supported only by his royal volunteers: but this attack, as rash as it was useless, did not succeed, and he was forced to fall back to Sisteron.

The second corps, restrained by the presence of the Duke of Angoulême, had lost but a small number of soldiers. The order to advance had just been given, when the Prince received the most disheartening news from all parts at once.

On one hand he was informed of the defection of the regular troops under General Ernouf, and his forced retreat to Sisteron.

On another he heard, that General Grouchy was advancing to meet him with a formidable force.

From a third source of intelligence he learned, that the royal party at Nismes, and at Toulouse, had dispersed without resistance: that M. Vitrolles, the head of the committee of insurrection, had been arrested; and that the patriots, and the troops of the 9th division, united under the orders of General Gilly, having marched to take him in the rear, had retaken the bridge of St. Esprit by assault, and passed the Rhone.

In fine, despatches from Turin announced to him, that he must no longer reckon upon any assistance from the Swiss, or upon the promises of the King of Sardinia.

The Prince in consequence ordered a retreat to be sounded, and retired to Valence.

The Emperor, who, according to custom, took the trouble to compose himself the articles in the Moniteur relative to this little war, gave the following account of the evacuation of Valence.

"*Valence, the 7th of April.* The Duke of Angoulême has made a sad figure here. The alarm bell sounded throughout Dauphiny, and numerous battalions of the national guards departed for Lyons. The Duke of Angoulême, informed of their arrival, set off helter skelter with the four thousand insurgents, who are under his orders. The troops of the line, informed by our citizens, that we were engaged in the cause of the nation against a few privileged families, of the people against the nobility, and in short of the revolution against the counter-revolution, suddenly changed sides. The army however reckons three traitors, who appear to have taken the part of the enemies of their country: they are Generals Ernouf, Monnier, and D'Aultannie." He forgot General Loverdo.

The Emperor was equally careful, to make public the correspondence, that was intercepted: and as some announced *the intention of separating the chaff from the wheat, and throwing it into the fire;* others, *of hanging all the rebels, without exception, and without mercy;* and, in fine, others, *invited Spain, Switzerland, and the King of Piedmont, to come and reduce France to reason;* they contributed not less powerfully than the success of the imperial army, to detach from the cause of the Bourbons every Frenchman, who was an enemy to treachery, hanging, and foreigners.

General Grouchy, informed of the retreat of the Duke of Angoulême, sent some light troops in pursuit of him. Most of the chasseurs of the 14th, and of the artillerymen, joined the imperialists. The volunteers of the south, who had hitherto set no bounds to their presumptuous hopes, now found none to their fears. As cowardly in adversity, as they were arrogant in prosperity, they abandoned their general at the approach of danger; and all, with the exception of a few hundreds of brave fellows, sought safety in flight.

The Duke of Angoulême, surrounded by the feeble remnants of their battalions, and by the 10th of the line, which still remained faithful, continued his retrograde march night and day; and traversed in silence the places, which his army had made ring with the shouts of victory but a few days before. The mountaineers, who had suffered so much from the exactions and ill treatment of the royal volunteers, now repeated in their turn "Wo to the vanquished!" and did not allow a moment's rest to the Duke of Angoulême and his followers. Pressed on one side by the columns of Grouchy, on the other by the troops of General Gilly; shut in, without hope of succour, between the Drôme, the Rhone, the Durance, and the mountains, the Duke of Angoulême had only two resources: one was, to abandon his army, and get over the mountains to Marseilles or Piedmont; the other, to submit, with his companions in misfortune, to the law of the conqueror.

The Prince would not separate his fate from that of his army. He consented to surrender. Baron de Damas and General Gilly regulated the conditions of the capitulation. It was agreed, that the Prince should disband his army, and have liberty to embark at Cette. As soon as this intelligence was announced by a telegraphic despatch, it was immediately made known to the Emperor by the Duke of Bassano, who prevailed on him, though opposed by several distinguished persons, to return an answer, by the same mode of conveyance, approving of the capitulation. At the same instant a second despatch announced, that General Grouchy refused to sign the treaty, unless he had the consent of the Emperor, and the Duke of Angoulême was deemed a prisoner. Upon this the Duke of Bassano hastened to transmit the first orders of Napoleon, and delayed informing him of the impediment to the ratification, till night rendered any new orders by telegraph impracticable. Being made acquainted with this noble daring of his minister, instead of reprimanding him, the Emperor dictated to him the following letter:

"M. le Count Grouchy, the ordinance of the king, dated on the 6th of March, and the declaration signed at Vienne on the 13th by his ministers, would authorize me to treat the Duke of Angoulême, as that ordinance, and that declaration, would have had me and my family treated: but, persevering in that disposition, which induced me to ordain, that the members of the Bourbon family might have free egress from France, my intention is, that you give orders for the Duke of Angoulême to be conducted to Cette, where he shall be embarked, and that you watch over his safety, and prevent him from receiving any ill treatment. You will only take care to recover the money that has been taken from the public offices, and to require the Duke of Angoulême to engage to restore the diamonds of the crown, which are the property of the nation[90]. You will at the same time make known to him the provisions of the laws of the national assemblies, which have been renewed, and which apply to those members of the Bourbon family, who shall re-enter the French territories," &c.

While awaiting the decision of Napoleon, the Duke of Angoulême was strictly watched. He supported this fresh disgrace with firmness and tranquillity. The Marquis de Rivière, informed of his detention, threatened Count Grouchy, if he did not restore him to liberty, to surrender Marseilles to the English, and raise up all Provence. These empty threats had no effect. The fate of the duke did not depend on Count de Grouchy: it was in opposition to his own feelings, that he had ventured to lay a sacrilegious hand on this prince; and he prayed sincerely, that the decision of the Emperor would allow him to break his chains.

As soon as the decision reached him, the general hastened to insure the Duke of Angoulême the means of embarking speedily; and with religious zeal took the necessary measures, for his being treated on the passage with due respect.

The prince, on his arrival at Cette, embarked immediately, and sailed for Cadiz.

His capitulation and departure soon led to the submission of Marseilles: and, thanks to the prudence and firmness of the Prince of Essling, governor of that division, the royal standard was hauled down, and the tricoloured flag hoisted in its stead, without any disturbance or effusion of blood.

The Emperor named General Grouchy marshal of the empire; not because he entertained any great admiration of his conduct, for he was aware, that he had but faintly pressed the Duke of Angoulême; but in order to give some splendor to the disgrace of the prince, and discourage the royalists in other parts of France. Resolving at the same time to punish the treason committed by the 10th at the passage of the Drôme, he decreed, that this regiment should wear a piece of crape on its colours, till it had washed in the blood of the enemy those arms, which it had stained with the blood of Frenchmen[91].

By the telegraph the Emperor was informed of the submission of Marseilles, and the entire pacification of the south, just as he was going to review the national guard of Paris. It was always in similar circumstances, that great news reached the Emperor: it seemed as if fortune, attentive to please him, sought to enhance her gifts by bestowing them *apropos*.

Ever since his arrival he had been intending to have this review, but the successive inspections of the troops of the line had prevented him. Some persons did not fail to ascribe this delay, so easily to be accounted for, to his fear of the sentiments and bayonets of the legions of Paris. Meantime some grenadiers of the royal ex-volunteers indulged in threats and imprecations against him. This was enough to terrify some of the alarmists of the court; and they requested Napoleon to mix a few battalions of his guards in the review, by way of precaution. The Emperor rejected their entreaties, and was angry at their fears: nevertheless, they caused him to be attended, without his knowledge, by ten or a dozen grenadiers, who were directed not to lose sight of him for a moment.

While the Emperor was walking his horse along the ranks, his escort had followed him without his paying any attention to it: but when he set off at a gallop, he perceived, that his grenadiers were galloping after him, and stopped. "What do you do there?" said he to one of them: "Go about your business!" The old grumbler[92], who knew that apprehensions were entertained for the life of his general, appeared disposed not to obey. The Emperor then took hold of him by his hairy cap, and, giving it a hearty shake, repeated with a smile his order to him to retire: "Go all of you away: I am surrounded by none but good Frenchmen; I am as safe with them as with you." The national guards, who heard these words, cried out spontaneously, "Yes, yes, Sire, you are right; we would all defend your life at the expense of our own." Encouraged by the familiarity which the Emperor displayed towards them, they quitted their ranks, and crowded round him: some pressed his hands, others kissed theirs to him; all expressed their satisfaction and attachment by continued shouts of "Long live the nation! Long live the Emperor!"

After this unexpected scene, the Emperor proceeded with his review: he then caused a circle of officers to be formed, alighted, and addressed them nearly in the following terms:

"Soldiers of the national guard of Paris, I am well pleased to see you. Fifteen months ago I formed you for the preservation of tranquillity in the capital, and for its security. You have fulfilled my expectations. You have shed your blood in defence of Paris; and if hostile troops entered your walls, the blame falls not on you, but on treason, and above all on that fatality, which attaches itself to our affairs under adverse circumstances.

"The royal throne was not adapted to France: it gave the people no security for its most valuable interests; it was imposed upon us by foreigners. I am arrived, equipped with all the strength of the people and of the army, to obliterate this stain, and restore the honour and glory of France to all their lustre.

"Soldiers of the national guard, this very morning the telegraph of Lyons has informed me, that the tricoloured flag is waving at Antibes and at Marseilles. The discharge of a hundred cannon on our frontiers will proclaim to foreign nations, that our civil discords are at an end: *I say foreign nations, because we yet know of none that are enemies.* If they assemble their troops, we will assemble ours. All our armies are composed of brave men, who have distinguished themselves in various battles, and who will display to foreigners a barrier of iron; while numerous battalions of grenadiers and chasseurs of the national guards will secure our frontiers. I shall not interfere with the affairs of foreign nations: wo to those governments, that shall interfere with ours! Misfortunes have tempered anew the character of the French people: it has resumed that youth, that vigour, which astonished Europe twenty years ago.

"Soldiers, you have been obliged to wear colours proscribed by the nation. But the national colours remained in your hearts: you now swear, to take them always for your rallying signal, and to defend the imperial throne, the only and natural guarantie of our rights; you swear never to suffer foreigners, in whose country we have appeared repeatedly as masters, to interfere with our constitution or government. In fine, you swear, to sacrifice every thing to the honour and independence of France."

This oath was pronounced with enthusiasm. The national guard showed, that it was not afraid of being taken at its word.

Apprehensions had been entertained, that the guards, who had long borne the Parisians a grudge for having surrendered so promptly in 1814, would indulge in some offensive reproaches: but Napoleon had enjoined his grenadiers to maintain silence; and, in order to complete the reconciliation, he caused it to be cemented by a dinner, to which the imperial guards invited the national guard and the garrison of Paris.

Fifteen thousand soldiers of every description assembled at the *Champ de Mars* under the eyes of the people of Paris: the joyous songs of the soldiers and citizens answered each other by turns, and gave a truly national character to this festival.

When the repast was over, a numerous crowd of soldiers, officers, and national guards, set off for the Tuileries, carrying the bust of Napoleon crowned with laurels. When they arrived before his Majesty's windows, they saluted him with thousands and thousands of acclamations; and then they repaired to la Place Vendôme, where they devoutly deposited at the foot of the monument raised to the glory of our armies the image of the hero, who had led them to victory. The Emperor, as soon as he was informed of it, ordered me to write to the minister of the police, to have the bust removed in the night. "It is not after bacchanalian orgies," said he, proudly, "that my image should be placed on the column."

Every body, in fact, knows, that the statue of Napoleon, by which this monument was formerly surmounted, had been pulled down in the early days of the restoration; and it was not for individual and unauthorized citizens to repair this affront.

A few royalists, at the head of whom figured M. de Maubreuil and M. Sostène de la Rochefoucault, were guilty of this profanation. M. de Rochefoucault, whose family had shared so largely in the gifts and favours of Napoleon, himself put a rope about the neck of his benefactor, with intention to have it dragged through the mud by some vagabonds, whom he had hired: but the statue mocked his endeavours; and the only fruit he reaped from them was the reprobation of honest men, and the contempt of foreigners[93].

The column itself was long offensive to the jealous eyes of the enemies of our glory. They conspired its destruction; and would have accomplished it, had they dared. History, which leaves nothing unpunished, will brand, I trust, these unworthy Frenchmen, these new Vandals, with eternal disgrace. It will inscribe their names, and their sacrilegious wishes, on the foot of the immortal column, which they wanted to overturn. No doubt it will also tell, that the federates, the half-pay officers, and all the partisans of Napoleon, whom some have been pleased to represent as madmen, as robbers, respected during the hundred days the statue of Henry IV.; though this statue, placed within reach of their blows, and constructed of frail materials, would have fallen with the slightest shock.

Napoleon had said to the national guard of Paris, "We yet know of none that are enemies:" and these words were true. It had been remarked, that the foreign troops concentrated themselves on our frontiers, but none of their dispositions appeared hostile, and Napoleon might still reasonably hope, that his care to maintain peace would not be fruitless.

On the very day of his entry into Lyons, he had hastened to commission Prince Joseph, to declare to the Austrian and Russian ministers at the Helvetic diet, that he was ready to ratify the treaty of Paris.

When he arrived in the capital, he found that the foreign ministers, particularly Baron de Vincent, the Austrian minister, and M. Boudiakeen, Russian chargé d'affaire, had not yet quitted it, for want of passports.

He caused the departure of M. de Vincent and M. de Boudiakeen to be delayed; and directed the Duke of Vicenza to see them, and assure them anew of his pacific disposition.

Baron de Vincent at first refused all kind of communication or conferences; but at length he consented to meet M. de Vicenza at the house of a third person. They had a conference together at Madame de Souza's. M. de Vincent did not conceal the resolution of the allies, to oppose Napoleon's retaining the throne: but he hinted, that in his opinion there might not be the same repugnance to his son. He engaged, however, to make known the sentiments of Napoleon to the Emperor of Austria; and consented to take charge of a letter for the Empress Marie Louise[94].

M. de Boudiakeen, after having equally refused the conference proposed by the Duke of Vicenza, finished also with accepting it. It was agreed, that they should meet at the house of Mademoiselle Cauchelet, lady of the bedchamber to the Princess Hortense.

M. de Jaucourt had forgotten to take out of the port-folio of foreign affairs a secret treaty, by which England, Austria, and France, had mutually engaged to oppose, peaceably or by force, the dismemberment of Saxony, which Russia and Prussia openly conspired.

The Emperor thought, that this treaty might perhaps alienate these two powers from the Bourbon interest, and generate distrust and discord between the allies. He directed the Duke of Vicenza, to show it to the Russian minister; and represent it to him as a fresh proof of the ingratitude, with which the court of the Tuileries repaid the numerous benefits of Alexander. The existence of this triple alliance was wholly unknown to M. de Boudiakeen, and appeared to cause him as much surprise as dissatisfaction. But he declared, that he was too well acquainted with the principles of his sovereign, to venture to flatter himself, that the circumstance of this treaty, or any other, could produce a favourable change in his disposition. He promised, however, to make a faithful report to him of the conference he had had with M. de Vicenza; and to express to him the desire, manifested by the Emperor Napoleon, of becoming again the ally and friend of Russia.

The Emperor, in order to give more efficacy to his proposals, directed the Princess Hortense, to confirm them in person to the Emperor Alexander. He also caused letters to be written to Prince Eugene, and to the Grand Duchess Stéphanie of Baden, to request them, to renew the same assurances to that sovereign, and to neglect no means of detaching him from the coalition.

In fine, the Emperor directed overtures to be made to the cabinet of London, by means of a person pointed out by the Duke of Otranto; and in order to gain the suffrage of the parliament, and give the English ministry a pledge of his good intentions beforehand, he abolished the slave trade by a spontaneous decree.

After having taken these indirect steps, Napoleon thought his duty as well as his dignity required him, to give a solemn and authentic character to the manifestation of his pacific intentions.

Accordingly he wrote to the foreign sovereigns a letter couched in the following terms:

"Sire, my brother,

"You will have heard in the course of last month of my return to the French coast, my entering Paris, and the departure of the Bourbon family. The true nature of these events must now be known to your Majesty: they are the work of an irresistible power, the work and the unanimous will of a great nation, who knows its duties and its rights. The dynasty, which force had bestowed on the French people, was not formed for them: the Bourbons would not accommodate themselves either to their sentiments, or to their manners. France could not but separate itself from them. Her voice called for a deliverer: the expectations, that had induced me, to make the greatest of all sacrifices, had been frustrated. I came, and from the spot where I touched the shore I was conducted by the love of my people to the bosom of my capital. The first wish of my heart is, to repay such great affection by the maintenance of an honourable tranquillity. The re-establishment of the imperial throne being necessary to the happiness of the French, nothing can be more pleasing to my thoughts, than to render it at the same time advantageous to the consolidation of the tranquillity of Europe. Sufficient glory had crowned the standards of the different nations by turns; the vicissitudes of fate have occasioned a sufficient succession of great successes and great defeats: a nobler career now opens itself to sovereigns, and I am the first to enter it. After having exhibited to the world the spectacle of great battles, it will be more pleasing, henceforth to know no rivalry but that of the advantages of peace, no strife but the sacred striving after the happiness of nations. France takes a pleasure in frankly proclaiming this noble end of all her wishes. Jealous of her own independence, the invariable principle of her politics will be the most absolute respect for the independence of other nations. If such be the personal sentiments of your Majesty, as I am happy to persuade myself, the general tranquillity is ensured for a long time to come; and justice, sitting on the confines of states, will be sufficient alone to guard their frontiers.

"Paris, the 4th of April."

The Duke of Vicenza received orders, personally to express to the foreign ministers the sentiments, with which the Emperor was animated: but the couriers, who carried his despatches, could not reach the places of their destination; one was arrested at Kehl, another at Mayence; a third, sent off for Italy, could not get beyond Turin; the communications were interrupted. The arrangements of the declaration of the congress of Vienna of the 13th of March were acted upon already.

This declaration, transmitted directly by the emissaries of the King to the prefects of the frontier cities, and distributed by the royalists, was in circulation at Paris. The inferior papers had announced its appearance, and united in asserting, that such an act was unworthy of the allied sovereigns, and could only be the work of calumny and malevolence.

However, when it became impossible to question its legitimacy, it was necessary to come to the resolution of no longer making a mystery of it to the French people; and accordingly the following account was given of it in the Moniteur on the 13th of April.

"Council of Ministers.

"*Sitting of the 29th of March.*

"The Duke of Otranto, minister of the general police, states, that he is about to read to the council a declaration, dated Vienna the 13th, which is supposed to have been issued by the congress:

"That this declaration, as it contains an incentive to the assassination of the Emperor, appears to him apocryphal: that, if it should prove genuine, it would be unexampled in the history of the world: that the libellous style, in which it is written, gives room to suppose, it ought to be classed among the papers fabricated by party-spirit, and by those pamphleteers, who of late years have foisted themselves uncommissioned into all state affairs: that it pretends to be signed by the English ministers; but it is impossible to suppose, that the ministers of a free nation, and particularly Lord Wellington, could have taken a step inconsistent with the legislation of their country, and with their own characters: that it pretends to be signed by the ministers of Austria; but it is impossible to conceive, whatever political dissensions may subsist between them, that a father could call for the assassination of his son: that, contrary to every principle of religion and morality, it is derogatory to the honourable character of the sovereigns, whose mandates are thus compromised by the libellists: that this declaration has been known several days, but, from the considerations abovementioned, it could not be considered otherwise than as deserving the profoundest contempt: that it was not deemed fit to engage the attention of the ministry, till official reports from Metz and Strasburg made known, that it had been brought into France by couriers from the Prince of Benevento; a fact confirmed by the result of the investigation that took place, and the interrogatories put: in fine, that it is proved, that this paper, which could not have been signed by the ministers of Austria, Russia, and England, was issued by the legation of the Count of Lille at Vienna; which legation had added to the crime of provoking assassination that of falsifying the signature of the members of the congress.

"The pretended declaration of the congress, the reports from Metz and Strasburg, as well as the investigation and interrogatories conducted by order of the minister of the general police, which ascertain, that the said declaration proceeded from the plenipotentiaries of the Count of Lille at Vienna, will be sent to the presidents of the sections of the council.

"Declaration.

"The powers, who signed the treaty of Paris, assembled in Congress at Vienna, being informed of the escape of Napoleon Bonaparte, and of his entering France by force of arms, owe to their own dignity, and to the interests of society, a solemn declaration of the sentiments, with which this event has inspired them.

"By thus infringing the convention, which settled him in the island of Elba, Bonaparte has destroyed the only legal title he had to his situation in life (*auquel son existence se trouvait attachée.*) By re-appearing in France, with the design of disturbing and subverting it, he has deprived himself of the protection of the laws, and has made manifest to the universe, that there can be neither peace nor truce with him.

"The powers declare in consequence, that Napoleon Bonaparte has thrown himself out of all the relations of civilized society; and that, as an enemy and disturber of the world, he has rendered himself obnoxious to public vengeance.

"At the same time they declare, that, firmly resolved to maintain unbroken the treaty of Paris of the 30th of March, 1814, and the arrangements sanctioned by that treaty, as well as those they have decreed, or may yet decree, for completing and consolidating it; they will employ all their means, and unite all their efforts, to prevent the general peace, the object of the wishes of all Europe, the constant aim of their labours, from being disturbed anew; and to guard it from every attempt, that would threaten to replunge nations into the disorders and calamities of revolutions.

"And though intimately persuaded, that all France, rallying round its legitimate sovereign, will annihilate without delay this last attempt of a criminal and impotent delirium, all the sovereigns of Europe, animated with the same sentiments, and guided by the same principles, declare, that if, contrary to all calculation, any real danger whatever should arise from this event, they will be ready to furnish the King of France and the French nation, or any other government that may be attacked, with the succours necessary to restore the public tranquillity, as soon as they shall be demanded, and to make common cause against all, who may attempt to disturb it.

"The present declaration, inserted in the register of the congress assembled at Vienna, in the sitting of the 13th of March, 1815, shall be made public.

"Done and certified as true by the plenipotentiaries of the eight powers, who signed the Treaty of Paris, at Vienna, the 13th of March, 1815.

Here follow the signatures in the alphabetical order of the courts.

"Austria	The Prince de Metternich, The Baron de Wessemberg.
"Spain *(Espagne)*	P. Gomez Labrador.
France	The Prince de Talleyrand, The Duke D'Alberg, Latour Dupin, The Count Alexis de Noailles.
Great Britain	Wellington, Clancarty, Cathcart, Stewart.
Portugal	The Count Palmela, Saldanha, Lobo.
Prussia	The Prince de Hardenberg, The Baron de Humboldt.

Russia	The Count de Rasoumowski,
	The Count de Stakelberg,
	The Count de Nesselrode.

Sweden   Lowenhielm."

This declaration, which no doubt will hereafter excite the astonishment of posterity, was commented upon and victoriously refuted by the Emperor himself. Count Boulay, to whom the following report is ascribed, had no farther share in it, than condensing it a little, and softening some of its expressions.

Report of the committee of presidents of the council of state.

"In consequence of the reference made to it, the committee, composed of the presidents of the sections of the council of state, has examined the declaration of the 13th of March, the report of the minister of the general police, and the papers added to them.

"The declaration is in an unusual form, composed in such strange terms, and expresses such anti-social ideas, that the committee was led to consider it as one of those supposititious productions, by means of which despicable men endeavour to impose upon people's minds, and mislead the public opinion.

"But the verification of the examinations taken at Metz, and of the interrogatories of the couriers, admit no doubt, that the declaration was sent by members of the French legation at Vienna; and consequently it must be considered as adopted and signed by them.

"It is under this last point of view, that the committee imagines it ought first to examine this production, which has no precedent in the annals of diplomacy, and in which Frenchmen, men invested with the most respectable of public characters, begin with a sort of outlawry, with a provocation to assassinate the Emperor Napoleon.

"We say with the minister of the police, that this declaration is the work of the French plenipotentiaries: because those of Austria, Prussia, Russia, and England, could not have been capable of signing a paper, which the sovereigns and people, to whom they belong, will be eager to disavow.

"And in the first place these plenipotentiaries, most of them coadjutors in the treaty of Paris, know, that Napoleon was there acknowledged as retaining the title of Emperor, and as sovereign of the island of Elba: they would have mentioned him by these titles, and would not have deviated, either in matter or in manner, from the respect they impose.

"They would have felt, that, agreeably to the laws of nations, a prince, however trifling the extent or population of his state, enjoys, as far as regards his political and civil character, the rights belonging to every sovereign prince in respect to the most powerful monarch; and Napoleon, acknowledged under the title of Emperor, and in quality of a sovereign prince, by all the powers, was no more amenable to the congress of Vienna than any of them.

"The forgetfulness of these principles, impossible to be supposed in plenipotentiaries, who weigh the rights of nations maturely with wisdom and consideration, has nothing astonishing in it when manifested by French ministers, whose conscience reproaches them with more than one act of treason, in whom fear has engendered rage, and whose remorse leads their reason astray.

"Such men as these may have risked the fabrication and the publication of a piece like the pretended declaration of the 13th of March, in the hope of stopping the progress of Napoleon, and misleading the French people with regard to the real sentiments of foreign powers.

"But they cannot judge like these powers of the merits of a nation, which they have misunderstood, betrayed, and delivered up to the arms of foreigners.

"This nation, brave and generous, revolts against every thing that bears the marks of cowardice and oppression: its affections are heightened, when the object of them is threatened or affected by a great injustice; and assassination, which the commencement of the declaration of the 13th of March is intended to excite, will find not a single hand to execute it, either among the twenty-five millions of Frenchmen, the majority of whom attended, guarded, and protected Napoleon from the Mediterranean to the capital; nor among the eighteen millions of Italians, the six millions of Belgians or inhabitants of the banks of the Rhine, and the numerous nations of Germany, who, on this solemn occasion, have not pronounced his name without respectful remembrance; nor a single individual of the indignant English nation, whose honourable sentiments disavow the language, that those men have dared to attribute to the sovereigns

"The people of Europe are enlightened; they judge the rights of Napoleon, the rights of the allied princes, and those of the Bourbons.

"They know, that the convention of Fontainbleau was a treaty between sovereigns. Its violation, the entrance of Napoleon into the French territory, like any other infraction of a diplomatic act, like any hostile invasion, could only bring on an ordinary war; the result of which can only be, to the person, that of being conqueror or conquered, free or a prisoner of war; to possessions, that of being lost or preserved, diminished or increased; and that every thought, every threat, every attempt, against the life of a prince at war with another, is a thing unheard of in the history of nations, and of the cabinets of Europe.

"In the violence, the rage, the forgetfulness of principle, that characterize the declaration of the 13th of March, we recognize the envoys of the same prince, the organs of the same councils, who, by the ordinance of the 6th of March, also put Napoleon out of the pale of the law, also invoked for him the daggers of assassins, and also promised a reward to whoever would bring his head.

"Yet what has Napoleon done? By his confidence he has honoured the men of all nations, who were insulted by the infamous office to which they were invited: he has shown himself temperate, generous, a protector, even toward those who had devoted his head to destruction.

"When he spoke to General Excelmans, marching toward the column that closely pressed Louis Stanislas Xavier; to General Count Erlon, who was to receive him at Lille; to General Clausel, who was going to Bourdeaux, where the Duchess of Angoulême was; to General Grouchy, who marched to put a stop to the civil disturbances excited by the Duke of Angoulême; every where, in short, orders were given by the Emperor, that their persons should be respected, and sheltered from all attack, from all danger, from all violence, during their progress on the French territories, and to the moment of their quitting them.

"Contemporary nations and posterity will judge, on which side respect has been paid in this grand conjuncture to the rights of nations and of sovereigns, to the laws of war, the principles of civilization, and the maxims of law civil and religious: they will pronounce between Napoleon and the house of Bourbon.

"If, after having examined the pretended declaration of the congress in this first point of view, we discuss it in its relations to diplomatic conventions, to the treaty of Fontainbleau of the 11th of April, ratified by the French government, we shall find, that their violation is imputable only to those very persons who charge it on Napoleon.

"The treaty of Fontainbleau has been violated by the allied powers, and by the house of Bourbon, in what regards the Emperor Napoleon and his family, in what affects the rights and interests of the French nation:

"1st. The Empress Marie Louise and her son were to obtain passports and an escort, to enable them to repair to the Emperor: but, far from performing this promise, the wife was separated by force from her husband, the son from his father, and this under painful circumstances, when the strongest mind finds it necessary to seek consolation and support in the bosom of its family and domestic affections.

"2d. The safety of Napoleon, of the imperial family, and of their suite, was guarantied (Art. 14 of the treaty) by all the powers: yet bands of assassins were organized in France under the eyes of the French government, and even by its orders, as the solemn proceedings against the Sieur de Maubreuil will shortly prove, to attack both the Emperor, his brothers, and their wives: this first branch of the plot failing of the expected success, a tumult was planned at Orgon, on the road taken by the Emperor, in order to make an attempt against his life by the hands of some brigands: one of the cut-throats of Georges, the Sieur Brulart, raised for the purpose to the rank of major-general, known in Brittany, in Anjou, in Normandy, in la Vendée, throughout all England, by the blood he has shed, was sent to Corsica as governor, in order to prepare and insure the crime; and, in fact, several solitary assassins attempted, in the island of Elba, to gain, by the murder of Napoleon, the culpable and disgraceful salary which was promised them.

"3d. The duchies of Parma and Placentia were given in full propriety to Marie Louise, for herself, her son, and his descendants: yet, after long refusal to put them into possession, the injustice was consummated by an absolute spoliation, under the illusory pretext of an exchange without valuation, without proportion, without sovereignty, without consent; and the documents existing in the office of foreign affairs, of which we have had an account presented to us, prove, that it was at the instance and through the intrigues of the Prince of Benevento, that Marie Louise and her son were despoiled.

"4th. A suitable establishment, out of France, had been given to Prince Eugene, the adopted son of Napoleon, who has done honour to France, where he was born, and gained the affection of Italy, where he was naturalized; yet he has obtained nothing.

"5th. The Emperor had stipulated (Art. 3 of the treaty) in favour of his brave soldiers the preservation of their salaries from the Napoleon fund (*sur le mont Napoléon*); he had reserved out of the extraordinary domain, and the funds remaining of the civil list, the means of recompensing his servants, and of paying the soldiers, that attached themselves to his fate. The whole was taken away and kept back by the ministers of the Bourbons. An agent of the French soldiers went in vain to Vienna, to claim for them the most sacred of all property, the price of their valour and their blood.

"6th. The preservation of the property, movable and immovable, of the Emperor's family, is stipulated by the same treaty (Art. 6); yet it has been despoiled of both: in France, with force of arms, by commissioned brigands; in Italy, by the violence of military commanders; in both countries by seizures and sequestrations solemnly appointed.

"7th. The Emperor Napoleon was to receive two millions of francs a year, and his family two millions and a half, agreeably to the distribution fixed by Art. 6 of the treaty: but the French government has constantly refused to fulfil these engagements, and Napoleon would have soon seen himself reduced to the necessity of dismissing his faithful guard, for want of the means of ensuring its pay, if he had not found in the grateful remembrances of the bankers and merchants of Genoa and Italy the honourable resource of a loan of twelve millions, which was offered him.

"8th. In fine, it was not without a motive, that certain persons were desirous of separating from Napoleon, by any means, the companions of his glory, models of attachment and constancy, unshaken guaranties of his life and safety. The island of Elba was secured to him in full property (Art. 3 of the treaty): yet the resolution to deprive him of it, desired by the Bourbons, and solicited by their agents, had been taken at the Congress.

"And if Providence in its justice had not interposed, Europe would have seen attempts made against the person, the liberty of Napoleon, banished for ever at the mercy of his enemies, far from his family, separated from his servants, either to St. Lucie, or to St. Helena, which was assigned him as a prison.

"And when the allied powers, yielding to the imprudent wishes, or cruel instigations, of the agents of the house of Bourbon, have stooped to violate a solemn contract, on the faith of which Napoleon had absolved the French nation from its oaths; when himself, and all the members of his family, saw themselves menaced and attacked in their persons, in their property, in their affections, in all the rights stipulated in their favour as princes, and even in those secured by the laws to simple citizens; how ought Napoleon to act?

"Ought he, after having endured so many insults, and suffered so many acts of injustice, to consent to the complete violation of the engagements entered into with him; and, resigning himself to the fate prepared for him, abandon also to their fearful destiny, his wife, his son, his relations, and his faithful servants?

"Such a resolution seems to require more than human strength of mind: yet Napoleon was capable of taking it, if the peace and happiness of France could have been purchased by this new sacrifice. He would again have devoted himself for the French people, from whom, as he wishes to declare in the face of all Europe, he makes it his glory to hold every thing, to whom he refers every thing, and to whom alone he will hold himself responsible for his actions and devote his life.

"It was for France alone, and to save her from the calamities of an intestine war, that he abdicated the crown in 1814. He restored to the French people the rights he held from them; he left them free to choose a new master, and to found their liberty and happiness on institutions, that would protect both.

"He hoped, that the nation would preserve all it had acquired by five and twenty years of glorious fighting; and the exercise of its sovereignty in the choice of a dynasty, and in stipulating the conditions, on which it should be called to the throne.

"He expected from the new government respect for the glory of the armies, and for the rights of the brave; the guaranty of all the new interests, interests generated and maintained during a quarter of a century, resulting from all the civil and political laws, observed and revered during that time, because they are identified with the manners, habits, and wants of the nation.

"Far from all this, every idea of the sovereignty of the people has been discarded.

"The principle, on which all public and civil legislation has been founded since the revolution, has been equally discarded.

"France has been treated as a revolted country, reconquered by the armies of its ancient masters, and subjugated anew to a feudal domination.

"A constitutional law has been imposed on France, as easy to be eluded as revoked; and in the form of royal ordinances simply, without consulting the nation, without even hearing those bodies, become illegal, the phantoms of national representation.

"The violation of this charter has been checked only by the timidity of the government; the extent of the abuses of its authority has been limited only by its weakness.

"The disjointing of the army, the dispersion of its officers, the exile of several, the debasement of the soldiers, the suppression of their endowments, the privation of their pay or pensions; the reduction of the pay of the legionaries, the despoiling them of their honours, the pre-eminence given to the decorations of the feudal monarchy, the contempt of the citizens, designated anew under the name of *tiers-état* (third estate); the spoliation of the purchasers of national property, prepared and already begun, the actual diminution of value of such as was obliged to be sold; the return of the feudal system in its titles, privileges, and useful rights, the re-establishment of tramontane principles, the abolition of the liberties of the Gallican church, the annihilation of the Concordat, the re-establishment of tithes, the reviving intolerance of an exclusive form of worship; the domination of a handful of nobles over a people accustomed to equality: are what the ministers of the Bourbons have done, or wished to do, for the people of France.

"It was under such circumstances, that the Emperor Napoleon quitted the island of Elba: such were the motives of the resolution he took, and not the consideration of his own personal interests, so trivial in his opinion compared with the interests of the nation, to which he has devoted his existence.

"He has not brought war into the bosom of France: on the contrary, he has extinguished the war, which the possessors of national property, constituting four fifths of the landholders throughout France, would have been compelled to make upon their despoilers; the war, which the citizens, oppressed, degraded, humiliated by the nobles, would have been forced to declare against their oppressors; the war, which the Protestants, the Jews, and the people of different sects, would have been obliged to maintain against their persecutors.

"He came to deliver France; and as a deliverer he has been received.

"He arrived almost alone; he travelled two hundred and twenty leagues, without meeting any obstacle, without a battle; and has resumed without resistance, in the midst of the capital, and of the acclamations of an immense majority of the citizens, the throne relinquished by the Bourbons; who, from among the army, their own household, the national guards, or the people, could not raise a single person in arms, to endeavour to maintain them in it.

"Yet, replaced at the head of the nation, which had already chosen him three times, and has just elected him a fourth time by the reception it gave him on his march, and his triumphant arrival; of that nation, by which, and for the interest of which, he wishes to reign;

"What is the desire of Napoleon? What the French people desire, the independence of France, peace within, peace with all nations, the execution of the treaty of Paris, of the 30th of May, 1814.

"What is there, then, changed in the future state of Europe, and in the hope of repose promised it? What voice is raised, to demand those succours, which, according to the declaration, are to be granted only when claimed?

"There is nothing changed, if the allied powers recur, as we have a right to expect from them, to just and temperate sentiments; if they acknowledge, that the existence of France in a respectable and independent state, as far from conquering as from being conquered, from domineering as from being held in subjection, is necessary to the balance of great realms, as well as to the guaranty of smaller states.

"There is nothing changed, if, not attempting to compel France to resume with a dynasty, which she can no longer desire, the feudal chains she has broken, and to submit to the seigneurial or ecclesiastical pretensions, from which it has emancipated itself, those powers do not attempt to impose on her laws, to interfere in her internal concerns, to assign her a particular form of government. to give her masters suited to the interests and passions of her neighbours.

"There is nothing changed, if, while France is occupied in preparing the new social compact, that shall guaranty the liberty of her citizens, and the triumph of those generous ideas, that prevail in Europe, and can no longer be stifled; she be not compelled, to call off her attention from these pacific ideas, and from the means of domestic prosperity, to which the people and their chief are desirous of devoting themselves in happy concord, in order to prepare for battle.

"There is nothing changed, if, while the French nation demands nothing, but to remain at peace with all Europe, an unjust coalition do not oblige her to defend, as it did in 1792, her will, and her rights, and her independence, and the sovereign of her choice."

This eloquent refutation, full of irrefragable facts, and reasonings not to be refuted, was no longer necessary. French honour had judged and condemned the Congress of Vienna and its Declaration.

When this declaration appeared, France grew pale: she was astonished, affrighted at the calamities, which the future boded; and groaned at the idea of being exposed to a war for the sake of one single man.

This first impression over, her pride, her virtue, felt indignant, that the allies should dare to conceive the thought, that she would yield to their menaces, and cowardly consent, to give Napoleon up to them.

Had Napoleon been no more than a simple citizen, the attempt to violate by authority the rights of men and nations in his person would have been sufficient, to induce the French, or at least all worthy of the name, to think themselves obliged to protect and defend him.

But Napoleon was not merely a simple citizen, he was the head of the French nation: it was for having aggrandized it by his conquests, and ennobled it by his victories, that he was proscribed by foreigners; and the most timid as well as the most generous made it their sacred duty to place him under the safeguard of the nation, and of French honour.

Thus the declaration of the Congress, instead of intimidating France, heightened its courage; instead of separating Napoleon from the French, drew still more close the bands that united them; instead of calling down on his head the public vengeance, rendered him more estimable and more dear in the eyes of the people.

If Napoleon, availing himself of these generous sentiments, had said to the French: "You have restored to me the crown, foreigners are desirous of tearing it from me; I am ready, either to defend it, or to lay it down; say which I shall do:" the whole nation would have understood Napoleon, and would have risen in a body, to cause the sovereign of its heart and its choice to be respected.

But Napoleon had other ideas: he considered the declaration of the Congress merely as a paper adapted to the circumstances of the day, the object of which was, at the time when it was subscribed by the allies, to support the courage of the royalists, and to restore to the Bourbons the confidence and moral strength they had lost.

He thought, that his entrance into Paris, and the entire pacification of the South, would have completely changed the state of things; and he hoped, that foreign nations would ultimately acknowledge him, when they were convinced, that he had been re-established on the throne by the unanimous consent of the French, and that his ideas of conquest and dominion had given place to the real desire of respecting the tranquillity and independence of his neighbours, and of living in harmony with them.

In fine, he considered, that prudence would induce the allies, as it was their interest, not to engage in a war, the results of which could not be favourable to them: "They will feel, that they will not this time have to do with the France of 1814; and that their successes, if they gain any, will be no longer decisive, but will merely serve to render the war more obstinate and bloody; while, if victory favour me, I may become as formidable as ever. I have for me Belgium and the Rhenish provinces, and with a tricoloured flag and a proclamation I could revolutionize them in four-and-twenty hours."

The treaty of the 25th of March, by which the great powers, renewing the arrangements of the treaty of Chaumont, engaged themselves anew not to lay down their arms, as long as Napoleon should be on the throne, appeared to him merely the natural consequence of the act of the 13th of March, and of the erroneous opinions the allies had formed of France. He thought, that it would not alter the state of the question; and resolved, notwithstanding this treaty, and the affronting manner in which his first overtures were received, to endeavour repeatedly to make the voice of truth, of reason, and of peace, heard at Vienna.

Baron de Stassart, late auditor to the council of state and prefect, had been made chamberlain of Austria, or of Bavaria, since the restoration. He was at Paris. The Emperor, hoping he might be able to reach Vienna under favour of his quality of chamberlain, charged him with a mission for the Empress Marie Louise, and fresh despatches for the Emperor of Austria. Napoleon at the same time had recourse to other means: he was aware of the intimacy and connexions of MM. D. de St. L** and de Mont** with Prince Talleyrand; and persuaded, that M. de Talleyrand would procure for them authority to repair to Vienna, he resolved, to send them thither. He did not deceive himself with the idea, that they would accept their mission for any other purpose than that of more easily serving the royal cause; but he paid little regard to their intrigues with the King, provided they delivered and brought back with exactness the despatches, that should be entrusted to them[95].

About the King, however, and what passed at Ghent, he took little concern: his anxious eyes were turned to Vienna; and convinced of the influence, that M. de Talleyrand might exert there, he particularly directed M. ****, to offer him his favour, and money also, if he would abandon the Bourbons, and employ his talents and experience for the benefit of the imperial cause.

The Emperor, who did not cease to hope, that his exertions, time, and reflection, might effect some changes in the resolutions of the allies, heard with extreme displeasure, that the King of Naples had commenced hostilities.

This prince had long been dissatisfied with the complaisance, with which the allied sovereigns listened to the protests of France, Savoy, and Spain: and, though his crown had been guarantied to him by a solemn compact with Austria, and by the formal declarations of Russia and England, he foresaw, that the doctrine of legitimacy would carry the point against the faith of treaties, and that Austria, though interested in not allowing another crown to be transferred to the house of Bourbon, would be obliged to submit to the unanimous will of the other powers.

Thus the fear of being driven from the throne, and the resolution to maintain himself in it, possessed Joachim, when the news of the successful landing of Napoleon reached Naples.

The horror with which the Austrian sway inspired the Italians, the attachment they retained to Napoleon, and the joy they displayed on hearing of his departure from the island of Elba, persuaded the King, that he should find no difficulty in raising Italy; and he flattered himself with bringing the allies, either by force of arms, or by way of negotiation, to guaranty to him irrevocably the possession of his kingdom.

Desirous on the other hand of securing the protection of Napoleon, in case of failure of success, he secretly despatched an emissary to congratulate him; and announce, that, with a view of seconding his operations, he was about to attack the Austrians, and, if his wishes were answered by victory, he would soon join him with a formidable army: "in fine," he wrote, "the moment of atoning for the wrong I have done your Majesty, and of proving my attachment, is now arrived; I will not let it escape."

This letter, which I deciphered, reached the Emperor at Auxerre; and he immediately enjoined the King, to continue his preparations, but wait for his giving him the signal, before he commenced hostilities. The natural impetuosity and impatience of this Prince did not allow him, to wait for the answer of Napoleon, and when his despatches arrived, the gauntlet had been thrown down.

The better to disguise his intentions, Joachim had summoned the ambassadors of Austria and England, immediately on hearing of the landing of Napoleon, and had assured them, that he would remain faithful to his engagements. When he had assembled his army (put in motion under pretence of reinforcing his troops in the March of Ancona), he fell unexpectedly on the Austrians; and announced to the Italians, by a proclamation dated at Rimini the 31st of March, that he had taken up arms to liberate Italy from a foreign yoke, and restore its ancient freedom and independence.

"Italians," said he to them, "the moment is arrived, when the great decrees of destiny are to be fulfilled. Providence at length calls you, to become an independent people: one cry resounds from the Alps to the straits of Scylla, the independence of Italy. By what right would foreigners rob you of your independence, the first right, and the first good, of all nations?

"Formerly masters of the world, you have expiated this fatal glory by an oppression of twenty centuries. Let your glory now be, to have no more masters.

"Fourscore thousand Italians hasten to you under the command of their king. They swear not to rest, till Italy is free. Italians of all countries, second their magnanimous efforts ... let those, who have borne arms, resume them, let the unpractised youth exercise themselves in the use of them, let all the friends of their country raise up one generous voice for liberty.

"Can England refuse you her suffrages, she whose noblest claim to glory is to spend her blood and treasure for the independence and freedom of nations?

"I call on all the brave, to come and fight with me; I call on all men of enlightened understandings, to prepare, while the passions are silent, the constitution and laws, that ought henceforward to govern happy and independent Italy."

This proclamation, to the great astonishment of Italy and France, did not once mention the name of Napoleon. It kept the most profound silence respecting his return, his intercourse with Joachim, and the hopes their combined efforts must inspire.

Joachim however was not ignorant of the ascendancy, which the name of Napoleon had on the spirit and courage of the Italians. But he knew also, that this name was odious to the English, and dared not invoke it, for fear of displeasing them. He thought he was sufficiently powerful of himself, to act independently of the Emperor; and that it would be enough, if he showed himself in arms to the Italian nation, and offered it independence, to raise it at his pleasure. He deceived himself: all his strength was borrowed from Napoleon: personally he enjoyed no weight, no influence, in Italy. The Italians could not forgive him for having betrayed his brother-in-law and benefactor in 1814, or for having revealed to Austria the patriotic conspiracy of Milan in 1815[96].

Thus prejudiced, they durst not confide in him; his intentions appeared doubtful, his promises vague, his resources uncertain; and they remained quiet spectators of the combat.

It is not, in fact, by concealments, that people are reduced or hurried away: to subjugate them, it is necessary, to convince their hearts and their understandings; and the heart and the understanding comprehend no language but the straight forward voice of truth. Unhappily this language was no longer known to Murat. Since his accession to the throne, he had adopted the system of dissimulation and duplicity, which pretty generally characterise Italian politics. These narrow politics, which support themselves by cunning and temporizing, were incompatible with the French blood, that circulated in his veins; and the continual conflicts, that arose between his novel inclinations and his natural petulance, were incessantly rendering his words and actions at variance, and leading him into devious paths, where he could not fail, to go astray and meet his ruin.

Nevertheless, such is the magic power of the sacred words of liberty and our country, that Murat did not utter them in vain. Bologna and a few cities declared for him; and a number of young Italians ran to enlist under his standards. Victory favoured their first steps; but Napoleon did not deceive himself: the moment had been ill-chosen, he foresaw the defection or ruin of Murat, and what passed beyond the Alps no longer inspired him with any thing but disgust. From that time he turned his attention with more ardor than ever to the means of struggling alone against his adversaries, whose proceedings began to assume a threatening appearance.

The royal government, partly through fear, partly from economy, had disorganized the army, reduced the regiments one half, changed their denominations, and dispersed the soldiers among new battalions.

Napoleon re-established the regiments on their ancient footing; restored to them their glorious surnames of Invincible, Incomparable, Terrible, One to Ten, &c. &c., which they had acquired and merited in the field of battle. He recalled to their standards the brave men who had been banished from them; and the army, which was scarcely fourscore thousand strong, soon reckoned on its lists near two hundred thousand fighting men.

The marines[97] and guards of the coasts, who so brilliantly signalized their courage in the plains of Lutzen and Bautzen, were united under the command of their officers, and formed a body of fifteen or eighteen thousand men, who were appointed to protect our maritime establishments, or, in case of necessity, reinforce the active army.

The cavalry of the imperial guard and the old grenadiers opened their ranks to ten thousand soldiers selected from the flank companies; the light artillery was re-organized; and the young guard received an addition of several regiments.

But it was not sufficient to restore to the army the forces, of which it had been deprived; it was equally necessary, to repair its destitution: the foot wanted arms and clothing, the cavalry had neither saddles nor horses.

The Emperor looked to all these things.

Levies and purchases of horses were made at once in all the departments.

The gendarmerie, by giving up the ten thousand horses belonging to it, which it replaced immediately, supplied the heavy cavalry with so many horses already trained, which in ten days rendered its numerous squadrons complete.

Spacious manufactories of clothing, arms, and equipage, were opened at once in all parts.

The Emperor caused an account of the number of workmen, and the produce of their labour, to be delivered to him every morning. He knew how long it took a tailor to finish a soldier's dress, a wheelwright to construct a carriage, or an armourer to fit up a musket. He knew the quantity of arms, in a good or bad state, contained in the arsenals. "You will find," he wrote to the minister at war, "in such an arsenal, so many old muskets, and so many broken up. Set a hundred men at work there, and arm me five hundred men a week." Such was the extent and variety of Napoleon's genius, that he soared without effort to the loftiest abstractions of the art of governing, and descended with the same facility to the minutest details of management.

Extraordinary commissioners were employed at the same time to direct the repairing and fortifying of the frontier towns. They employed themselves day and night on this important business. But the slightest delay appeared to the Emperor an age of expectation, and frequently he put his hand to the work himself. He was perfectly acquainted with the nature of the fortifications of every place, the number of men it ought to contain, and the approaches necessary to be defended; and in a few hours he settled what the most experienced engineer would have found it difficult to conceive and determine in several days. And let it not be supposed, that the works he thus ordered bore any marks of precipitancy. At the head of his topographical cabinet he had one of the first engineer officers in France, General Bernard; and this general, too brave, too loyal, to be a flatterer, could never enough admire the profound knowledge the Emperor possessed of the art of fortification, and his happy and prompt application of it.

The zeal and joint efforts of these committees, and of the Emperor, produced, in a short time, effects truly miraculous. All France seemed an intrenched camp. Napoleon, in the articles he wrote[98], frequently gave an account of the progress of his armament, of the fortified places, and of the works of defence. I will transcribe here one of these articles, which, exclusive of the merit of depicting the aspect of France at that period, in a better manner than I could, appears to me well adapted to convey an idea of the fervid activity of Napoleon, and the immensity of the objects his eye embraced.

"All the strong places on the northern frontier, from Dunkirk to Charlemont, are furnished with ordnance, provision, and stores: the sluices are put into order, and the country will be inundated at the first hostile movement: field-works have been laid out in the forest of Mormale: measures are taken for throwing up intrenchments in the different passes of the forest of Aregonne: all the strong places of Lorraine are prepared: intrenchments are formed at the five passes of the Vosges: the fortresses of Alsace are equipped: orders are given for the defence of the pass of Jura, and all the frontiers of the Alps. The passes of the Somme, which are in the third line, are putting into order. In the interior, Guise, la Ferté, Vitry, Soissons, Château Thierry, and Langres, are equipping and fortifying. Orders have been issued even for constructing works on the heights of Montmartre and Ménilmontant, and furnishing them with three hundred pieces of ordnance: they will be formed at first of earth, and the solidity of permanent fortifications will be given them in succession.

"His Majesty has ordered, that Lyons should be put into a state of defence: a *tête-de-pont* will be established at Broteaux. The drawbridge at La Guillotière is replacing. The space between the Saône and the Rhone will be fortified: some redoubts are preparing to be constructed in advance of this space. A redoubt will be constructed on the height of Pierre en Size, to support a work, that closes the city on the right bank. The heights, that command the quarter of St. Jean, on the right bank of the Saône, will be defended by several redoubts: a train of eighty pieces of cannon, with the necessary stores, is sent off for Lyons. Sisteron and the bridge of St. Esprit will be placed in a state of defence. Eight armies or corps of observation are formed: namely

"The army of the North;

"The army of the Moselle;

"The army of the Rhine;

"The corps of observation of the Jura, which is assembling at Befort;

"The army of the Alps, which is assembling at Chambery;

"The corps of observation of the Pyrenees, which is assembling at Perpignan and at Bordeaux;

"And the army of reserve, which is assembling at Paris and at Laon.

"The old soldiers are every where on the march, animated with the greatest enthusiasm, and come to complete our hundred and twenty regiments of infantry. The purchases made for remounting the cavalry have been going on rapidly for this month, and will soon render our seventy regiments of cavalry fully complete. Regiments of volunteer cavalry are forming in many parts: Alsace has already furnished two regiments of lancers, of a thousand men each. We have reason to think, that this example will be followed in Brittany, Normandy, and Limousin, the province in which the greatest number of horses are bred.

"Parks of artillery, forming more than a hundred and fifty batteries, are already harnessed, and on the march for the different armies. The corps of artillery for the defence of Lyons is composed of two companies formed in the school of Alfort. The corps for serving the three hundred pieces of ordnance, that will be placed on the heights of Paris, will consist of twelve companies of marine artillery, two companies of invalids, two companies of the school of Alfort, two companies of the polytechnic school, two companies of the school of St. Cyr, and six companies of foot artillery.

"Corps of partisans and free corps are forming in a great number of departments. An adjutant-general, stationed with each general commanding in chief, will conduct the correspondence with these corps; which, if the enemy be rash enough to penetrate into our territories, will fall upon his communications in the mountains and forests, and find support in the fortified towns.

"The organization of the levy in mass of Alsace, Lorraine, the county of Messin, Franche Comté, Burgundy, Dauphiny, and Picardy, is prepared.

"All the cities will arm in defence of their vicinity: they will follow the example of Chalons sur Saône, Tournus, and St. Jean de Losne. Every unfortified town even would betray the national honour, if it surrendered to light troops, and did not make the best defence its means will allow, till the arrival of infantry and artillery in such force, that its resistance would cease to be prescribed by the laws of war.

"Every thing is in motion in all parts of France. If the coalition persist in the designs they have announced of making war on us, if they violate our frontiers, it is easy to foresee, what fruits they will reap from their attempt on the rights of the French nation: all the departments will emulate in zeal those of Alsace, the Vosges, Franche Comté, Burgundy, and the Lyonese; every where the people are animated with a patriotic spirit, and ready to make any sacrifice, to maintain the independence of the nation, and the honour of the throne."

In fine, to complete his means of resistance and attack, the Emperor remodelled the national guard, and divided it into three thousand one hundred and thirty battalions, forming a body of two millions two hundred and fifty thousand men. All the national guards from twenty years old to forty were classed in active companies of light infantry and grenadiers, and fifteen hundred of these companies, or a hundred and eighty thousand men, were immediately placed at the disposal of the minister at war, to form the garrisons of the frontier places, and reinforce the armies of reserve.

The general officers sent to the frontier departments, to accelerate the raising and departure of this national militia, had need only to show themselves, to accomplish their mission. Every citizen aspired beforehand to the honour of making a part of it; and in the provinces of the east, the north, and the centre, it was found necessary to form supernumerary companies[99]. The father would have renounced his son, the wife her husband, the girl her betrothed lover, if they had been deaf to the voice of honour and their country. The mothers themselves, who at other times had so bitterly deplored the departure of their children, encouraged them, like the Spartans, to march against the enemy, and fall, if it must be so, in the sacred cause of their country. This picture is not an exaggeration, it is faithful, it is true. Never was a more beautiful spectacle exhibited to the eyes of any man, to whom the glory and independence of his country were dear, than that of the enthusiasm and martial joy, with which the warlike inhabitants of Alsace, Lorraine, Burgundy, Champagne, and the Vosges, were animated. The roads were covered with waggons loaded with young warriors, who hastened, gaily singing, to the post of honour assigned them by Napoleon: the population of the towns and villages received them on their way with applauses, which inflamed their minds with fresh ardor, and made them enjoy by anticipation the praises and acclamations, that their friends, parents, and fellow-citizens would lavish on them at their return.

France seemed to call aloud, to see her eclipsed greatness restored. She had recovered all her energy: an evident proof, that the strength of a nation is always the work of the prince, by whom it is governed. It is he, who enervates the public spirit, and bastardizes his subjects, by the effeminacy of his government: or it is he, who inspires them with the love of their country, with priding themselves in it, and leads them to undertake, whatever can augment its glory and its power.

To draw still more closely the bonds of union between the French people, and impart greater intensity to their patriotism, Napoleon authorized the re-establishment of popular clubs, and the formation of civic confederations. This time his expectations were not answered by success. The major part of the clubs were filled with men, who formerly composed the revolutionary tribunals and societies; and their imprecations against kings, and their liberticide motions, made the Emperor fear, that he had revived the spirit of anarchy.

The sentiments manifested by the federates equally disquieted him. He perceived, that he did not occupy the first place in their thoughts and affections; that the primary wish of their hearts was liberty; and, as this liberty was in his eyes synonimous with republicanism, he exerted all his endeavours to moderate, restrain, and repress, the development of these patriotic associations. Perhaps there were men among the federates, whose principles might be dangerous, and their intentions criminal: but in general they consisted of pure patriots, who had taken up arms to defend the imperial government, and not to overturn it.

Napoleon had never been able to surmount the aversion, which he felt for the veterans of the revolution. He dreaded their constancy, and their daring spirit; and he would have thought himself in danger, if not lost, had they become consolidated, and resumed their ascendancy. This panic fear was the cause, that he did not reap from the confederations the advantages he promised himself; and which they would unquestionably have afforded him, if he had not clogged their wings. It was also the cause of his committing a perhaps still greater fault, that of putting a stop to the popular movements, that had shown themselves in most of the departments. In the critical state in which he found himself, and into which he had drawn France, he should not have disregarded any means of security; and the most efficacious, the most analogous to his situation, was indisputably that of engaging the people most intimately in his fate, and in his defence. It was necessary, therefore, while preventing them from spilling a single drop of blood, to let them compromise themselves with some of those incorrigible ultras, who had harassed, ill-treated, and insulted them, since the restoration. The people would then have been more sensible, that it was no longer the personal cause of Napoleon alone, that they had to defend; and the dread of chastisement, and of the yoke, would have restored to them that ancient enthusiasm, which had proved so fatal to the first coalition.

The moderation adopted by Napoleon on this occasion was honourable, but not politic. He conducted himself, as he might have done at a time, when all parties, confounded together and reconciled, acknowledged him for their sole and only sovereign. But things had changed: he had no longer the whole of France in his favour; and hence it was necessary, that he should conduct himself rather as the head of a party, than as a sovereign; and that he should display as it were all the vigour and energy of the leader of a faction. Energy unites men, by taking from them all uncertainty, and hurrying them with violence toward their object. Moderation, on the contrary, divides and enervates them, because it leaves them to their own irresolution, and allows them leisure, to listen to their interests, their scruples, and their fears.

The attention paid by the Emperor to his military preparations did not prevent his continuing to occupy himself on the welfare of the state, and endeavour more and more to conciliate the confidence and affection of the public.

Already, in other days, he had drawn out from its ruins the ancient University. A new basis, more broad, more extensive, more majestic, had raised this noble institution to a level with the age, and with France. But the first stage of education did not answer the efforts made to improve it, and to diffuse it among the younger classes of society.

M. Carnot, in a report that combined the most pleasing philanthropy with the most sage and lofty views, taught the Emperor the advantages of the methods of Bell and Lancaster, and the monarch and the minister made a present to France, to morality, to humanity, of the system of mutual instruction.

The Emperor, on removing his eyes from this interesting youth, the hope of the country, turned them to those old soldiers, who had formerly been its pride and support.

A royal ordinance had expelled from their asylum a considerable number of invalids, and had taken from them a portion of their endowments: a decree restored them to their rights; and a visit, which the Emperor paid these veterans in glory, added a kindness to the benefit.

He also repaired to the Polytechnic school. It was the first time of his showing himself to its pupils. Their love of perfect liberty, their inclination for republican institutions, had long alienated from them the affections of the Emperor: but the striking bravery they had displayed under the walls of Paris had restored to them his esteem and friendship; and it was satisfactory to him (these are his own words), to have such a fine occasion of reconciling himself with them.

The suburb of St. Antoine, that cradle of the revolution, was not forgotten. The Emperor traversed it from one end to the other. He had the doors of all the workshops opened to him, and examined them very minutely. The numerous workmen of the manufactory of M. Lenoir, who retained a grateful remembrance of what the Emperor had done for their master and for themselves, loaded him with expressions of their attachment. The commissary of police of the quarter had followed Napoleon into this manufactory; and, willing to set the example, opened his mouth to its utmost extent, to holla as loud as he could bawl "Long live the Emperor!" but, by a terrible slip of the tongue, a very distinct "Long live the King!" on the contrary issued from it. This caused great confusion: but the Emperor, turning to him, said in a rallying tone: "So, Mr. Commissary, you are determined then not to get rid of your bad habits." This sally was the signal for a general laugh: and the commissary, plucking up his spirits, convinced Napoleon by many a vigorous "Long live the Emperor!" that we never lose any thing by a little patience.

The Emperor was accompanied only by three officers of his household. It was impossible for them to defend him from the approaches and caresses of the people: the women kissed his hands; the men squeezed them, till they made him cry out; both expressed to him in a thousand ways, which I cannot transcribe, the difference they made between him and his predecessor. At all times he had been much beloved by the class of workmen and artisans. He had enriched it: and interest is the prime mover of regard among the people, as well as among the great[100].

The Emperor received a great number of petitions during his excursions. Unable to read them all, he ordered me, to examine them carefully, and give him an account of them. He loved to repay the confidence that the people reposed in him; and frequently granted to the request of an obscure and unknown citizen, what he would perhaps have refused to the entreaties of a marshal or a minister. The utility of these familiar communications between the nation and the sovereign was not confined, in his eyes, to the solitary interests of the petitioner. He considered them as efficacious means of coming at the knowledge of abuses and acts of injustice, and of keeping the depositaries of authority within the limits of their duty. He was fond of encouraging them, that the phrase, If the Emperor knew it, or The Emperor shall know it, might solace the heart of the oppressed, and make the oppressor tremble.

In former days he had appointed a special commission, to receive petitions, and give them suitable effect. This benefit not appearing to him sufficiently complete, he would have them subjected to a preliminary examination, under his own eye. He decided himself the method to be followed: and directed me, to make known to him every day, without disguise, the complaints, wants, and wishes, of the French people. I made it a point of duty, of honour, to execute this task in a proper manner, and to become the zealous protector of those who had none. Every morning I laid before the Emperor an analytical report of the requests capable of demanding his attention: he examined them with care, made marginal notes on them with his own hand, and sent them to his ministers with a favourable decision, or an order to verify them, and give him an account of the result.

In fine, to fulfil, as much as in him lay, the public expectation, the Emperor made numerous changes in the laws relating to the consolidated taxes (*droits réunis*), which, while they diminished the impost, freed it from its abuses and tyrannical forms, and rendered it less odious, and more supportable. These beneficial meliorations, though incomplete, were received with gratitude; and the Emperor was thanked for his endeavours to reconcile the interests of individuals with the wants of the public treasury.

But the satisfaction Napoleon derived from the happy effects of his solicitude was frequently disturbed by the disquietude and perplexity, which the cabals and manœuvres of the royalists occasioned him. "The priests and the nobles," said he one day in a fit of ill-humour, "are playing a deep game. If I were to let loose the people upon them, they would all be devoured in the twinkling of an eye[101]."

By a decree of the 25th of March, he had already ordered the ministers of the King, and the civil and military officers of his household, as well as of those of the princes, as also the chiefs of the Chouans, of the Vendeans, and of the royal volunteers, to remove to a distance of thirty leagues from Paris. This prudent precaution was but imperfectly executed. M. Fouché, to secure himself a refuge in the King's party, had sent for the principal of the proscribed persons to his house; expressed to them how much he felt interested for their situation, and the efforts he had made, to prevent their banishment; and finally authorised them pretty generally, to remain at Paris.

The Emperor, not aware that their audacity was owing to the protection of his minister, watched for an opportunity of intimidating them by an act of severity. While things were in this state, a M. de Lascours, a colonel, was arrested at Dunkirk, where he had introduced himself as an emissary from the King. Napoleon, deceived by the similarity of the name, supposed this officer to be the person, who pretended, in 1814, to have received orders, to blow up the powder magazine at Grenelle, and refused to execute them. "I should be sorry," said he, "to sacrifice by way of example a worthy man; but an impostor like this deserves no pity. Write to the minister at war, to have him taken before a military commission, and tried as an instigator to civil war, and to the overturning of the established government."

The Emperor, turning towards me, added: "How is it, that the absurd fable of this man has not been contradicted?"—"Sire," I answered, "Gourgaud has often assured me, that all your officers had publicly avowed their sentiments on it; and that it had been the intention of several generals, and particularly of general Tirlet, to unmask this odious lie to the King; but...." "Enough," said the Emperor, "I make no account of intentions: send the order, and let me hear no more of him."

I lost sight of this business: but I have since learned, that M. de Lascours was acquitted.

If M. de Lascours had been so unfortunate, as to fall a victim to his zeal, the Emperor would have been accused of barbarity; yet he was neither cruel nor sanguinary, for cruelty must not be confounded with severity. I know but one single act, the result of the most fatal counsels, for which, alas! he may be reproached by posterity[102]. Who besides have been the victims of his pretended ferocity? Will the death of Georges, and his obscure accomplices, be considered as a judicial murder? Are the infernal machine and its terrible ravages forgotten? Georges, at the head of the Chouans, was a misled Frenchman, to be pitied, and to be spared. Georges, at the head of a band of assassins, was undeserving of pity, and the cause of morality, as well as of humanity, demanded his punishment.

Will it be said, that Pichegru was strangled by his orders? The designs of Pichegru were so clearly substantiated, and the laws so clear, that he could not escape the scaffold: why, then, should he cause him to be murdered? The greatest criminals themselves do not commit useless crimes. Were apprehensions entertained of the disclosures he might make?... What could he disclose to the French people? That Napoleon aspired to the throne? Of this no one was ignorant.

A man, that Napoleon had reason to dread, was Moreau: was his life attempted? Yet it was less dangerous, to assassinate him, than to send to a tribunal, where guilt presided, a warrior at that time so dear to France and to the army.

No, Napoleon was not cruel, he was not sanguinary. If he were sometimes inexorable, it was because there are circumstances, in which the monarch must shut his heart to compassion, and leave the law free to act: but, if he knew how to punish, he was also capable of pardoning; and, at the moment when he gave up Georges[103] to the sword of justice, he spared the lives of Messrs. de Polignac and the Marquis de Rivière, whose courage and zeal he respected.

The Emperor did not stop at the rigorous trial, to which he had delivered over the person of M. de Lascours: by a decree, dated the 18th of March, and published the 9th of April, he ordered the condemnation, and the sequestration of the property of

The Prince of Benevento,

The Duke of Ragusa,

The Duke of Alberg,

The Abbé de Montesquiou,

The Count de Jaucourt,

The Count de Bournonville, and

The Sieurs Lynch,

Vitrolles,

Alexis de Noailles,

Bourienne,

Bellard,

La Roche-Jaquelin, and

Sostène de la Rochefoucault[104];

All of whom, as members of the provisional government, or agents of the royal party, had concurred in the subversion of the imperial government, previous to the abdication of Napoleon.

This decree, though supposed to have originated at Lyons, first saw the light at Paris; and was, as I have just said, the result of the ill humour, into which the plots of the royalists had thrown Napoleon. The terms, in which it was originally couched, too clearly attested its source: the first article said; "are declared traitors to their country, and shall be punished as such, &c."

It was I, who wrote this decree, from the dictation of the Emperor. When I had finished it, he ordered me, to go and get it signed by Count Bertrand, who had countersigned the decrees of Lyons. I went to the marshal. He read the decree, and returned it to me, saying: "I will never sign it: this is not what the Emperor promised us; they who advise him, to take such measures, are his bitterest enemies; I will speak to him about it." I related this firm and courageous answer to Napoleon word for word. He ordered me, to return to the grand Marshal, to endeavour to overcome his repugnance, and, if he still persisted, to bring him to him. Count Bertrand instantly followed me, with head erect, into the Emperor's closet. "I am astonished," said Napoleon to him in a dry tone, "that you make such difficulties about it to me. The severity I wish to display is necessary for the good of the state." — "I do not think so, Sire." — "I do, I tell you: and it is my business alone to judge of it. I did not ask your advice, but your signature, which is only a matter of form, and cannot in any way compromise you." — "Sire, a minister, who countersigns the act of a sovereign, is morally responsible for that act; and I should think myself wanting in my duty to your Majesty, and perhaps to myself, if I were weak enough to set my hand to such measures. If your Majesty choose to reign by the laws, you have no right, arbitrarily to pronounce, by a simple decree, sentence of death, and forfeiture of property, against your subjects. If you choose to act as a dictator, and to have no law but your own will, you have no need of the addition of my signature. Your

Majesty has declared, by your proclamations, that you would grant a general amnesty. I countersigned them most cordially; and I will not countersign the decree, that revokes them." — "But you well know, I always told you, that I never would pardon Marmont, Talleyrand, and Augereau; and that I promised only to overlook, what had passed since my abdication. I know better than you, what I ought to do, to keep my promises, and ensure the tranquillity of the state. I begun with being indulgent, even to weakness and the royalists, instead of appreciating my moderation, have abused it: they bestir themselves, they conspire, and I ought and will bring them to their senses. I would rather have my blows fall on traitors, than on men who are misled. Besides, all those who are on the list, Augereau excepted, are out of France, or in concealment. I shall not seek for them: my intention is to terrify them more than harm them. You see, therefore," continued the Emperor, softening his voice, "you have not rightly considered the business: sign this for me, my dear Bertrand: you must." — "I cannot, Sire. I request your Majesty's permission, to submit my observations to you in writing." — "All that, my dear sir, will make us lose time: you are startled, I assure you, without any reason; sign, I tell you; I request you, you will do me pleasure." — "Permit me, Sire, to wait, till your Majesty has seen my observations." The marshal went away. This noble resistance did not offend the Emperor: the language of truth and honour never displeased him, when it issued from a pure heart.

General Bertrand delivered to Napoleon a statement of his reasons. It did not alter his resolution; it only determined him, to give it a legal form.

The Emperor, persuaded that General Bertrand would equally retain his opinion, would not have this new decree presented to him, and it appeared without being countersigned.

The effect it produced justified the apprehensions of the grand Marshal. It was considered as an act of despotism and vengeance; as the first infraction of the promises made to the nation. The murmurs of the public were echoed even within the walls of the imperial palace. Labedoyère, at a moment when Napoleon was passing by, said loud enough to be heard, "If the system of proscriptions and sequestrations begin again, all will soon be over."

The Emperor, according to his custom on such occasions, affected to be perfectly satisfied with himself, and appeared no way apprehensive of the storm. Being at table with several personages and ladies of distinction belonging to the court, he asked the Countess Duchâtel, if her husband, who was director-general of the domains, had executed the order for sequestrating the estates of Talleyrand and company. "There is no hurry for that," answered she drily. He made no reply, and changed the conversation.

The persons about him are incessantly reproached, with having basely crouched to his will and opinions: this anecdote, and many others that I might relate, prove, that all of them at least did not deserve this reproach. But, supposing it to be just with regard to some, is it as easy, as is commonly thought, to overcome the will of a sovereign?

From pride, and perhaps from a conviction of superiority, Napoleon did not readily endure counsel.

In affairs of state, he imposed upon himself the law of consulting his counsellors, and his ministers. Endowed by nature with the faculty of knowing every thing, or of divining every thing, he almost always took an active part in the discussion: and I must say, to the honour of the Emperor, his ministers, and his counsellors, in common, an inexpressible degree of confidence, frankness, and independence, prevailed in these discussions, highly animated as for the most part they were. The Emperor, far from being shocked when any one contradicted him, endured, nay provoked contradiction and adopted without resistance the advice of his opponents, when he thought it preferable to his own opinion.

When the question concerned those grand decisions, that influence the fate of empires, the case was different. He listened for a certain time to the objections of his ministers: but, when his attention had reached its bounds, he interrupted them, and supported his own opinion with so much fire, force, and perseverance, that he reduced them to silence.

This silence was less the effect of their passive obedience to the intentions of the monarch, than the result of the lessons taught by experience. They had seen, that the most rash, the most incomprehensible, I had almost said the most senseless, enterprises of Napoleon were invariably crowned with success; and they were convinced, that reason could not contend against the inspirations of genius, and the favours of fortune.

In fine, Napoleon often consulted only his own will; and his ministers then knew nothing of his resolves, till they received orders, to carry them into execution.

Such was, and such always will be the situation of ministers, in a monarchy, where the Prince governs for himself; and more especially when this Prince, like Napoleon, owes his throne merely to the ascendancy of his genius and his sword.

Besides, the time of flatterers and flattery was past with Napoleon. Every one was interested in telling him the truth, and no one was sparing of it to him.

The security inspired by this rare and valuable veracity was strengthened by the arrival of Prince Joseph and Prince Lucien. The moderation of the one, and the patriotism of the other, were well known; and the care of maintaining the liberal and pacific intentions of the Emperor was laid on them both.

Prince Lucien had been deeply afflicted in 1814 at the misfortunes of his brother, and was eager to offer him his fortune and his services. This, generous offer did not entirely efface from the heart of Napoleon the remembrance, of their ancient differences, but it softened the asperity of them; and it might be foreseen, that their enmity would not be eternal.

As soon as Prince Lucien heard of the entry of Napoleon into Paris, he wrote him a letter of congratulation. "Your return," said he, "fills up the measure of your military glory. But there is another glory still greater, and above all more desirable, civil glory. The sentiments and intentions, which you have solemnly promulgated, promise France, that you know how to acquire it," &c.

Prince Lucien, however, notwithstanding his desire of revisiting that country, the cause of which he pleaded, did not venture to approach it. But the invasion of the King of Naples having rendered his services necessary to the Sovereign Pontiff, the gratitude he owed to the Holy Father triumphed over his apprehensions. He departed under the title of secretary to the Pope's nuncio, and crossed the Alps without any obstacle. Arrived in the French territory, he wrote to Napoleon, to inform him of his mission, and to ask if his coming to Paris would be agreeable to him. Napoleon's first feeling was that of hesitating to receive him: his second, that of opening to him his arms. The intention of the Prince was to return quickly to Home, whither he was called by the concerns entrusted to him: but the interruption of the communications did not allow this. Obliged to return to Paris, he laid aside his incognito. His return was then publicly announced, and made an advantageous and agreeable impression on every mind.

A few days before, the Emperor had made the acquisition of another personage; less illustrious, it is true, but equally renowned for his patriotism and intelligence: I mean M. Benjamin Constant.

Napoleon, knowing the experience and reputation of this learned civilian, sent for him, to converse with him "on liberty and the constitution." Their conversation continued more than two hours. The Emperor, willing to attach M. Constant to his party, employed all his means of seduction; and I leave it to those Frenchmen, and those foreigners, who have had access to him, to say, whether it were possible to resist him.

When he wished to fix any one in his train, he studied and penetrated with extreme sagacity his way of thinking, his principles, his character, his ruling passions; and then with that familiar grace, that affability, that force and vivacity of expression, which gave so much value and such a charm to his conversations[105], he insinuated himself imperceptibly into your heart, made himself master of your passions, gently excited them, and artfully flattered them: then, displaying at once the magic resources of his genius, he plunged you into intoxication, into admiration, and subdued you so rapidly, so completely, that it seemed the effect of enchantment.

Thus M. Benjamin Constant was subjugated: he arrived at the Tuileries with repugnance, he quitted the palace an enthusiast.

The next day he was named counsellor of state: and this favour he owed to no base submissions, as his enemies have pretended, but to his learning, and to the desire the Emperor had of giving to public opinion, and to M. B. Constant himself, a pledge of his having forgotten the past; a pledge so much the more meritorious, as the Emperor, independently of the Philippic launched against him by this writer on the 19th of March, had besides before his eyes a letter in his own hand to M. de Blacas, the subject and expressions of which were of a nature, to inspire Napoleon with something more than aversion for its author.

M. de Blacas had left in his boxes a great number of papers. The Emperor directed the Duke of Otranto to examine them. Of this he immediately repented, and sent for them again. Part fell to our share: the rest were delivered to the Duke of Vicenza. Their examination afforded nothing interesting. The Emperor, disappointed, accused M. Fouché of having removed the important papers. Those we inspected consisted only of private reports, and confidential and anonymous notes. The hatred of the revolution pervaded every line, every word. The writers did not dare to propose plainly the revocation of the Charter, and the abolition of the new institutions; but they declared without any circumlocution, that the dynasty of the Bourbons would never be secure with the existing laws; and that it was necessary, to distrust and get rid of the men of the revolution. More effectually to know and persecute these, M. de Blacas had caused to be disinterred from the archives of the cabinet, and of the ministers, the documents that might serve to make known their conduct ever since 1789, and he had directed biographical notices of each to be composed, which might easily have been taken for indictments drawn up by M. Bellart[106].

We found also a number of minutes of laws and ordinances, written by the hand of this minister, and attesting by their laborious corrections, how destitute he was of readiness and of imagination. Frequently he made three or four foul copies, before he could give any consistency or connection to his ideas. His familiar style was dry and turgid: if the style exhibit the man, how I pity M. de Blacas. He took extreme pains to vary, himself, the form of his appointments (rendez-vous): and the trouble he gave himself, to say the same thing in several different ways, wonderfully reminded us of the billet-doux of the Bourgeois Gentilhomme: "Belle Marquise, vos beaux yeux me font mourir d'amour; d'amour mourir me font, belle Marquise, vos beaux yeux[107]."

In fine, we collected from the cabinet of this minister an ample collection of royal denunciations, petitions, justifications, and confessions, of those men, who, like Lockard, are always "the most humble servants of circumstances."

These humble servants, when the Emperor returned from the island of Elba, did not fail to prostrate themselves before him anew. They assured him, after the example of a certain Marquis well known, that they had denied, insulted, calumniated him, only that they might remain faithful to him, without being suspected by the royal government: they conjured him, to grant them the happiness and glory of serving him; but he disdained their supplications, as he had disdained their insults: they gained nothing but his contempt. Always as devoid of shame as of faith, they were eager, immediately after the fall of Napoleon, to turn round anew, and carry back to the King their faded homage. Some, as M. the Count de M***, whose hands are still reeking with the blood of his assistants (*administrés*), contrived, with the help of their lying fidelity, to surprise his easy confidence. Others, as M. F***, became in their writings the virulent persecutors of men, whose lot they had envied, and whose support they had begged. All arrogated to themselves exclusively the title of pure royalists: the title of honest men.... I know them ... the mask, with which they cover themselves, the honours, the dignities, with which they are invested, cannot disguise them to my eyes.... Shall I name them? And the Emperor is accused of despising mankind! ah, where is the sovereign, that can esteem them?

Footnote 1: The misfortunes of that eventful day, and of the remainder of the campaign, were caused by the treachery of the Saxons and the defection of the Princes of the Confederation of the Rhine.

Footnote 2: Napoleon, according to the common report, was frequently heard to repeat, after his abdication, "I have been ruined by liberal ideas." I do not think that he ever expressed himself in this manner. I do not intend to doubt the irresistible force which liberal ideas have now acquired; but I do not think, that they contributed to effect the first downfal of the imperial throne. Nobody thought about liberal ideas at that period. France had been trained to the government of Napoleon, and his despotism gave rise to no complaints. She was not free in the manner according to which the nation now wishes to enjoy liberty. But the liberty which France then possessed was enough for the French. Napoleon would often exercise unlimited authority, but the country had only one master, and *he* was the master of all. If it is true that the French abandoned Napoleon in 1814, it was not because we were tired of Napoleon or discontented with his government, but because the nation was exhausted, discouraged, and demoralized by an uninterrupted succession of calamitous wars. The people would still have been delighted to obey him, but they had neither strength nor soul.

The real causes of the downfal of Napoleon are to be found in his hatred towards England, and in the continental system, which resulted from that hatred. This gigantic system, which oppressed all Europe, could not fail to raise the entire continent against Napoleon and France, and thus to bring on the ruin of both. "Rome," as it is said by Montesquieu, "extended her empire because her wars only followed in succession. Each nation, such was her inconceivable good fortune, waited till another had been conquered, before beginning the attack." Rome fell as soon as all the nations assailed and penetrated on every side.

Footnote 3: He arrived at Paris before his august brother, and by these pleasing expressions he replied to the addresses of congratulation presented to him by the municipality of Paris.

Footnote 4: Extracted from the Journal des Débats. The principal proprietor and editor of this paper was Monsieur Laborie, one of Talleyrand's creatures, and private secretary to the provisional government.

Footnote 5: This expression was one of those of which the ministers made the worst use. If they were told that any magistrate, any officer, any functionary, whom they had turned out, had fulfilled his duties with honour and distinction, that he was loved and regretted by the people, they answered, "he is a dangerous character," and there was an end of the business.

Footnote 6: When Dupont capitulated to the Spaniards, the insurgents refused to acknowledge the Emperor. Dupont therefore only took the title of general in the French service.

Footnote 7: I speak only of acting and thinking beings. In all countries there is to be found a class of cyphers, who are so careless, stupid, or selfish, that they belong to no party, and indeed to no nation.

Footnote 8: The accusation that a spirit of mutiny prevailed amongst them cannot be refuted more effectually than by quoting the expressions used by M. de Montesquiou on the 14th of March. "In the last two months," said he, "not one of the soldiers or officers belonging to the corps of the old guard composing the garrison of Metz, has been once reprimanded."

Footnote 9: The Chouans never allowed the opportunity of committing murder to escape them. They carried their muskets as they walked by the side of the plough, and the furrows which they trod were frequently sprinkled with blood. The priests who had taken the oaths, and the purchasers of national domains, were particularly the objects of the refinements of their cruelty. They seldom entered a town without plundering the inhabitants, and without slaughtering those who had been pointed out to their vengeance.— Lacretelle, Précis de la Revolution.

Footnote 10: M.M. David and Falconnet. In order to appease the public indignation, a summons was issued against these writers, it being stated in the process that they had endeavoured to excite civil war. There was no difficulty in guessing that this proceeding was a farce, and that by overcharging the crime it was the intention of the government to favour the acquittal of the accused, and accordingly they were acquitted.

Footnote 11: Before the revolution it was customary for "les grands seigneurs" to obtain what were called "lettres de surséance," by means of which they avoided the payment of their debts, and defeated their creditors.

Footnote 12: This proposal was not carried into execution.

Footnote 13: There are times when a government may attack general principles without danger. But men and their personal interests can never be assailed with impunity. Personal interest is the prime mover of public opinion and feeling; and however degrading the truth may appear, it is not to be disputed. After a great national catastrophe this baleful egotism is particularly evident. Dignified passions become extinct for want of fuel; and the human mind, destitute of external occupation, works inward upon itself, and begets selfishness, the true pestilence of the soul. When this disease affects a nation, the government is lost if it attacks the interests of individuals.

Footnote 14: By means of ordonnances the ministers legislated according to their pleasure in matters which ought only to have been regulated by the law, so that the greater part of the bills presented to the chambers "had been already enacted and executed in the shape of ordonnances; and the legislature had no other function except that of giving a legal sanction to the arbitrary decrees of the ministers." —Censeur.

Footnote 15: Even in Paris several persons were ill treated and bayoneted, because they refused to pull off their hats and kneel, whilst the processions were passing by.

Footnote 16: Under the reign of Napoleon, if a priest had ventured to utter any opinion contrary to the system of government, he would have been immediately removed.

Footnote 17: I cannot express their thoughts more forcibly than by copying the passage, which I have quoted in my text, from the View of the Revolution by Lacretelle.

Footnote 18: From his early youth, it may be even said from his days of boyhood, Napoleon felt an inward presentiment that he was not destined to live in mediocrity. This persuasion soon taught him to treat others with disdain, and to entertain the highest opinion of himself. Scarcely had he obtained a subaltern command in the artillery, when he considered himself as the superior of his equals, and the equal of his superiors. In his 20th year he was placed at the head of the army of Italy. Without appearing to be in the slightest degree surprised by his elevation, he passed from a secondary station to the chief command. He immediately treated the old generals of the army—they who were so proud of the laurels—with an air of dignity and authority, which placed them in a situation which was probably new to them. But they did not feel humiliated, and their inferiority seemed to result as a matter of course, for the ascendancy exercised by Napoleon was irresistible; and he was thoroughly endued; with that instinct of authority, that talent of ensuring obedience, with those faculties which are usually confined to those who are kings by birth. Napoleon could probably have attained to supreme authority in any country in the world. Nature had formed him for command, and she never creates such men for the purpose of leaving them in obscurity. It seems, according to the remark of a writer whose name I have forgotten, that she is proud of her own work, and that she wishes to offer it to admiration, by placing it at the head of human society.

Footnote 19: The continental system induced Napoleon to exercise a real tyranny over Europe. We do not pretend to deny the fact; but we only wish to add, that this exterior despotism always induced a belief amongst foreigners, that Napoleon, who tyrannized so violently over nations which did not belong to him, must necessarily be the tyrant of his own subjects.

Footnote 20: The Emperor thus addressed the Spanish Cortes; when assembled at Bayonne.

Footnote 21: Napoleon was accused of having aspired to universal monarchy. In all ages, this desire has been imputed to powerful and ambitious sovereigns. Let us confess that no monarch was ever better justified in yielding to the seductions of this brilliant phantom than Napoleon. From the summit of his throne he held the reins which guided the greater part of

Europe, whose docile monarchs instantly obeyed any direction which he chose to give them. At the first word, at the slightest signal, their subjects were arrayed beneath the imperial eagle. Their continual intercourse with us, the obligation of obeying Napoleon, an obligation imposed upon them by their own princes, had accustomed them to consider the Emperor as their chieftain. But whatever ambition may have been attributed to Napoleon, his good sense restrained him from aspiring to universal monarchy. He had another plan; he intended to re-establish the eastern and western empires. It would now be useless to reveal the lofty and powerful considerations by which this grand and noble idea was suggested to Napoleon. Then, France might have been allowed to grasp again the sceptre of Charlemagne: but now, we must forget that we have been the masters of the world.

Footnote 22: Neither the nature nor the extent of these aids has been well understood out of France. Napoleon revived our industry by the loans, which he never hesitated to grant to any enterprising manufacturer who needed capital; and this assistance was always liberal and well-timed.

Footnote 23: Louis XIV., who has been so much praised for his liberality, only distributed 52,300 francs per annum to the literati and artists of France, and 14,000 francs to foreigners.

Footnote 24: The soldiers identified the name of Napoleon with their country and their honour. When the accession of Louis XVIII. put an end to the sufferings and captivity of those who were imprisoned in England, they returned to France, cursing the cause of their liberty, and exclaiming, "Vive l'Empereur!" Even in the deserts of Russia, neither threats of ill treatment, nor promises of assistance offered to the French prisoners at the moment when they were starving, could extort a single complaint against Napoleon.

Footnote 25: Marshal Soult had just succeeded General Dupont.

Footnote 26: M. Comte, one of the acute and courageous editors of the Censor, was chosen by the general as his "counsel." General Fressinet was his advocate. (According to the forms of the French courts of judicature, the counsel assists by his advice, the advocate pleads.) This officer, equally distinguished by his firmness, his talents, and his bravery, was afterwards punished and exiled on account of the generous assistance which he gave on this important occasion to General Excelmans, his fellow soldier and friend.

Footnote 27: It has been alleged, but without foundation, that he retained his taste for military exercises. Not one review took place during his residence at Porto Ferrajo; arms seemed to have no attractions for him.

Footnote 28: It is well known that there was not a single individual of note in the service, either of his allies or of his enemies, whose strong and weak points were not perfectly understood by Napoleon.

Footnote 29: This officer is the person who is named in the declaration made on the 15th of March to the prince of Essling, then governor of the 8th military division, by Monsieur P*****, who landed with Napoleon from the Isle of Elba, and was arrested at Toulon by order of the prefect of the department of the Var.

Footnote 30: At Malmaison the Emperor asked me what had become of M. Z***. I answered that he had been killed on Mount St. Jean: "Well," answered the Emperor, "he is happy. But pray did he tell you that he had been at Elba?"—"Yes, Sire; he even entrusted me with the narrative of his voyage, and of the conversations which he had with your Majesty."—"You must give me this narrative: I will take it with me: it will help me in the composition of my memoirs."—"Sire, it is no longer in my possession."—"What have you done with it? you must get it back, and let me have it to-morrow."—"I have deposited it with a friend, who happens to be absent from Paris."—"So the narrative will be handed about at the mercy of the world."—"No, Sire. It is inclosed in an envelope, and deposited in a box of which I keep the key; but if I should not be able to deliver it to your Majesty, before your Majesty's departure, it will yet come to your knowledge, for I intend to publish it according to the last wishes of M. Z***, unless your Majesty forbids me."—"No; I allow you to print it, only leave out whatever may tend to compromise those who have displayed their attachment towards me. If Z*** has made a faithful report of all that passed, the people will know that I sacrificed myself for their good; and that it was not the love of power which brought me again into France, but that I yielded to the desire of restoring to the French those gifts which are dearest to great nations—independence and glory. Take care lest they should get hold of your manuscript—they will falsify it. Send it to England to *****; he will print it; he is devoted to me, and he may be very useful to you. M. *** will give you a letter for him: do you understand me?"—"Yes, Sire."—"But do your utmost to recover your manuscript before my departure. I see that you are anxious to keep it, and I will leave it with you. I only wish to read it." The Emperor read the manuscript, and he returned it to me, saying, "Z*** has told the truth, and nothing but the truth; keep his manuscript for future generations."

Footnote 31: On cherche à plaire même à des matelots quand on a besoin d'eux.

Footnote 32: As only six were noted in the "feuille de bord" they took an extra sailor, in order that there might be six on board after my landing, otherwise, on landing, they would have been obliged to account for the sailor whom I represented.

Footnote 33: The time required for sailing from one port to another is pretty well ascertained; if this period is exceeded, and no sufficient reason can be assigned for the delay, it is assumed that the vessel may have touched at some infected port; and, by excess of caution, they compel you to undergo the lesser quarantine. The lesser quarantine is also ordered as a punishment when the master of a vessel does not behave with due respect and submission to the health officers.

Footnote 34: I had believed, according to the statements in the ministerial journals, that the sea was covered by French and English ships, by which all vessels and passengers, proceeding to the island, were intercepted. I did not meet with a single ship of this description. The ports were placed under a "surveillance," equally brutal and tyrannical but the sea was free. All vessels went in and out of Porto Ferrajo without experiencing the slightest obstacle.

Footnote 35: The corvette commanded by Captain Campbell.

Footnote 36: Napoleon usually liked to intimidate and disconcert those who approached him. Sometimes he feigned that he could not hear you, and then he would make you repeat in a very loud tone what he had heard perfectly well before. However, he was really deaf in a slight degree. At other times he would overwhelm you with such rapid and abrupt interrogatories, that you had not time to understand him, and were compelled to give your answers in confusion. He used then to laugh at your embarrassment; and when he had driven you out of your presence of mind and confidence, he amused himself at your expense.—Note of the author of the work.

Footnote 37: "Ma gloire est faite à moi. Mon nom vivra autant que celui de Dieu!!!"

Footnote 38: I obtained this information in the course of my voyage.

Footnote 39: This narrative evidently shows, that the revolution of the 20th of March was not the effect of a conspiracy. but, strange to say, the work of two men, and a few words.

The share that M. Z*** had in the return of Napoleon will, perhaps, call down upon his head the censures of those who judge events only from their results. Will this opinion be well founded? Are men responsible for the caprice of fate? Is it not to fortune, rather than to M. Z***, that we must impute the disastrous end of this revolution, begun under such happy auspices?

More fortunate than Napoleon, M. Z*** was killed on Mount St. Jean, the moment when our troops penetrated thither amidst the plaudits of the army. He was permitted to draw his last breath on the standards, which the conquerors of Ligny had just snatched from the English; and, far from foreseeing that his visit to the island of Elba would at some future day be a reproach to his memory, he died with the persuasion, that victory had irrevocably fixed his destiny, and that his name, cherished by the French, cherished by the hero whom he had restored to them, would be for ever hallowed by the gratitude of France, become once more the great nation.

I shall not prematurely rob his manes of this consoling illusion; I shall not inform them, that ... no! it will be time enough hereafter to disturb their repose, and I shall await the attack before I begin the defence.

Footnote 40: The flotilla of Napoleon consisted of the brig Inconstant, carrying twenty-six guns and four hundred grenadiers, and six other light vessels, on board which were two hundred foot, two hundred Corsican chasseurs, and about a hundred Polish light horse. The feluccas and the brigs had been so fitted up, as to show no signs of the troops, and to have the appearance of mere merchantmen.

Footnote 41: People are pretty generally of opinion, that the escape of the Emperor from the Island of Elba was favoured by Captain Campbell. I do not think so: but every thing leads to the belief, that this officer had received orders from his government, not to prevent such a step. — (Note by the author of the Memoirs.)

Footnote 42: The passages between two sets of inverted commas are copied from the official account published on the 22d of March. This account was drawn up by Napoleon, and I thought I could not do better than borrow his words.

Footnote 43: They had fled precipitately as far as Basil.

Footnote 44: The cockade adopted by Napoleon, as sovereign of the island of Elba, was white and amaranth powdered with bees.

Footnote 45: The passages marked with two sets of inverted commas continue to be extracts from the official account.

Footnote 46: The public papers, since the second restoration, have not failed to assert, that the troops of the Emperor disgracefully pillaged the communes through which they passed. This imputation, like many others, is a cowardly slander. The Emperor had recommended to his grenadiers, and it is well known that they never disobeyed him, to exact nothing from the inhabitants; and in order to prevent the least irregularity, he took care himself to arrange the means of ascertaining every thing that was furnished, and paying for it. He had given this in charge to an inspector in chief of reviews, M. Boinot, and a commissary at war, M. Ch. Vauthier, for whose zeal and integrity he had the highest esteem. Whatever was furnished was paid for on delivery by the treasurer, M. Peyruse, or an account authenticated by M. Vauthier, and at the prices fixed by the mayors themselves.

Footnote 47: This mode of proceeding, worthy of the barbarous ages, was a new infraction of the law of nations, and of the constitutional laws of France, on the part of the ministry. No article of the charter conferred on the monarch the right of life and death over his subjects; and consequently he had no authority to proscribe those who accompanied and assisted Napoleon. If they were considered as robbers, it was the office of the tribunals to judge and to punish them.

Neither was he authorized, to order Napoleon to be murdered. He had preserved the title of Emperor, legally enjoyed the prerogative of sovereignty, and might make war or peace as he pleased.

The title of Emperor of the French, which he arrogated to himself, could not be a title to proscription. George III., previous to the treaty of Amiens, styled himself King of France and Navarre. Had he made a descent in arms on our territory, would any one have had a right, to proclaim him out of the pale of the law, and order the French people to murder him?

Footnote 48: These four generals had agreed, to repair together to Paris. The troops of Count d'Erlon, quartered at Lisle, deceived by supposititious orders, were on their march, when they were met by the Duke de Trévise, who was going to take the command of his government. He interrogated them, perceived the plot, and ordered them back.

Count Lefevre Desnouettes, ignorant of this unlucky circumstance, put in motion his regiment, which was in garrison at Cambrai. When he reached Compiègne, he did not find the troops he expected, and showed some hesitation. The officers of his corps, and particularly Major Lyon, questioned him, and finally abandoned him.

On the other hand, the brothers Lallemand, one of whom was general of artillery, had marched to Fère with a few squadrons, intending to seize the park of artillery. The resistance they met from General d'Aboville disconcerted them, and, after they had attempted in vain to seduce the garrison, they fled, but were shortly after arrested.

It was supposed, that this rising in arms had been concerted with Napoleon; but I know from good authority, that it was solely the result of an evening spent at General ***'s. A few bowls of punch had heated their brains; they complained of their situation; they were indignant, that a handful of cowardly emigrants should prescribe laws to them; they were persuaded it would be easy to displace them; and, proceeding from one step to another, they concluded by agreeing to march to Paris, and compel the King to change his ministry, and banish from France all those whom the public voice denounced as enemies to the charter, and disturbers of the public tranquillity and happiness. Such was their true and only object.

Footnote 49: The chancellor, no doubt, had forgotten the proscription, that delivered over to death all those Frenchmen who joined or assisted Bonaparte.

Footnote 50: It is asserted, that on this occasion a conference took place, at which M. Lainé, MM. de Broglie, la Fayette, d'Argenson, Flaugergue, Benjamin Constant, &c. were present, where it was decided, that the King should be required in the name of the public safety:

1. To dismiss MM. de Blacas, Montesquiou, Dambray, and Ferrand:

2. To call to the Chamber of Peers forty new members, chosen exclusively from men of the revolution:

3. To confer on M. de la Fayette, the command of the national guard: and

4. To despatch patriotic commissioners, to stimulate the attachment, the zeal, and the fidelity of the troops.

Footnote 51: The double sets of inverted commas are still used to distinguish passages extracted from the official account.

Footnote 52: He had travelled from Cannes to Grenoble partly on horseback, but chiefly on foot.

Footnote 53: It was a great oversight, to send the Count d'Artois to face Napoleon. It was easy to foresee, that, if this prince should fail in a city of a hundred thousand inhabitants against eight hundred men, the business would be decided.

Footnote 54: Marshal Macdonald was not so happy. Two hussars, one of whom was drunk, pursued him, and would have arrested him, if he had not been extricated by his aide-de-camp.

Footnote 55: Those who have been about Napoleon's person know, that he recommended to his secretaries, and the officers of his household, to take notes of what he said and did on his journeys. A number of notes of this nature must have been found at the Tuileries, most of which contained particulars that were highly interesting. I preserved mine, and from them I have composed, in great measure, the present work.

Footnote 56: The Bourbons.

Footnote 57: The newspapers of the day asserted, that Napoleon, though he had in his pocket the proclamation of Augereau, filled with reproaches and invectives, had thrown himself into his arms, and heard the cutting reprehensions of the marshal, without saying a word.

Footnote 58: He had retired to Switzerland.

Footnote 59: The author of a libel entitled Les Quinze Semaines, "The Fifteen Weeks," asserts. that shouts were heard of "Death for ever! Guilt for ever! Down with virtue! Down with God!" Such a charge requires no refutation: I mention it here only to show, to what a point the spirit of party, and the rancorous passions, have misled writers, who call themselves royalists. It has been equally asserted, that the people plundered and destroyed a number of shops and warehouses. This, too, is false: no disorder occurred, except in Bellecour Square, where the people broke the windows and tables of the Bourbon coffee-house, known to be the place where the ultra-royalists assembled; and this disorder was quieted and suppressed immediately.

Footnote 60: He attempted to harangue the Chalonese, but they allowed him only time to take to his heels.

Footnote 61: I dare not positively affirm it, for in my memorandums I have confounded together Chalons, Avalon, &c.

Footnote 62:

ORDERS OF THE DAY.

The Marshal Prince of the Moskowa, to the troops of his Government.

Officers, non-commissioned officers, and soldiers!

The cause of the Bourbons is lost for ever. The legitimate dynasty, which the French nation has adopted, is about to re-ascend the throne: it belongs to the Emperor Napoleon alone, our sovereign, to reign over our fine country. Whether the nobility of the Bourbons take the step of expatriating itself again, or consent to live among us, is no concern of ours. The sacred cause of liberty, and of our independence, will no longer suffer from their fatal influence. They have endeavoured to debase our military glory; but they have found themselves mistaken. This glory is the fruit of labours too noble for us to lose the remembrance of it. Soldiers! those days are no more, when nations were governed by stifling their rights. Liberty is at length triumphant and Napoleon, our august Emperor, is about to confirm it for ever. Henceforth let this lovely cause be ours, and that of all Frenchmen: let all the brave fellows, whom I have the honour to command, be thoroughly imbued with this grand truth.

Soldiers! I have often led you to victory; I am now going to conduct you to that immortal phalanx, which the Emperor Napoleon is conducting to Paris, and which will be there in a few days, and our hopes and our happiness will be for ever realized. Long live the Emperor!

> Lons le Saulnier, the 13th of March, 1815.
> The marshal of the empire,
> Prince of the Moskowa.

Footnote 63: He alluded to the installation of the council of state, where the chancellor actually dropped on one knee, to ask and receive the King's orders.

And to the city entertainment, where the prefect, his wife, and the municipal body, waited at table on the King and his suite, consisting of forty ladies of the old court, and only four ladies of the new nobility, two of whom were the wives of the marshals on duty.

Footnote 64: M. Gamot, prefect of Auxerre, had married the sister of Madame Ney.

Footnote 65: It is indisputable, in fact, that a general insurrection, provoked by the oppressive and senseless conduct of the government, was ready to burst out, at the moment when Napoleon re-appeared.

It is known, that France, wearied, disgusted, and discontented with the new order of things, wished heartily for a new revolution; and people had united and concerted measures for preparing the crisis, and causing it to turn to the advantage of the country.

Some of the malecontents maintained, that the first step should be, to shake off the insupportable yoke, under which they were groaning, and then see what was to be done: the majority formally declared for the immediate recall of the Emperor, and were desirous, that emissaries should be deputed to him, or that vessels should be sent, to take him off from the island of Elba.

The necessity of a change was unanimously agreed upon, and they were endeavouring to settle the rest, when the sudden arrival of Napoleon put an end to the discussion.

After the 20th of March, the Emperor was made acquainted with these projects of insurrection; and knew that certain chiefs hesitated about having any thing to do with him. "The leaders," said he, "wished to take the business into their own hands, and labour for themselves; now they pretend, that they opened the way for me to Paris: I know better; it was the nation, the people, the soldiers, and the sub-lieutenants, who did all. It is to these, and to these only, that I owe every thing."

Footnote 66: A nickname given to the emigrant officers.

Footnote 67: He had just been appointed to the command of the advanced guard.

Footnote 68: Napoleon had already given similar orders to General Cambronne. The following is his letter, which I reproach myself with not having quoted. "General Cambronne, to you I entrust my noblest campaign: all the French expect me with impatience: every where you will find none but friends: do not fire a single musket; I will not have my crown cost the French a drop of blood."

Footnote 69: Napoleon was a fatalist, and superstitious; and made no secret of it. He believed in lucky and unlucky days. We might be astonished at this weakness, if we did not know, that it was common to the greatest men both of ancient and modern times.

Footnote 70: This was Napoleon's favourite compliment. The fonder he was of a person, the more he gave him, and the harder he struck.

Footnote 71: The Duke of Vicenza, convinced of the inutility of the efforts Napoleon might make, to establish any diplomatic connexion with foreign powers, refused to accept the post. The Emperor offered it to M. Môlé. M. Môlé objected, that he was an entire stranger to diplomacy, and requested Napoleon, to make another choice. Napoleon and his other ministers were then so pressing with the Duke of Vicenza, that he considered it his duty to yield. He would have preferred the Emperor's giving him a command in the army, where he would at least have found an opportunity of usefully serving his country and the Emperor.

The ministry of the interior, intended at first for M. Costaz, was also offered to M. Môlé, and ultimately given to M. Carnot, at the recommendation of the Duke of Bassano.

The Emperor was not pleased with the obstinate refusals of M. Môlé: he was fond of his name, and valued his talents. He had intended to appoint him governor of the Imperial Prince; and it was to this intention that M. Môlé was chiefly indebted for the high rank, to which he had been so rapidly raised.

Nevertheless M. Môlé solicited and obtained the general superintendance of highways and bridges, a post which he occupied in 1813, before he was appointed minister of justice.

Footnote 72:

"Make him, nor think his genius check'd,
A herald, or an architect." —Gay.

Footnote 73: General Le Tort's address to the King.

Footnote 74: "In all ages the poor have suffered for the faults of the great."

Footnote 75: He constantly refused the emoluments and allowances of considerable offices, attached to the rank of major-general of the guards. The appointments of a lieutenant-general and aide-de-camp appeared to him, to pay him more than his services deserved.

Footnote 76: I cannot avoid remarking the beauty of this passage.

Footnote 77: The king departed with such suddenness, that he had not time to carry away his private papers. In his writing table was found his family port-folio. It contained a great number of letters from Madame the Duchess of Angoulême, and from some of the princes. Napoleon cast his eye over several of them, and gave me the port-folio, with orders, that it should be scrupulously preserved. Napoleon would have respect paid to royal majesty, and to every thing that pertained to the person of kings.

The king habitually used a small table, that he had brought from Hartwell. Napoleon took pleasure in writing on it for a few hours: he afterwards ordered it to be removed, and the greatest care to be taken of it.

The Merlin's chair used by the king, not being suited to Napoleon, whose limbs and health were in full strength and vigour, was banished to the back closet. Some person being found sitting in it, when the Emperor passed through unexpectedly, he gave him an angry look, and the chair was removed.

One of his valets de chambre, thinking to please him, ventured to place over his mantel-piece some insulting caricatures of the Bourbons: these he disdainfully threw into the fire, and severely enjoined the valet, never in future to be guilty of such an impertinence.

Footnote 78:

"If we sometimes play the fool,
Reason should resume her rule."

Footnote 79: I have been assured, that Napoleon in his youth composed a history of Paoli, and of the war of liberty: may he realize the design of writing the history of his own reign, for the instruction of future ages! This reign is so fertile in extraordinary events, and unforeseen catastrophes, and displays to our view such numerous examples of human vicissitudes, that its history may supply the place of all others, and become itself alone a lesson for kings and people.

Footnote 80: This decree, and all those previously dated from the palace of the Tuileries, contained no title but simply that of "Emperor of the French." The "&c. &c.," noticed with anxiety in the proclamations and decrees from Lyons, were suppressed. They had been inserted without reflection, without object, and merely from custom. The Emperor, too, would not have his familiar letters continue to be concluded in the usual form: "On which I pray God, to have you in his holy keeping, &c." "All those antiquated things," said he, "must be laid aside; they are well enough for kings by the grace of God."

Footnote 81: Never, in fact, at any period of the revolution, did writers enjoy such complete liberty and impunity. The seizure of the Censeur Européen, which made such noise, was the work of M. Fouché. The Emperor knew nothing of this infringement of the law, till it had been carried into effect; and he immediately ordered, that the copies seized should be returned to the editors of the Censeur, and that they should be at liberty to circulate them freely.

Footnote 82: The audience was to take place at noon; and at nine o'clock his Majesty had not prepared his answers. They were dictated in haste, and we had scarcely time to copy them out fairly.

Footnote 83: I am speaking here only of the addresses of bodies corporate, and of certain generals and prefects.

Footnote 84: We have no single word in our language answering to this: it implies one who undertakes works of different kinds, including our architect and civil engineer.—Tr.

Footnote 85: It was this mission, that became the source of the disgrace, in which the marshal lived, till the day of his being recalled to the army. The Emperor had ordered him, to set off immediately: he answered, that he could not go, till he was paid some twenty thousand francs, which were owing to him. The Emperor, swearing, ordered them to be paid.

The next day General Le Courbe, to whom the Emperor had just entrusted an important command, wrote to him, to demand several favours, and in addition a hundred and fifty thousand francs, as arrears of pay, in order to discharge his debts.

Two other generals, less known, were equally desirous of being paid for their services. He was disgusted at their claims. "Do these men think," said he, "that I throw away my money? I am not inclined to suffer myself to be plundered like Henry IV; if they be not inclined to fight, let them put on petticoats, and go and take an airing."

Footnote 86: I regret, that I did not learn his name.

Footnote 87: The fortress in which the garrison was quartered.

Footnote 88: She set off in the evening for Pouillac; where, having bidden adieu to the volunteer cavalry, who had escorted her, she went on board an English vessel, and sailed for England on the 2d of April.

Footnote 89: Report of General Ernouf.

Footnote 90: The diamonds that were sought to be obtained in exchange for the Duke of Angoulême were worth fourteen millions. The Duke of Otranto proposed to the Emperor, to throw M. de Vitrolles into the bargain, if they were restored; to which the Emperor readily consented. The Duke of Otranto opened a negotiation on this point, which had no farther result, than procuring him an opportunity of corresponding more at his ease with Ghent.

Footnote 91: It was discovered by the Duke d'Albufera, that this supposed treason was the consequence of the mistake, which I have related above, and the decree was not carried into effect.

Footnote 92: A nickname given by Napoleon to his old grenadiers.

Footnote 93: The Emperor Alexander, in particular, expressed the most generous indignation.

Footnote 94: M. de Vincent set out before this letter was written, and it was entrusted to his secretary. The Emperor of Austria ordered it to be delivered into his hands, and contented himself with informing the Empress Marie, that he had received news of her husband, and that he was well.

Footnote 95: It was a laughable singularity, that, of all the double-faced men employed by the Emperor, there was no one, in whom he had more confidence, than he had in M. de Mont**. He had formerly ill-treated, persecuted, and banished him: he knew, that he detested him, and was the most intimate, the most devoted friend of M. de Talleyrand: but he knew also the bent of M. de Mont**'s mind; and he thought, that he would feel an infinite pleasure, in executing his mission well, and humming [rouer] M. de Talleyrand, who flattered himself, that he had never been hummed by any person. I know not whether M. de Mont** found it pleasant, or not, to take in M. de Talleyrand; what I know is, that he justified the expectations of Napoleon, and brought back to him intact the letters, that were delivered to him by M. de Mont**.

Footnote 96: I know not whether the fact be true: but, true or false, it had the same effect on the minds of the Italians.

Footnote 97: Les marins. Properly, perhaps, the seamen, whom Napoleon took from the ships of war, and converted into soldiers.—Tr.

Footnote 98: For the Moniteur, I presume.—Tr.

Footnote 99: I cannot avoid here making a comparison. On the 15th of March, the Count d'Artois wished to form a legion from the light infantry and grenadiers of the national guard of Paris. He reviewed the twelve legions, harangued them, and announced, that he would march at the head of the volunteer national guards: a hundred and fifty turned out.

Napoleon from his closet called the national guard to the defence of the imperial cause: 150,000 men took up arms, and hastened to battle.

What must we conclude from this coldness on the one hand, and this enthusiasm on the other? I leave the question to be answered by those, who pretend, that the revolution of the 20th of March obtained the assent only of a handful of factious persons.

Footnote 100: The reverses of Napoleon's fortune had been so rapid, that the possessors of great places, and of great preferment, had not had time to retrench their way of living. When the Bourbons were recalled, they were obliged to come to a reckoning with their means, and all these extravagant expenses ceased at once.

On the other hand, the new court, in order to distinguish itself from the imperial court, substituted the most offensive simplicity for the useful pomp of Napoleon. The richest emigrants imitated this pernicious example; and, as Napoleon remarked, the luxury of the table was almost the only kind, on which encouragement was not spared. The result of this economical system was, that the produce of our manufactories remained unemployed, and industry was suddenly paralyzed.

Thus commerce, which had loudly called for peace, was almost totally annihilated by it: and the manufacturers, the mechanics, the merchants (those of the sea-ports excepted), greatly regretted those *happy* times, when we were at war.

In fact, it must be admitted, that our industry was indebted to the war, and to our conquests, for its progress, and its prodigious increase. The war, by depriving us of the products of the English manufactories, had taught us, to manufacture for ourselves. The continual prohibition of these articles protected our rising manufactures from the danger of competition; and allowed them to engage with safety in the trials and expenses necessary for equalling or surpassing in perfection foreign manufactures. In all parts of the empire were seen manufactories for spinning and weaving cotton; and this branch of trade, almost unknown before, employed three hundred thousand work people, and produced goods to the value of more than two hundred and fifty millions.

The other products of our industry equally received improvements and extension; and France, in spite of the conscription, reckoned in its numerous workshops nearly twelve hundred thousand workpeople.

If this flourishing state of our continental trade were the effect of the enlargement of our territory, and the scope the war had given to our industry, we must say, that it was also the result of the succour, encouragement, and honorary distinctions, which Napoleon knew how to bestow appropriately on our manufacturers; and the return for those enormous sacrifices he made, to create, repair, and keep in order, those superb roads, and those numerous canals, which rendered the communications between France, and the countries subjected to its empire, equally easy, safe, and pleasant.

Footnote 101: These words, and several others that I have quoted, prove Napoleon not to have been ignorant of the use he might make of the people. If he did not have recourse to them, no doubt it was because he feared, that the remedy might prove worse than the disease.

Footnote 102: Napoleon, during the hundred days, entertained for a moment the design of issuing a demi-official note on the arrest and death of the Duke of Enghien.

The following memorandums are taken from papers, from which the note was to have been compiled.

Reports from the police had informed Napoleon, that there were conspiracies of the royalists beyond the Rhine, and that they were conducted and supported,

1st, by Messrs. Drake and Spencer Smith, the English ministers at Stutgard, and at Munich;

2dly, by the Duke d'Enghien and General Dumourier:

The central point of the former was at Offenbourg; where were some emigrants, some English agents, and the Baroness de Reich, so noted for her political intrigues:

The central point of the latter was given out to be at the castle of Ettenheim, where the Duke d'Enghien, Dumourier, an English colonel, and several agents of the Bourbons, resided.

The hundred and twenty thousand francs given by the minister Drake to the Sieur Rosey, chef de bataillon, to excite an insurrection,

The declarations of Mehée;

And the reports of M. Sh***, prefect of Strasbourg, and brother-in-law of the Duke de Fel....; leave no doubt of the existence of the intrigues at

Offenbourg and Ettenheim, to which M. Sh*** ascribes in particular the agitation, and symptoms of discontent, that prevail at Weissembourg, and in several parts of Alsace.

On the other hand, the conspiracy of the 3d of Nivôse had just broken out. The discoveries made by the servant of Georges, and by other individuals, led to the belief, that the Duke d'Enghien had been sent by England to the borders of the Rhine, in order to place himself at the head of the insurrection, as soon as Napoleon was made away with.

The necessity of putting an end to these plots, and strike terror into their instigators by a grand act of reprisal, squared in an incredible degree with the political considerations, that led Napoleon to attempt a bold stroke, in order to give the revolution, and the revolutionists, those guaranties, which circumstances demanded:

Napoleon, named consul for life (I borrow here the language of the Manuscript from St. Helena), felt the weakness of his situation, the ridiculousness of his consulship. It was necessary to establish something solid, to serve as a support to the revolution. The republicans were alarmed at the height, on which circumstances had placed him: they were suspicious of the use he might make of his power: they dreaded his renewing an antiquated royalty by the help of his army. The royalists fomented this rumour, and took a delight in representing him as an ape of the ancient monarchs: other royalists, more adroit, whispered about, that he was enamoured of the part of Monk, and that he would take the pains to restore the power, only to make a present of it to the Bourbons, when it should be in a proper state to be offered them.

Ordinary minds, unacquainted with his powers, credited these reports; they sanctioned the tales of the royalist party, and decried him to the people, and to the army; for they began to suspect him, and his attachment to their cause. He could not allow such an opinion to pass current, because it tended to unhinge every thing. It was necessary, at all events, to undeceive France, the royalists, and Europe at large, in order that they might know, what they had to reckon upon in him. A persecution of reports in detail never produces any thing but a bad effect, for it does not attack the root of the evil.

The death of the Duke d'Enghien would decide the question, that agitated France; it would decide the character of Napoleon beyond return; in fine, it might intimidate and punish the authors of the plots incessantly contriving against his life, and against the state: accordingly he determined on it.

He sent for Marshal Berthier, and this minister directed General Ord**, by an order which the Emperor dictated, and which I have *seen*, to set off post for Strasbourg; to cause General Lev** to place under his orders fifteen boatmen, three hundred dragoons from the garrison of Schelstadt, and thirty gendarmes; to pass the Rhine at Rheinan, to proceed to Ettenheim, to surround the town, and *to carry off the Duke d'Enghien, Dumourier, an English colonel, and all the persons in their suite.*

> The Duke d'Enghien,
> General Thumery,
> Colonel de Grunstein,
> Lieutenant Schmidt,
> Abbé Weinburn, and five other inferior persons, were arrested by a chef d'escadron of the gendarmerie, named Ch**, who was charged with this part of the expedition.

Then, and then only, it became certain, that Dumourier was not at Ettenheim. General Thumery had been mistaken for him. This mistake, occasioned by the similarity of their rank, and some likeness of sound between their names, which the Germans pronounced nearly alike, had heightened the importance and criminality of the pretended plots at Ettenheim in the mind of Napoleon, and had the most fatal influence on his determination.

The Duke d'Enghien was brought from Strasbourg to Paris, and carried before a military commission.

The Empress Josephine, the Princess Hortense, fell at Napoleon's feet in tears, and conjured him to spare the life of the Duke d'Enghien. Prince Cambacérès and the Prince of Neufchâtel strongly remonstrated to him on the horrible inutility of the blow he was about to strike. He appeared to hesitate, when the information was brought him, that the prince was no more.

Napoleon had not expected so speedy a catastrophe. He had even given orders to M. Réal, to repair to Vincennes, to interrogate the Duke d'Enghien: but his trial and execution had been hastened by Murat; who, urged by some regicides, at the head of whom was M. Fou***, thought he should render a service to Napoleon, to his family, and to France, by insuring the death of a Bourbon.

The Prince de T***, whom the Emperor often publicly reproached with having advised the seizure and death of the Duke d'Enghien, was directed to pacify the court of Baden, and to justify the violation of its territory in the eyes of Europe. M. de Caulincourt being at Strasbourg, the Emperor thought him more proper than any other person, to follow up a negotiation, if the turn of affairs should require it; and he was directed to send to the minister of Baden the despatch of the Prince de T***. But there was no need of having recourse to negotiations: the court, far from complaining of the violation of its territory, expressed itself well contented, that the step taken had saved it the disgrace of consenting, or the embarrassment of a refusal.

This is an exact and true recital of the circumstances, that preceded, followed, and accompanied, the carrying off and death of the last of the house of Condé.

The seizure of the Duke d'Enghien was long imputed to M. de Caulincourt, and is still imputed to him by persons uninformed of the truth.

Some assert, that he arrested him with his own hands:

Others, that he gave orders for the seizure of his person: both these imputations are equally false.

He did not arrest the Duke d'Enghien, for his seizure was executed and consummated by chef d'escadron Ch***.

Neither directly, nor indirectly, did he give orders for seizing the prince: for the particular mission, to carry him off, was confided to General Ord**, and this general had no orders to receive from M. de Caulincourt his equal, perhaps even his inferior.

What made it be supposed, at a time when it was not possible to explain the facts, that M. de Caulincourt had been employed to seize the Duke d'Enghien, or cause him to be seized, was, that M. de Caulincourt received, at the same moment as General Ord**, orders to repair to Strasbourg, to cause the emigrants and English agents, who had fixed the seat of their intrigues at Offenbourg, to be carried off. But this mission, for which it would be requisite to take measures in concert with General Ord**, and perhaps even to assist him in case of need; for a simultaneous proceeding was necessary, that one expedition might not cause the failure of the other; this mission, I say, though analogous to that of General Ord**, had no real connexion with it.

Their objects were different:

That of one was to carry off the Duke d'Enghien from Ettenheim;

That of the other, to seize the conspirators at Offenbourg, which was eight or ten leagues distant.

Perhaps it will be objected, that M. de Caulincourt was not ignorant of General Ord**'s being directed, to seize the Duke d'Enghien. Be it so: I cannot perceive the consequence, attempted to be drawn from this. But what I have seen in the cabinet, and what I attest, is, that the order given to M. de Caulincourt said nothing of Ettenheim, and that the name of the

Duke d'Enghien was not even mentioned in it: it related solely, in the first place, to the construction of a flotilla, that was preparing on the Rhine; and, secondly, to the expedition of Offenbourg; an expedition that terminated, as no doubt is still remembered, in the laughable flight of the minister Drake and his agents.

I have thought it my duty as a Frenchman and an historian, to enter into these details, and destroy for ever an error, which malevolence and the spirit of party have laid hold of, in order to tarnish the political life of one of the men, who do the greatest honour to the imperial government and to France.

M. de Caulincourt would not have been less irreproachable, had he committed the fatal seizure ascribed to him: he would have done his duty, as General Ord** did his. A soldier is not the judge of the orders he is to execute. The great Condé, covered with the laurels of Rocroy, Fribourg, Norlinguen, and Lenz, was arrested, in spite of the faith pledged to him, in the apartments of the King; yet neither his contemporaries, nor posterity, have charged Marshal d'Albret with this arrest as a crime.

Footnote 103: I have been assured, that Georges was three times offered his pardon by Napoleon, if he would promise, not to engage in any conspiracy again; and that it was not till after his third refusal, that his sentence was ordered to be carried into execution.

Footnote 104: Marshal Augereau, Duke de Castiglione, was also in this list. His name was struck out at the request of the duchess, and in consideration of the proclamation, which he published on the 23d of March.

Footnote 105: These conversations with persons, whose merit and opinion Napoleon esteemed, were always pleasing, instructive, interesting, always marked with strong thoughts, and bold, ingenious, or sublime expressions. With persons indifferent to him, or whose nullity he discerned, his phrases, scarcely begun, were never finished: his ideas turned only on insignificant, common-place matters, which, by way of amusing himself, he was apt to season with biting sarcasm, or jokes more whimsical than witty.

This explains the contradictions between the different opinions given of Napoleon's understanding by foreigners introduced at his court.

Footnote 106: Attorney-general to the king, employed on certain occasions, to prosecute political crimes and misdemeanors.

Footnote 107: "Beautiful Marchioness, your beautiful eyes make me die of love; of love make me die, beautiful Marchioness, your beautiful eyes."